Oxford School *Shakespeare*

HENRY IV
PART I

edited by
Roma Gill, OBE
M.A. *Cantab.*, B. Litt. *Oxon*

OXFORD
UNIVERSITY PRESS

OXFORD
UNIVERSITY PRESS

Great Clarendon Street, Oxford OX2 6DP

Oxford University Press is a department of the University of Oxford.
It furthers the University's objective of excellence in research,
scholarship, and education by publishing worldwide in

Oxford New York

Auckland Cape Town Dar es Salaam Hong Kong Karachi
Kuala Lumpur Madrid Melbourne Mexico City Nairobi
New Delhi Shanghai Taipei Toronto

with offices in

Argentina Austria Brazil Chile Czech Republic France Greece
Guatemala Hungary Italy Japan Poland Portugal Singapore
South Korea Switzerland Thailand Turkey Ukraine Vietnam

Oxford is a registered trade mark of Oxford University Press
in the UK and in certain other countries

© Oxford University Press 1984

Reprinted in this new edition 2008

British Library Cataloguing in Publication Data available

ISBN: 978 0 19 832091 3

10 9 8 7 6 5 4 3 2 1

Typeset by Herb Bowes Graphics, Oxford
Printed by Bell and Bain Ltd., Glasgow

Paper used in the production of this book is a natural, recyclable
product made from wood grown in sustainable forests. The
manufacturing process conforms to the environmental
regulations of the country of origin.

Illustrations by Shirley Tourret
Cover Photograph by
Dominic Photography

For Joanna

Oxford School Shakespeare
edited by Roma Gill

A Midsummer Night's Dream
The Taming of the Shrew
Romeo and Juliet
Othello
As You Like It
Hamlet
Macbeth
King Lear
Julius Caesar
Henry V
The Merchant of Venice
The Winter's Tale
Henry IV Part I
Antony and Cleopatra
Twelfth Night
The Tempest
Much Ado About Nothing
Richard II
Measure for Measure
Coriolanus
Love's Labour's Lost

Contents

Introduction

A 'History' Play

Born to be king

The King of England is a unique personage. He does not achieve
position by effort and intelligence; he does not win it by power a
force; and he is not elected by the people that he will rule. He is b
to be king – chosen by God for that special purpose; and he is 'Gc
substitute, His deputy anointed in His right'. That quotation is fr
Shakespeare's play *Richard II*, and it states the official Elizabet
view of the monarchy. Such doctrine was taught in the schools,
churches – and even the theatres.

The Elizabethans were afraid of rebellion. The country v
enjoying an uneasy peace under Elizabeth I, and the politicians w
anxious to maintain this peace. The Queen was threatened by th
(chiefly Roman Catholics) who disputed her right to the throne, s
was essential for her supporters to warn the English people of
dangers of rebelling against a divinely ordained ruler. The history
England provided plenty of examples.

Inspired by history

Shakespeare was not the only dramatist to write plays on 'historie
subjects; but he certainly wrote *more* than anyone else, so it is safe
infer that he was fascinated by his country's past, and that
recognized the lessons which the past might give to the future. I
greatest inspiration came from the events that followed the crisis
1399, when Henry Bolingbroke deposed King Richard II and usurp
his crown. Shakespeare wrote eight plays around this subject, and th
seem to form two groups of four (i.e. two 'tetralogies'), although
plays were not written in the chronological order of the reigns whi
they describe. The first tetralogy – the group of plays that Shakespe
wrote first – consisted of the three *Henry VI* plays with *Richard III*;
second group starts with *Richard II*, continues with the two *Henry*
plays, and comes to a triumphant conclusion with *Henry V*.

The moral lesson

The moral lesson that can be drawn from the eight plays is the ve
orthodox teaching that it is wrong to rebel against God's true kin

even though he is not a good ruler; and God will punish such rebellion – but He will do so in His own time. Henry Bolingbroke wears Richard's crown, but it does not bring him happiness: he never feels secure, and he is always conscious of his guilt. At his death his son takes the crown, becoming (legitimately) Henry V; but Shakespeare still insists on the guilt of the rebellion, and before his most famous victory, at Agincourt, Henry V prays

> Not today, O Lord!
> O not today, think not upon the fault
> My father made in compassing the crown!

The 'fault' was not punished at Agincourt – nor, indeed, in the whole reign of King Henry V, whom the Elizabethans regarded as a great national hero. After the death of Henry V, however, the country endured great suffering under the weak King Henry VI and the tyrant Richard III; order and harmony were restored at the accession of Henry Tudor – King Henry VII – in 1485.

A rightful heritage?

Shakespeare could assume that his sixteenth-century audiences would be familiar with some English history – even if they knew no more than the brief outline I have sketched here. To make sure that they understood the circumstances of Bolingbroke's usurpation of the English crown, he puts the details into the mouths of the rebels, who frequently seek to justify their actions by recalling the events which immediately preceded the death of Richard II.

These events were the subject of Shakespeare's play *Richard II*, which opened when the young Bolingbroke was sentenced to exile by the King. Old John of Gaunt, Bolingbroke's father, died; and the King confiscated his property – the land and goods which properly belonged to the eldest son. This theft gave Bolingbroke an excuse to break his exile and return to England. Members of the Percy family, outraged by the King's action, pledged their support to the injured heir, so long as he was trying to reclaim his own property. But the dukedom of Lancaster – his rightful heritage – was not enough for Bolingbroke, whose ambition reached to Richard's crown. Eventually Richard was compelled to resign – but he insisted that he was, and always would be, the true king:

> Not all the water in the rough, rude sea
> Can wash the balm off from an anointed king.

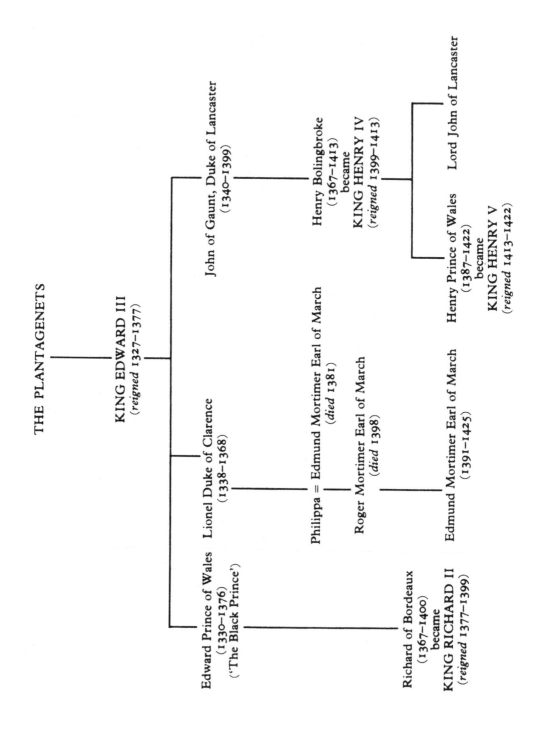

THE PLANTAGENETS

KING EDWARD III
(*reigned* 1327–1377)

Edward Prince of Wales
(1330–1376)
('The Black Prince')

Richard of Bordeaux
(1367–1400)
became
KING RICHARD II
(*reigned* 1377–1399)

Lionel Duke of Clarence
(1338–1368)

Philippa = Edmund Mortimer Earl of March
(*died* 1381)

Roger Mortimer Earl of March
(*died* 1398)

Edmund Mortimer Earl of March
(1391–1425)

John of Gaunt, Duke of Lancaster
(1340–1399)

Henry Bolingbroke
(1367–1413)
became
KING HENRY IV
(*reigned* 1399–1413)

Henry Prince of Wales
(1387–1422)
became
KING HENRY V
(*reigned* 1413–1422)

Lord John of Lancaster

The MORTIMERS and the PERCYS

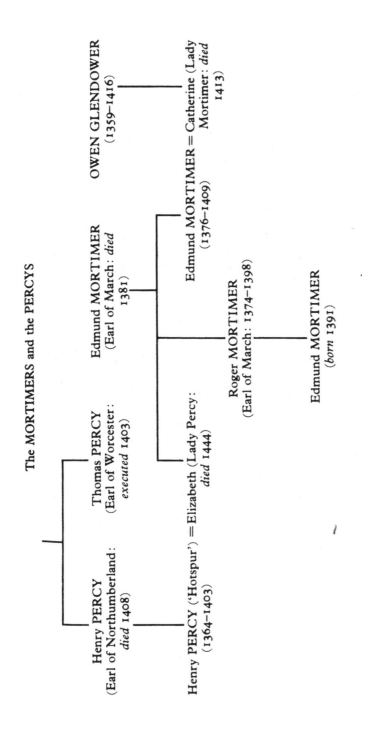

OWEN GLENDOWER
(1359–1416)

Edmund MORTIMER
(Earl of March: *died*
1381)

Thomas PERCY
(Earl of Worcester:
executed 1403)

Henry PERCY
(Earl of Northumberland:
died 1408)

Edmund MORTIMER = Catherine (Lady
(1376–1409)   Mortimer: *died*
1413)

Roger MORTIMER
(Earl of March: 1374–1398)

Henry PERCY ('Hotspur') = Elizabeth (Lady Percy:
(1364–1403)   *died* 1444)

Edmund MORTIMER
(*born* 1391)

Leading Characters in the Play

King Henry IV   This is a very worried man. When he was plain Henry Bolingbro[ke] he was exiled from his native country – England – but returned (aft[er] his father's death) to claim his inheritance. Soon afterwards, [he] deposed the King, Richard II, and usurped his throne. Now he h[as] two great problems. He is afraid that he too may lose his throne a[nd] kingdom; and he is distressed because his elder son and heir, t[he] Prince of Wales, seems to be a riotous, irresponsible young man.

Prince Hal   The Prince of Wales is having a good time. He and his friends a[re] usually found in taverns, and he seems to have no sense of the prop[er] behaviour for a prince. But gradually we learn that Hal is not a me[re] 'playboy'.

Hotspur   This is the nickname of Henry Percy, son of one of the King's ch[ief] opponents. He is young and impetuous (as the nickname suggest[s]) but he is also a very valiant warrior who has already won a gre[at] reputation for himself. He has an exaggerated sense of milita[ry] honour, which he values above everything else.

Sir John Falstaff   A most complex character. He is a fat knight, who eats too muc[h,] drinks too much, and spends most of his time in the tavern. He ha[s a] great sense of humour – and makes fun of himself, as well as laughi[ng] at the other characters. He is also a liar, a thief, and a coward. Falsta[ff] has no historical counterpart, but the original name of this charact[er] was 'Oldcastle' – which suggests that Sir John Oldcastle, a Lollard wh[o] was hanged for heresy in 1417, might have provided the inspiratio[n] for the frequent biblical quotations and Puritan speech mannerism[s] which Shakespeare's character uses to comic effect.

Synopsis

ACT 1

SCENE 1   King Henry tells his supporters of his desire for peace. His plans for a crusade to the Holy Land are interrupted by news of attacks from the Scots and the Welsh. Hearing of the valiant exploits of Hotspur (Harry Percy), Henry wistfully wishes his son, Prince Hal, showed the same qualities, even though Percy is currently proving awkward to the King.

SCENE 2   Away from the responsibilities of court, Prince Hal jests with his drinking companion, Falstaff. When Poins joins them a robbery is planned but one which will backfire on Falstaff. A soliloquy by Hal reveals his realization he must leave this dissolute life behind.

SCENE 3   The King confronts Hotspur and the other rebels. Despite Hotspur's attempts to explain his actions, the King will not be pacified. The King gives them an ultimatum, leaving Hotspur and his companions determined to defy the King.

ACT 2

SCENE 1   Carriers at an inn in Rochester make preparations for their journeys, whilst robbers Gadshill and Chamberlain prepare for a robbery.

SCENE 2   On a highway, a gang of robbers, including Falstaff, hold up some travellers. The robbers in turn are robbed by Prince Hal and Poins, both in disguise.

SCENE 3   Hotspur ignores warnings within a letter, and determines to join the rebellion against the King. He brushes off the concerns of his wife, refusing to share his plans with her.

SCENE 4   Hal and Poins amuse themselves in a tavern as they await the arrival of Falstaff. Falstaff's outrageous lies about the robbery are countered by the Prince revealing the truth. When summoned to court, Hal and Falstaff comically improvise the meeting with his father. When a sheriff arrives seeking Falstaff, Hal promises to make good the losses.

ACT 3

SCENE 1   In Wales, the rebels Hotspur and Owen Glendower clash over the

Henry IV Part 1: Commentary

SCENE 1   The play's first scene takes place in the Palace of Westminster, and we might expect to find the splendour of a royal palace combined with the vitality of the political heart of England. But the King's first speech has neither splendour nor vitality. King Henry is weary – a fact that is conveyed by the words he uses (such as 'shaken' and 'wan with care') and also by the rhythm of the lines. He speaks of the peace that has been achieved, but it is a 'frighted peace' – an insecure period waiting for the next outbreak of war, 'To be commenc'd in stronds afar remote'. The King is determined, however, that there shall be no more *civil* war – never again will England 'daub her lips with her own children's blood'. This personification of England introduces into the play an idea that was always popular with the Elizabethans: they believed that there was a similarity (or 'correspondence') between the human body and the state or country (which was the 'body politic').

Another favourite Elizabethan notion appears when King Henry compares the opposed armies to 'the meteors of a troubled heaven'. Disturbances in the universe – such as storms, thunder, and lightning, or meteors – were said to reflect, or even foretell, major events happening on earth: a character in Shakespeare's *Julius Caesar* declares that 'The heavens themselves blaze forth the death of princes'. This idea recurs frequently in *Henry IV Part 1*.

Now that the King and his country are enjoying peace – even though it is a 'frighted peace' – it is possible for Henry to look forward to a project which is very dear to his heart: he longs to lead a crusade to the Holy Land, so that his Christian soldiers will 'chase these pagans [the Turks] in those holy fields'. This will not be a holiday but a pilgrimage, in which Henry Bolingbroke can try to atone for his sin in usurping the throne of England and causing the death of the rightful king, Richard II. He has cherished this plan for at least a year ('our purpose now is twelve month old'); but he is still frustrated.

When Westmoreland tells of the Council meeting which was interrupted because new fighting had broken out, we (audience or readers) become more conscious of the tense political situation. In Wales 'the noble Mortimer' has suffered defeat, and further north 'the gallant Hotspur' has been doing battle with 'brave Archibald', th Earl of Douglas. This news must bring gloom – but there is fres information: the Scots have been defeated, and Hotspur has won y another 'gallant prize'.

When Westmoreland agrees that Hotspur has made a nob conquest, he uses an unfortunate expression: 'It is a conquest for prince to boast of'. The word 'prince' reminds King Henry of his ow son, Prince Hal, who is a great disappointment to his father. This is th first comparison of Hotspur and Prince Hal, and it should prepare ι for one of the most important aspects of *Henry IV Part 1*: through th constant contrast of the two, Shakespeare is able to examine th personalities of both (but especially of the Prince of Wales); and he als seems to be posing the question: 'What are the qualities that make good king?'

SCENE 2   In the first scene King Henry spoke of his son's 'riot and dishonour the second scene shows what he means by this. In a very relaxe atmosphere (quite unlike the formality which precedes it), Prince Hal i chatting to his best friend, Sir John Falstaff. Their conversation is light hearted, and full of jokes (especially puns – which play with the tw meanings of a word). Falstaff (see p. 000) has a very quick, inventiv mind; it is usually he who begins the word-play, and the young Princ tries hard to match the older man's wit. But when Falstaff suggests a illegal action – robbing travellers on the way to London – the Prince i unwilling to join his friend. He does, however, agree to the propos: made by Poins that the two of them should waylay Falstaff after hi robbery. In this way the young Prince can have the fun of law-breakinç and yet do no harm.

The scene ends with a soliloquy in which Prince Hal – who is no* alone on the stage – speaks aloud his thoughts. He knows that hi companions are not suitable friends for a prince, and that his ow behaviour attracts serious criticism. But for the time being, he intend to have his fun and 'awhile uphold The unyok'd humour of [their idleness'. Eventually, however, he will reform and 'throw off' his presen 'loose behaviour' in such a way that he will be praised and admired fo his reformation.

It is not easy to be sure how Shakespeare intends us to react to thi speech. Some people regard Hal as a cold, scheming hypocrite, who ha no real feeling for those whom he calls his friends and is simply makinç use of them until it pleases him to drop them and forget all about them I personally feel that Hal must be a very *lonely* young man: his positio as heir to the throne sets him apart from other men, and however much he wants to be like them, he can never escape from his heritage. Even when he is at ease, laughing with Falstaff, some of the jokes refer to his inescapable future: 'were it not here apparent that thou art heir apparent . . .'. Prince Hal knows that he must soon reject his friends and take upon himself the responsibilities of his position – but not yet! He feels unready – and certainly unwilling – to leave his youthful, irresponsible lifestyle; perhaps he is trying to justify to himself the reasons for his failure to reform?

The verse of this soliloquy makes a sharp contrast with the prose in which the rest of this scene is written, and the contrast emphasizes the importance of Hal's thoughts. It is in fact the only speech of its kind in the whole play. We never again see so deeply into Hal's mind and heart – and no other character shows such depth of thought and feeling.

SCENE 3   The scene and mood change again when we meet the third set of characters in the play – those who will soon show themselves as rebels against the King. As he promised at the end of Scene 1, King Henry has sent for Hotspur, and now the angry King confronts his mutinous subjects – the Earls of Northumberland and Worcester, and young Hotspur. The King reminds them that he is their ruler, 'Mighty and to be fear'd'; and in response Worcester reminds the King that he achieved his position only with their assistance. This short exchange recalls the past revolt, when Bolingbroke deposed Richard II; and it also prepares for what is to come.

The Earl of Northumberland is not so antagonistic towards the King, and both he and his son (Hotspur) try to pacify their enraged monarch. Hotspur tries to explain the circumstances of his refusal to surrender the prisoners, and his speech brings a lightness – even comedy – into a tense situation. But the King's suspicions are not so easily satisfied. He repeats his demand for the prisoners, and also, even more forcefully, his refusal 'To ransom home revolted Mortimer'. Hotspur is passionate in his defence of Mortimer as a loyal and valiant soldier who had fought nobly for the King. Tempers rise again, and Henry leaves the stage with a threat: 'Send us your prisoners, or you will hear of it'.

After the King has gone, Hotspur demonstrates the fiery spirit that has earned his nickname. Apparently the young man is ignorant of Edmund Mortimer's claims to the throne (see p. 000), and of the part played by his own uncle and his father (Worcester and

Northumberland) in establishing Henry Bolingbroke as King of England. Now he refers to the deposed Richard as 'that sweet lovely rose', and contrasts the present king by referring to 'this thorn, this canker Bolingbroke'. The 'rose' imagery is significant, because in the elaborate system of 'correspondences' which the Elizabethans loved the *rose* was held to be head of the flower hierarchy – the 'king' among flowers – and therefore an appropriate emblem for the human king.

The passionate outburst also shows Hotspur's devotion to the ideals of 'honour' (which for him means military glory), which is in complete contrast to his uncle's cold, calculated scheming. Hotspur is slow to understand Worcester's intentions, but the older man is patient: he knows that the valiant Hotspur is essential to the scheme. At last Hotspur appears to comprehend – and of course he is eager to join in the fighting which must follow:

> O, let the hours be short
> Till fields, and blows, and groans applaud our sport.

ACT 2

SCENE 1   In the Elizabethan theatre there were no curtains to separate the audience from the stage, and no artificial lighting; consequently there were no sudden breaks (such as we are accustomed to nowadays) in the movement of the play. So Hotspur would leave at one side of the stage, following the conspirators with his longing for *action* – and at the other side of the stage there would appear the two Carriers, yawning and scratching their fleabites as they prepare for another day's work. When the robber Gadshill talks to the inn's Chamberlain we hear of another conspiracy, which is also carefully plotted.

SCENE 2   This scene flows smoothly into Scene 2, where Prince Hal and Poins play tricks on their fat friend, Sir John Falstaff. The knight's anger at the loss of his horse turns to boyish delight when he can join in the robbery (although he seems to do little more than encourage the real thieves by shouting insults at their victims). When the disguised Prince and Poins attack the 'true thieves', there is no word from Falstaff, but the stage-direction in the earliest editions suggests that he is not quite so afraid as the others: '*They all run away, and Falstaff after a blow or two runs away too*'. But the best part of the joke will come when they all meet together at the tavern in Eastcheap.

SCENE 3   Before we can enjoy this comedy, however, we must return to the serious business of the play. The scene changes to the north of England, where Hotspur is reading a letter. It is clear that there are problems, but Hotspur dismisses these with humorous impatience. The writer of the letter (we never learn his identity) is refusing to join the rebels. He tries to persuade Hotspur that the undertaking is dangerous – but this does not deter the fiery young revolutionary who scoffs: 'Why, that's certain; 'tis dangerous to take a cold, to sleep, to drink'. But although we laugh with Hotspur, we also become aware of the foolishness of the rebellion, and of the danger which the rebels are in. Hotspur recognizes the danger – but pretends to laugh at it: 'Hang him, let him tell the King! We are prepared'.

This sounds like bold defiance – but when we hear the words of Hotspur's wife we realize that her husband is more anxious than he will admit. Lady Percy – Kate – is distressed because her husband shows symptoms of acute depression (although of course he will not admit that he is worried). He has no appetite for food, he sleeps badly, and he has no sexual desires – for the past two weeks Kate has been 'A banish'd woman from [her] Harry's bed', but she has heard him talking in his troubled sleep. Lady Percy's tenderness for her husband suggests that there is another aspect of Hotspur's character – one that the play has not so far revealed: as well as being hot-tempered and impetuous (but not without a sense of humour) he is a man who is dearly loved by his wife.

Hotspur, however, ignores Kate's pleadings; or else he does not hear them – his mind is fixed on the business he must now deal with, and he calls for his horse. But when the servant has left them alone, the husband and wife play a short scene of delightful intimacy, where Hotspur refuses to give serious answers to Kate's questions and she, in loving desperation, offers a lover's threat: 'I'll break thy little finger, Harry'.

Their parting shows a rather more mature Hotspur than we have seen before. He teases Kate, but explains that this is not a time to spend in making love; he loves and trusts his wife – but he believes that women are weak and may be easily tempted: 'constant you are, But yet a woman'. But he promises that she shall join him, and they will not be separated for long: 'Today will I set forth, tomorrow you'.

SCENE 4   The gentle emotion of this scene gives way to some of the finest comedy in the whole play – in what is also (perhaps) the play's most serious scene. The opening is slow. Prince Hal has been drinking in

the tavern cellars at Eastcheap in London, where he and Poir
arranged to meet Falstaff and the other thieves after the robbery a
Gad's Hill. Hal is absurdly proud that he has won the approval of th
inn's apprentice-lads – the Drawers; but at the same time he realiz
that this kind of behaviour is degrading, very much beneath th
dignity of a future king: 'I have sounded the very base-string of
humility'.

Hal has devised a trick to play on the slow-witted apprentic
Francis. It is not a very clever joke; even Poins seems unable t
appreciate the fun, having to ask the Prince to explain what it is abor
('come, what's the issue?'). Hal, however, seems to be almost drunk
and certainly without any serious worries. When Falstaff enters th
fun begins. Pretending to ignore the Prince, the fat knight lamen
the state of the world, which is full of cowards who will not keep the
promises. When Hal at last interrupts him, Falstaff turns his attac
on the Prince. After a short verbal combat with Hal, Falstaff starts t
demonstrate his greatest accomplishment: he is the master of *lies*!

The comedy increases as the number of the 'rogues in buckrar
increases. All the time, Falstaff protests his honesty – if he is lying, h
is 'an Ebrew Jew', 'a bunch of radish', and 'no two-legged creature'. A
the time, of course, Prince Hal, with Poins (and the audience c
readers), knows the real truth.

When Falstaff makes an obvious mistake, the Prince challeng
his story: 'how couldst thou know these men in Kendal green when
was so dark thou couldst not see thy hand?' Anyone but Falsta
would certainly be embarrassed by such a question – but Sir John
not easily upset. By now it is very clear that he too knows what ha
happened: he is taking part in the joke to please the Prince, an
instead of trying to hide from 'this open and apparent shame', h
offers a comical reason for his behaviour: 'I was now a coward upo
instinct'.

The laughter is interrupted by the arrival of the King's messenge
bringing information that war has been declared, and summonir
Hal to the interview with his father when (as Falstaff knows) he wi
be severely reprimanded ('horribly chid') for his present conduc
There is a feeling that this is the last time the friends will be togethe
in such a relaxed, carefree, happiness. To make the most of it, Princ
Hal and Falstaff amuse themselves (and the spectators in the tavern
by acting in fun the scene which will soon become serious – th
Prince's interview with King Henry IV.

First, Falstaff plays the part of the King, reproaching Hal for hi unseemly conduct and unsuitable friends, but singling out for praise one 'virtuous man' who is 'A goodly portly man . . . of a cheerful look, a pleasing eye, and a most noble carriage'. This is Falstaff's defence of himself, expressed in eloquent prose which has many of the Elizabethan beauties of language (although, of course, the comedy of the situation turns these rhetorical devices into parody). But when Falstaff has finished speaking in self-defence, Hal 'deposes' him – taking from him the stool that was his 'throne' and the 'leaden dagger' that he used as a 'golden sceptre'. Now Hal speaks as though he were the King, and he makes an accusation of Falstaff – the 'old fat man' – with surprising violence. These different descriptions of Falstaff demand that we should reconsider our own views of the character. Is he simply 'old and merry' – a good companion who is always ready to share a drink and a joke? Or is he in fact a 'villainous abominable misleader of youth'?

Falstaff ends his defence of himself with a declaration which, though spoken apparently in fun, is received with the utmost seriousness. 'Banish plump Jack, and banish all the world'. The actor who plays the part of Prince Hal now has a very difficult choice to make: how shall he speak the Prince's next words? Whatever intonation he chooses, I think there should be a pause after 'I will'. The other characters wait in embarrassed silence to hear how Falstaff will turn *this* situation into comedy. And Falstaff himself (for the first – and only – time in the play) does not have a ready answer. He knows that with these words, Hal has pronounced a sentence of banishment on 'old Jack Falstaff'.

Before Falstaff can make any response, the tension of the situation is broken by the knocking at the door. The sheriff has come to charge Falstaff with the Gad's Hill robbery. For the time being, everything returns to its normal state: Falstaff hides; Hal protects his friend, and promises to settle the damage – and more: 'The money shall be paid back again with advantage'.

But there is a sense that, 'betimes in the morning', things will be very different.

ACT 3

SCENE 1   While we have been laughing in the tavern, the King's enemies have been gathering forces; now their leaders have met together in Wales.

Owen Glendower makes his first appearance in the play. The references to him in earlier scenes should have prepared us for a rather unusual character – he was described as 'irregular and wild' the play's first scene (line 40); and at another time King Henry spol of 'that great magician, damn'd Glendower' (Act 1, Scene 3, 82). Th man himself believes that he has magic powers, and tries to impre Hotspur by telling of the mysteries that surrounded his birth, and his wonderful skills: 'I can call spirits from the vasty deep'. He us 'call' in a technical sense (meaning 'conjure up'), but Hotspur refus to be impressed and responds with humorous commonsens pretending that 'call' has its usual meaning:

> Why, so can I, or can any man;
> But will they come when you do call for them?

This amusing interlude is the preface to some very serious busines

The rebels plan to divide between them the united kingdom England and Wales so that (after they have defeated King Henry I each of the three leaders (Mortimer, Hotspur, and Glendower) w rule over one-third of the land. An Elizabethan audience wou know immediately that it is very wrong to make any such division and the argument between Hotspur and Glendower gives a hint the kind of territorial disputes that would inevitably follow a partition. But for the moment the dispute is not serious, and the tw are easily calmed.

Glendower goes to find the ladies, leaving Mortimer an Worcester to reprove Hotspur for his lack of respect. The scene en with music, and the teasing tenderness of Hotspur and his wife, Kat

SCENE 2   Meanwhile in London the King has been making *his* preparations f war; and this is the day for the interview with his elder son, the Prin of Wales. Remembering the comedy of the mock-interview wit Falstaff, we become even more sensitive to the solemnity of th present scene.

King Henry speaks more in sorrow than anger as he reproach Hal for his wild behaviour; his distress and disappointment in h son make him believe that God is angry with him, and perhaps usir Hal as a means of punishing the 'mistreadings' of the past (i.e. h usurpation of the throne of England). Hal humbly asks for h father's forgiveness, confessing that there is *some* truth in th accusations made against him. The King grants pardon ('Go pardon thee!'), but insists upon giving a lecture to Hal, pointing ou the difference between his own conduct as a young man, and th present conduct of his son. He compares Prince Hal to the foolis

Richard II, whose crown Henry now wears: this should be a warning to the Prince, who will inherit the crown and must develop the sense of responsibility which will make him fit to wear it. Henry finally speaks of Hotspur, whose fine military career (like that of the King himself) seems to entitle him – rather than Prince Hal – to be the next heir to the throne:

> He hath more worthy interest to the state
> Than thou the shadow of succession.

This comparison seems to hurt Hal, especially when his father speaks of the advance of the rebels and of his feeling that Prince Hal, more than the Percy family, is his 'nearest and dearest enemy'. Hal reassures his father; and we can see that the time has come when (as he promised at the end of Act 1, Scene 2) he will 'throw off' his 'loose behaviour' and present himself as he really is – a worthy successor to Henry IV.

The King trusts his son at last; and the scene ends as he gives marching orders to meet the rebels at Shrewsbury.

SCENE 3   At the Boar's Head tavern, Falstaff is examining his life and (like Prince Hal) vowing to repent. But we cannot believe *him* as we believe the Prince: Falstaff's repentance is due to his 'hangover' after the heavy drinking of the previous night, and Bardolph observes that he is 'fretful'. Yet Falstaff is still in command of his inventive wit, and he cheers up when he starts abusing the redfaced Bardolph with amazing insults. For a short time Falstaff is in control of the situation, as he insults Bardolph and argues with the Hostess; but all the characters have to become sober again when Prince Hal enters with Peto. A stage-direction in the early editions describes how Falstaff should greet the Prince – '*playing upon his truncheon like a fife*'. This direction may have been written by Shakespeare himself, and it shows yet another quick move on the part of Falstaff. Just before the Prince's entrance, Falstaff was threatening to beat Hal: 'and he were here I would cudgel him like a dog'. Presumably he raised his 'truncheon' as he spoke the line; but on the arrival of the Prince he turns the weapon into an imagined musical instrument.

The same stage-direction instructs the Prince that he is to enter '*marching*'; and Falstaff immediately realizes what this means; 'Is the wind in that door, i'faith? Must we all march?'. Very quickly (but still with comedy) all the problems created by the Gad's Hill robbery are sorted out; the episode is finished. Arrangements are made for the

next, more serious, engagement; then Prince Hal leaves the tavern w
the heroic words:

> The land is burning, Percy stands on high,
> And either we or they must lower lie.

It is a fine battle-cry, and Falstaff applauds it. But he will not follow t
Prince until he has eaten his breakfast.

Act 4

SCENE 1   The fourth act is an act of *preparation*, in which we witness all t
different characters making their plans for war. The first scene is set
the rebel camp, where Hotspur and the Earl of Douglas are exchangi
compliments. In the first scene of the play we heard how Hotsp
encountered Douglas as an enemy and defeated him at the battle
Holmedon – but now the enmity is forgotten as the two warriors jo
forces against King Henry. Hotspur's pleasure in his new ally soon gi
way to disappointment when he hears – by letter – that his father
'grievous sick' and cannot join in the fighting. At first Hotspur is ang
thinking of the effect his father's absence will have; but he quic
decides how to turn this apparent loss of support into a positi
advantage to the rebels.

He maintains his confidence when news is brought of the Kin
approaching army, although this sounds very much more power
than his own forces. He asks scornfully about Prince Hal, 'The nimb
footed madcap Prince of Wales'. Vernon replies, giving a br
description of the splendid appearance of the King's army; and then
speaks about 'young Harry'. He seems to describe a very differe
character from the one we are already familiar with: this is the ne
reformed, Prince of Wales – a glamorous knight in glittering armo
who seems more like a Greek god ('feather'd Mercury') than a hum
being.

If he is dismayed by this account, Hotspur tries to hide his feelin
and urge his supporters to fight. But there is one more piece of b
news: the Welsh Glendower will not be fighting with the rebels becau
he is still unprepared for war – 'He cannot draw his power this fourte
days'.

Hotspur speaks brave words as he leaves the stage, but it is alrea
clear to him (and to us) that the rebellion is doomed to failure. Dougl
tells him to 'Talk not of dying'; but Hotspur makes no reply.

SCENE 2   The gloom of Scene 1 is quickly lightened at the start of Scene 2 when Falstaff gives an account of his conscription techniques, confessing at once that he has 'misused the King's press damnably'. The king's authority allowed him to conscript into his regiment any man he chose; and Falstaff chose only those men who were willing and able to bribe him so that he would release them from the service. Consequently his regiment now consists only of miserable wretches who are not even properly clothed. When Prince Hal sees them, he is horrified: 'I did never see such pitiful rascals'. But Falstaff has no pity, dismissing them contemptuously as 'food for powder'.

   It seems probable (since there is no stage-direction for them) that these poor 'scarecrows' do not appear on the stage. If the audience were to *see* them, the scene would lose much of its comedy – and Falstaff would lose some of the audience's sympathy. But the scene changes quickly; and we are back in the rebel camp again.

SCENE 3   While the rebels are arguing about the best time to start fighting, they are interrupted by the arrival of Sir Walter Blunt with a final offer of peace from the King. King Henry has asked for a full statement of their grievances, so once again we are reminded of the historical circumstances: the usurping of the crown by Henry Bolingbroke, and the murder of Richard II. The battle is postponed.

   The Archbishop of York is also one of the rebel 'confederacy', and in this short scene we learn from him that many of the King's opponents have not presented themselves on the battlefield at Shrewsbury. This is a very useful scene. The Archbishop and Sir Michael are not important characters, and so our attention is not at all distracted from what they say. They repeat the names of those who have joined Hotspur and the other rebels to fight against the King; and the Archbishop names the different leaders of King Henry's forces.

   In addition to this useful roll-call of the opposing sides, the Archbishop voices a fear for the future:

> if Lord Percy thrive not, ere the King
> Dismiss his power he means to visit us.

The fighting at Shrewsbury will bring *Henry IV Part 1* to an end; but this will not be the end of his troubles for King Henry IV: Shakespeare is in possession of enough material for *Henry IV Part 2*.

Act 5

SCENE 1   Now we are ready for the battle at Shrewsbury, where even
the weather seems to be disturbed by the preparations for war. But
before the fighting starts the King makes yet another offer of peace
and Worcester restates the grievances of the rebels. In the hope of
avoiding total war Prince Hal suggests a token combat, in which he
alone will fight with Hotspur; but the King can see that this would
not be an adequate solution. He makes his final peace offer.

Both the King and his son are shown to good advantage in the
debate with Worcester. Henry IV seems ready to forgive and forget
the faults of the rebels who have created this terrible situation of
'pellmell havoc and confusion'. Prince Hal is noble and modest in
praising Hotspur; he shows compassion when he refers to the
soldiers, in both armies, who will suffer if the fighting starts; and his
challenge to Hotspur is brave without being boastful. He speaks
wisely after the King's offer of peace, knowing that 'It will not be
accepted'. Falstaff tries to detain the Prince as he is leaving the stage,
but Hal refuses to waste time. After a quick joke, he is gone.

Falstaff is now left alone on the stage, contemplating the thought
of the battle which must soon be fought. During the course of the
play a great deal has been spoken about 'honour' – the kind that is
won by courage and strength in fighting. Hotspur, of course, is the
chief authority on the subject: the first time he appeared in the play
he extolled the subject with exaggerated terms of praise:

> By heaven, methinks it were an easy leap
> To pluck bright honour from the pale-fac'd moon . . .
>   (Act 1, Scene 3, lines 199 f)

Now Falstaff is going to say a few words on the matter, but he speaks
in prose. His language is simple and colloquial, contrasting sharply
with Hotspur's passionate rhetoric; and in the same way, Falstaff's
ideas about 'honour' are very different from those of the young man.
Hotspur will give all for 'honour' – but Falstaff can find no practical
value 'in that word "honour"' and so he dismisses the whole concept:
'Therefore I'll none of it'.

SCENE 2   As well as lightening the atmosphere, Falstaff's speech has allowed
the Earl of Worcester and his companion, Vernon, to cross the
battlefield from the King's camp. We meet them again as they are
approaching the tents of the rebels.

Worcester and Vernon are still discussing the King's 'liberal and kind offer' of peace, but Worcester does not trust King Henry. Perhaps he is right to be suspicious – but he is wrong not to tell the truth when he reports on his mission. He lies to them: 'The King will bid you battle presently'. When he tells Hotspur of the challenge to single combat with Prince Hal, it is clear that he intends to make Hotspur even more angry – and he almost succeeds in doing this. Hotspur wants to know *how* the challenge was made: 'How show'd his tasking? Seem'd it in contempt?'. But Worcester is prevented from answering by Vernon's quick interruption, and Vernon describes exactly how Prince Hal spoke his challenge: 'I never in my life Did hear a challenge urg'd more modestly'. He continues in his praise of the Prince, and his words seem to foretell not only the noble reformation of the Prince of Wales, but also his future greatness as King Henry V.

Hotspur is not worried by this praise of Hal; indeed, he seems almost amused at Vernon's enthusiasm, and he looks forward to the time when he will 'embrace [Prince Hal] with a soldier's arm' – and kill him. Now the battle must commence. Hotspur speaks a few words to the assembled troops, insisting that he does not have 'the gift of tongue'; at last he draws his sword, and with his family's war-cry of 'Esperance! Percy!' he leads the rebels into battle.

SCENE 3 We now witness the honourable (and dishonourable) deeds that are done in war. Blunt is protecting his King by his disguise, as well as by his fighting; Hotspur recognizes and praises the valour of an old enemy (Douglas) and a new one ('A gallant knight he was, his name was Blunt'); and Prince Hal will make a fresh charge against the 'vaunting enemies'. But Falstaff has 'led [his] ragamuffins where they are peppered', and he is proud of it! This was a fairly common practice: a corrupt captain would take his men into a dangerous situation and leave them there to be killed – and then keep their wages for himself.

Falstaff can still make us laugh, however; and we are once again compelled to question the ideal of military honour when Falstaff contemplates the dead body of the valiant Blunt, with the words 'I like not such grinning honour as Sir Walter hath. Give me life . . .'

SCENE 4 The division of the play into 'scenes' can sometimes be misleading. The stage-direction here (*Alarum. Excursions.*) shows that there is no real break between Scenes 3 and 4; the fighting is continuous, and in

the theatre the actors, flourishing their swords, cross constantly fro
one side of the stage to the other. When the conversation starts on
more, we find that the King and a few of his supporters have cor
together for a brief moment.

Both the sons of the King – Prince Hal and Lord John – have be
fighting bravely, and their father is proud and delighted. He fails
persuade Hal to retire to his tent, even though the Prince is wound
and bleeding. It is in this scene that the Prince of Wales will show l
true worth – as a son (when he rescues his father from the Earl
Douglas); as a knight (in his encounter with Hotspur); and as
friend (in his treatment of Falstaff).

In the interview with Prince Hal (Act 3, Scene 2) the King admitt
his fear that his son might even join the rebels and fight against him

> Thou . . . art like enough, through vassal fear,
> Base inclination, and the start of spleen,
> To fight against me under Percy's pay.   (124–

At that time, the Prince could use only *words* to express his loyalty
his father; but now his *sword* speaks even more powerfully for him.
is the complete reconciliation of father and son.

Now Prince Hal must meet Hotspur. At first the two a
cautiously polite – like two tigers, circling round each other befo
they start to fight. It is certainly a fight for mastery: much is at sta
in this duel, as both the combatants know:

> Two stars keep not the motion in one sphere,
> Nor can one England brook a double reign
> Of Harry Percy and the Prince of Wales.

Soon the time for courtesy is past, and Hotspur attacks Hal. Whi
they are fighting, Falstaff arrives on the scene and – as though he we
the spectator at a prize-fight – proceeds to shout encouragement
the Prince until he is himself surprised by a sudden attack from tl
Earl of Douglas. At almost the same moment, both Falstaff ar
Hotspur, mortally wounded, fall to the ground.

Hotspur speaks a few last words, lamenting the loss of his hono
– 'those proud titles' – more than the loss of his life. In the middle
a sentence, his voice breaks off and he dies. Prince Hal completes tl
sentence, clearly moved by the death of this 'great heart'. He does n
triumph over his dead enemy, but instead shows tend
magnanimity as he covers Hotspur's face with the 'favours' – the sil
or plumes – which he wears on his own helmet.

As the turns away from the dead Hotspur, Hal sees another body lying on the ground. His reaction is very interesting: 'could not all this flesh Keep in a little life?'. He makes one of his usual jokes about Falstaff's size, but the laughter has turned to grief. Yet Hal can find few words to speak of his friend; he has spoken so much – with deep feeling – about his enemy. His speech is rich with puns (on 'heavy', 'deer', and 'in blood'), which suggests that he is trying to conceal, rather than express, his sorrow.

But there is no need for sorrow! An audience watching the play (if not the readers of the book) can experience joyful surprise when the fat knight waits until the stage is empty, and then lumbers to his feet with words that (in Falstaff's usual manner) seize upon the Prince's puns and extend them: 'If thou embowel me today, I'll give you leave to powder me and eat me too tomorrow'. Once again, Falstaff turns a scene that would otherwise have been heroic – or even tragic – into comedy. He has a few words to say on the subject of 'valour' and these, together with his treatment of the dead Hotspur, insist that we make a comparison between Falstaff and the Prince of Wales, and examine our ideas of 'valour'.

Falstaff has already explained to the audience how he managed to extricate himself from a difficult situation when he was attacked by 'that hot termagant Scot', the Earl of Douglas. Characteristically, he escaped by means of falsehood – by *acting* a lie and pretending to be dead. Now, when he encounters Prince Hal and Lord John, he exaggerates the lie to monstrous proportions when he claims to have been merely resting, so that he could rise refreshed to fight for 'a long hour by Shrewsbury clock', killing Hotspur at the end of the hour. Lord John is astounded, but the Prince seems to be amused: he can still share a joke with Falstaff, even though he is now no longer the same 'lad of mettle' that he was in the tavern in Eastcheap (Act 2, Scene 4, 12).

A serious note returns as the play ends. King Henry IV confronts the defeated rebels, reproaching Worcester and condemning him to death. Prince Hal once more shows his great generosity of spirit when he requests life and freedom for the Earl of Douglas. The fighting is over: but the war is not yet won. King Henry must now divide the troops, sending one detachment northwards to York while he and the Prince Hal lead the other soldiers into Wales. The success at Shrewsbury has given the King confidence, so that he can at last promise

> Rebellion in this land shall lose his sway,
> Meeting the check of such another day.

Sir John Falstaff

Falstaff is the character who has always attracted more attention th
any of Shakespeare's other creations: even Queen Elizabeth I, it
reported, was so entertained by him that she demanded another p
in which she could see the fat knight in love. Shakespeare satisfied
by writing *The Merry Wives of Windsor*. All the great critics ha
written about Falstaff, but none has shown more sympathe
appreciation than Dr Samuel Johnson, the eighteenth-century edit
of Shakespeare's plays, and his account of Falstaff is printed on pa
xxx of this edition.

Falstaff is a very complex character, and a different aspect is sho
every time he appears. His quick wit, however, is constant: he ne
ceases to provoke laughter – which is very often directed at hims
and especially at his bulk. The first impression (when he appears
Act 1, Scene 2) is of a great, carefree, jester, who cares nothing for
dreary routine of everyday life. Prince Hal seems almost envious wh
he asks, 'What a devil hast thou to do with the time of day?'. Falstaf
relationship with the Prince is relaxed and easy; he seems to have
almost *fatherly* regard for the young man when he addresses him
'sweet wag', and plays verbal games with him – which he allows Hal
win, conceding victory with 'Thou hast the most unsavouriest simil
and art indeed the most comparative, rascalliest, sweet young prin

This admission of affection is speedily followed by a moc
reproach, when Falstaff chooses to see *himself* in the role of the you
innocent, led astray by the 'sweet young prince' who is now 'able
corrupt a saint'. Here Falstaff demonstrates another of his pecul
skills as he adopts a religious manner of speech (with freque
reference to the Bible). The comedy lies not only in the words, but
the contrast between the speech (full of sham piety) and the speak
(full of real mischief).

The lighthearted tone of this scene draws attention away from t
faults, crimes, and sins of Falstaff. His gluttony and drunkenness a
subjects for witty amusement; and his thieving activities a
dismissed as the work of 'Diana's foresters, gentlemen of the shad
To Falstaff, villainy is merely excitement – although he does see
rather sensitive when Hal introduces the subject of prison cloth
'What a plague have I to do with a buff jerkin?'.

The robbers' conspiracy is planned with the enthusiasm of boys who play at being highwaymen; and when Falstaff abuses the victims at Gad's Hill, it is impossible to feel sympathy for the defrauded travellers. Here the comedy resides in Falstaff's wonderfully inventive insults – 'whoreson caterpillars, bacon-fed knaves' – and also in the contrast of speech and speaker as the old man declares 'They hate us youth'.

Before the actual robbery, Falstaff speaks out to the audience, cursing Prince Hal for having stolen his horse, thus compelling him to shift his enormous weight on foot. Falstaff frequently delivers such speeches: they are not soliloquies in the usual sense, because the character is not speaking aloud his inner thoughts. Falstaff knows that he is being listened to, and his speech is intended to create an effect on the audience: it has much more in common with the 'patter' of a modern comedian (on stage or television) than with the sensitive broodings of a character like Hamlet – or Prince Hal when he murmurs to himself 'I know you all . . .' (Act 1, Scene 2, lines 197 ff.).

After the 'real' robbery, the Prince and Poins attack the robbers, who offer no serious resistance before they run away. In the Eastcheap tavern we wait to share in the grand joke that Poins has promised:

> The virtue of this jest will be the incomprehensible lies that this same fat rogue will tell us when we meet at supper: how thirty at least he fought with; what wards, what blows, what extremities he endured; and in the reproof of this lies the jest.
>
> (Act 1, Scene 2, 187–92)

Everything happens as Poins promised. Falstaff pours out lies, excuses, explanations, and insults, in an apparently endless explosion of invention whose climax comes when the Prince at last accuses him of cowardice. Hal, having given a brief account of the attack on the would-be robbers – two against four – charges Falstaff with having 'roared for mercy, and still run and roared'. He waits for an explanation – and it is quickly given: 'By the Lord, I knew ye as well as he that made ye'. And Falstaff wriggles (verbally) out of another dilemma with the grand defence that he was 'a coward on instinct'.

The episode can, I think, be taken in one of two ways. Perhaps Falstaff, like Bardolph and the others, *was* decived on Gad's Hill when the disguised Hal and Poins attacked them; and perhaps he is boasting about his valour in the encounter with the 'buckram men' and the 'knaves in Kendal green'. Certainly Bardolph and Peto were

genuinely afraid of their attackers, and they ran away in fear. B
neither of these is particularly intelligent, and they do what they a
told to do: Bardolph admits freely, 'I ran when I saw others run'. B
was *Falstaff* so easily deceived?

Perhaps he recognized the Prince and Poins (despite their 'vizar
and their 'cases of buckram'), and joined in the joke?

At Gad's Hill no one was seriously hurt: but this is not the case
Shrewsbury. Falstaff callously admits – again in a speech addressed
the theatre audience – that he has 'led [his] ragamuffins where th
are peppered', so that of his original conscripts 'there's not three
my hundred and fifty left alive', and these are so badly wounded th
they can have no hopes for the future – 'they are for the town's en
to beg during life'. And Falstaff will pocket the money intended f
the soldier's pay.

This is not a *sudden* change in Falstaff. Gradually, throughout tl
play, we have been shown that there is indeed an unpleasant side
his character: he can be selfish, and cruel. He tries to cheat tl
Hostess at Eastcheap, who laments 'you owe me money, Sir John, ar
now you pick a quarrel to beguile me of it' (Act 3, Scene 3, 68–9). F
boasts of his cleverness in conscripting (initially) only those me
who were able to buy themselves out of his army, acknowledging
without any shame – that he has 'misused the King's press damnabl
making more than three hundred pounds profit for himself.

Such a man – dishonest, selfish, and with no thought for tl
welfare, or even the lives, of those for whom he should be responsib
– is not a very suitable companion for the Prince of Wales, the futu
King of England. But Hal is perhaps thinking most of all abou
Falstaff when he muses at the end of Act 1, Scene 2

> I know you all, and will awhile uphold
> The unyok'd humour of your idleness.

In the hilarious scene in the tavern at Eastcheap, the Prince shov
that he understands what he has to do when he promises that he w:
indeed 'Banish plump Jack, and banish all the world'.

In this scene the Prince, when he speaks in the person of his fath
and denounces the 'old fat man', refers to Falstaff as 'that reverer
vice'. This description should make Falstaff's role perfectly clear – t
an Elizabethan audience!

Before the drama became commercialized, with the building c
theatres in London and the rise of the new profession of playwright
the people of England got much of their dramatic entertainme:

from groups of strolling actors. These wandered around the country, carrying their costumes and properties, and performing a small repertoire of short pieces often known as 'Morality Plays'. As the name implies, these plays were didactic, teaching some kind of moral; and most frequently they told of a young man (perhaps even called 'Youth') who had to make a choice between right and wrong – between a good life, which would lead to heaven, and a bad one, which became the pathway to hell. His choice was always made more difficult by the presence in the play of a figure called 'The Vice', whose function was to tempt the young man and lead him away from the life of virtue. Audiences would never have had any difficulty in identifying the Vice character (whatever his name in the play) because he always carried a short, cheap dagger, usually made of wood. The Vice was in fact a 'villainous abominable misleader of youth'; and these are the words used to describe Falstaff in Act 2, Scene 4.

Sir John Falstaff: an appreciation by Dr Samuel Johnson

But Falstaff, unimitated, inimitable Falstaff, how shall I descri**b**e thee? Thou compound of sense and vice; of sense which may **be** admired but not esteemed, of vice which may be despised but hard**ly** detested.

Falstaff is a character loaded with faults, and with those fau**lts** which naturally produce contempt. He is a thief, and a glutton, **a** coward, and a boaster, always ready to cheat the weak, and prey up**on** the poor; to terrify the timorous and insult the defenceless. At on**ce** obsequious and malignant, he satirizes in their absence those who**m** he lives by flattering. He is familiar with the Prince only as an age**nt** of vice, but of this familiarity he is so proud as not only to **be** supercilious and haughty with common men, but to think h**is** interest of importance to the Duke of Lancaster.

Yet the man thus corrupt, thus despicable, makes hims**elf** necessary to the Prince that despises him, by the most pleasing of **a** qualities, perpetual gaiety, by an unfailing power of exciting laught**er,** which is the more freely indulged, as his wit is not of the splendid **or** ambitious kind, but consists in easy escapes and sallies of levit**y,** which make sport but raise no envy.

It must be observed that he is stained with no enormous **or** sanguinary crimes, so that his licentiousness is not so offensive b**ut** that it may be borne for his mirth.

[176

Shakespeare's Verse

Blank verse

Shakespeare's plays are mainly written in 'blank verse', the form preferred by most dramatists in the sixteenth and early seventeenth centuries. Blank verse has a regular rhythm, but does not rhyme. It is a very flexible medium, which is capable – like the human speaking voice – of a wide range of tones. Easily the best way to understand and appreciate Shakespeare's verse is to read it aloud – and don't worry if you don't understand everything! Try not to be influenced by the dominant rhythm. Instead, decide which are the most important words in each line and use regular metre to drive them forward to the listeners. Shakespeare used a particular form of blank verse called iambic pentameter.

Iambic pentameter

In iambic pentameter the lines are ten syllables long. Each line is divided into pairs of syllables, or 'feet'. Each 'foot' has one stressed and one unstressed syllable – a pattern that often appears in normal English speech. Here is an example:

> **King**
> So sháken ás we áre, so wán with cáre,
> Find we a tíme for fríghted péace to pánt,
> And bréathe short-wínded áccents óf new bróils
> To bé commén'cd in strónds afár remóte:
> No móre the thírsty éntrance óf this sóil
> Shall dáub her líps with hér own chíldren's blóod;
> No móre shall trénching wár channél her fiélds,
> Nor brúise her flów'rets wíth the ármed hóofs
> Of hóstile páces.

Here the King speaks a verse which is completely regular, expressing his command of the situation and his personal dignity. The verse line sometimes contains the grammatical unit of meaning, thus allowing for a pause at the end of the line before a new idea is started: 'No more shall trenching war channel her fields'. At other times, the sense runs on from one line to the next – 'the armed hoofs/Of hostile paces'. This makes for the natural fluidity of speech, avoiding monotony but still maintaining the iambic rhythm.

Source, Text, and Date

The first part of *Henry IV* was entered in the Stationers' Register 1598, and printed soon afterwards. The play was probably writt and performed a year or two earlier. It may well have been revised Shakespeare, perhaps in 1597, when he changed the name of the knight from 'Oldcastle' to 'Falstaff' because the Lord Chamberla the patron of Shakespeare's company of actors, was descended fro the historical Oldcastle and objected to Shakespeare's portrayal of l ancestor. A trace of the earlier version can possibly be seen in Act Scene 2, where Prince Hal addresses his friend as 'my old lad of t castle' (line 44).

The Quarto edition of 1598 is a well printed text on which modern editions are based.

Henry IV Part 1

Characters in the Play

THE KING

Henry IV   *formerly* Henry Bolingbroke

THE KING'S SONS

Prince Hal   Henry Prince of Wales, *heir to the throne*
Lord John of Lancaster

THE KING'S ALLIES

Earl of Westmoreland
Sir Walter Blunt

REBELS AGAINST THE KING

Earl of Worcester	Thomas Percy
Earl of Northumberland	Henry Percy, Worcester's *brother*
Hotspur	Henry (Harry) Percy, Northumberland's *son*
Edmund Mortimer	Earl of March
Owen Glendower	
Earl of Douglas	Archibald
Archbishop of York	Richard Scroop
Sir Michael	*the* Archbishop's *friend*
Sir Richard Vernon	
Lady Percy (Kate)	Mortimer's *sister*, Hotspur's *wife*
Lady Mortimer	Mortimer's *wife, daughter of* Glendower

PRINCE HAL'S FRIENDS

Sir John Falstaff
Poins
Peto
Bardolph

AT THE TAVERN IN EASTCHEAP

Mistress Quickly   *Hostess of the tavern*
Francis   *Drawer*
Vintner

IN THE INN AT ROCHESTER

Gadshill   *A robber*
Two Carriers
Chamberlain
Ostler

Sheriff, Officers, Messengers, Travellers, Lords, Attendants

Act I

Act 1 Scene 1
King Henry is addressing his supporters.
He hopes that England will continue to
be peaceful, free from the horrors of
civil war. He intends now to lead an
army in a Crusade to Jerusalem, to fight
the pagans (Turks) who are in
possession of the Christian Holy Land.
Westmoreland, however, has brought
bad news of fresh aggression: the
Welsh and the Scots are now attacking
the English – and so the Crusade must
be postponed. The King's nephew,
Hotspur, is being difficult; but Henry
wishes that his own son were like
Hotspur in bravery.

    shaken: upset.
    wan: pale.
    frighted: frightened.
    pant: pause for breath.
    breathe . . . accents: speak
breathlessly.
    broils: quarrels.
    stronds: shores.
    The King hopes that the blood of
Englishmen will never again be shed in
their own motherland.
    trenching: digging trenches
(channels).
    flow'rets: little flowers.
    armed: iron-shod.
    opposed eyes: i.e. the eyes of
opposing armies.
    All of the same sort and
nationality.
    intestine: internal.
    close: meeting (in battle).
    mutual: united.
    well-beseeming: suitable.
    ranks: military order.

Scene 1 *London : the Palace of Westminster*

> *Enter the* King, Lord John of Lancaster,
> Earl of Westmoreland, Sir Walter
> Blunt, *with others*

    King
So shaken as we are, so wan with care,
Find we a time for frighted peace to pant,
And breathe short-winded accents of new broils
To be commenc'd in stronds afar remote:
5 No more the thirsty entrance of this soil
Shall daub her lips with her own children's blood;
No more shall trenching war channel her fields,
Nor bruise her flow'rets with the armed hoofs
Of hostile paces. Those opposed eyes
10 Which, like the meteors of a troubled heaven,
All of one nature, of one substance bred,
Did lately meet in the intestine shock
And furious close of civil butchery,
Shall now, in mutual well-beseeming ranks,

15   March all one way, and be no more oppos'd
Against acquaintance, kindred, and allies.
The edge of war, like an ill-sheathed knife,
No more shall cut his master. Therefore, friends
As far as to the sepulchre of Christ—
20   Whose soldier now, under whose blessed cross
We are impressed and engag'd to fight—
Forthwith a power of English shall we levy,
Whose arms were moulded in their mothers
        womb
To chase these pagans in those holy fields
25   Over whose acres walk'd those blessed feet
Which fourteen hundred years ago were nail'd
For our advantage on the bitter cross.
But this our purpose now is twelve month old,
And bootless 'tis to tell you we will go;
30   Therefor we meet not now. Then let me hear
Of you, my gentle cousin Westmoreland,
What yesternight our Council did decree
In forwarding this dear expedience.

Westmoreland

My liege, this haste was hot in question,
35   And many limits of the charge set down
But yesternight, when all athwart there came
A post from Wales, loaden with heavy news,
Whose worst was that the noble Mortimer,
Leading the men of Herefordshire to fight
40   Against the irregular and wild Glendower,
Was by the rude hands of that Welshman taken
A thousand of his people butchered,
Upon whose dead corpse there was such misuse
Such beastly shameless transformation,
45   By those Welshwomen done, as may not be
Without much shame retold or spoken of.

King

It seems then that the tidings of this broil
Brake off our business for the Holy Land.

Westmoreland

This match'd with other did, my gracious lord,
50   For more uneven and unwelcome news
Came from the north, and thus it did import:
On Holy-rood day, the gallant Hotspur there,
Young Harry Percy, and brave Archibald,

---

15   *all one way :* in the same direction.
16   *acquaintance:* friends.
17   *edge:* sword.
19–22   The King intends to recruit ('levy') an army ('power') of English soldiers and lead them as far as Jerusalem (to the tomb where Christ was buried).
20–21   Henry sees himself as a soldier of Christ, conscripted ('impressed') to fight under the sign of the cross (as soldiers marched behind the banners of their commanders).
27   *for our advantage:* Christians believe that Christ was crucified for the salvation of mankind.
        bitter: cruel.
28   'We have intended to do this for the past year'.
29   *bootless:* unnecessary.
30   *Therefor . . . now:* that is not why we are meeting now.
31   *Of:* from.
        gentle cousin: noble relation (Shakespeare uses the word 'cousin' to refer to any close relation: Westmoreland was in fact married to Henry's half-sister.)
32   *yesternight:* last night.
33   *expedience:* undertaking (which is important – 'dear' – to Henry's heart).

liege: lord.
haste: urgent business.
hot in question: being seriously
discussed.
We had already decided ('set
down') who should have the
responsibility (limit) for many of the
duties ('charge').
all athwart: interrupting,
upsetting.
post: messenger.
heavy: serious, worrying.
Whose worst: the worst of which.
irregular: lawless; Glendower
was fighting guerrilla warfare.
Whose . . . corpse: i.e. the bodies
of the thousand soldiers.
transformation: atrocity.
Brake: broke.
match'd with other: together with
other bad news.
uneven: unpleasant, disturbing.
thus it did import: this is what it
said.

Holy-rood Day: 14 September,
the day of the Christian festival
celebrating the Cross (rood) of Christ.
approved: of proven worth.
Holmedon: see map, p. xxxiv.
'So far as we could tell from the
way they were firing ('artillery' means
arrows and other missiles, as well as
guns) and from the way things seemed
likely to happen'.
them: i.e. the news.
pride of their contention: height of
their battle.
issue: outcome.
lighted: alighted.
Sir Walter's mud-stained clothes
seem to show all the different soils that
he has ridden through to get to London
and the King's palace ('this seat of
ours').
smooth: pleasant.
discomfited: defeated.
Balk'd: overthrown; a 'balk' is
the ridge between two furrows of a
ploughed field—the bodies were piled
in heaps, making furrows through
which their blood drained away.

That ever valiant and approved Scot,
55 At Holmedon met, where they did spend
A sad and bloody hour;
As by discharge of their artillery,
And shape of likelihood, the news was told;
For he that brought them, in the very heat
60 And pride of their contention did take horse,
Uncertain of the issue any way.
  King
Here is a dear, a true industrious friend,
Sir Walter Blunt, new lighted from his horse,
Stain'd with the variation of each soil
65 Betwixt that Holmedon and this seat of ours;
And he hath brought us smooth and welcome
 news.
The Earl of Douglas is discomfited;
Ten thousand bold Scots, two and twenty knights,
Balk'd in their own blood, did Sir Walter see
70 On Holmedon's plains; of prisoners Hotspur took
Mordake, Earl of Fife and eldest son
To beaten Douglas, and the Earl of Athol,
Of Murray, Angus, and Menteith:

74   *spoil*: prize.

75   *In faith*: indeed.

80   'A son who is always the subject when men are talking about honour'.

82   *minion*: darling, favourite.

86–7   There was a popular superstition that the fairies would sometimes steal a beautiful human baby from its cradle, leaving in its place a weak or ugly child (a changeling).

90   *let ... thoughts*: forget about him.

    coz: the abbreviation of 'cousin'.

92   *surpris'd*: captured.

93   *To ... use*: for his own advantage (i.e. so that Hotspur can keep the ransom money instead of giving it to the King).

94   *Mordake*: the earl was of royal blood, so Hotspur was obliged to surrender him to the King.

96   Worcester is spoken of as a planet which, however it appears ('in all aspects') is always hostile ('Malevolent').

97–8   Taught by his uncle, Hotspur is proud and disdainful: he is like a cock, which will preen ('prune') its feathers and erect its comb ('crest') when it intends to fight.

103   *so ... lords*: inform the Council of these facts.

106   'Than I can say in my present anger'.

And is not this an honourable spoil?
75 A gallant prize? ha, cousin, is it not?

Westmoreland   In fai
It is a conquest for a prince to boast of.

King
Yea, there thou mak'st me sad, and mak'st me s
In envy that my Lord Northumberland
Should be the father to so blest a son;
80 A son who is the theme of honour's tongue,
Amongst a grove the very straightest plant,
Who is sweet Fortune's minion and her pride;
Whilst I, by looking on the praise of him,
See riot and dishonour stain the brow
85 Of my young Harry. O that it could be prov'd
That some night-tripping fairy had exchang'd
In cradle-clothes our children where they lay,
And call'd mine Percy, his Plantagenet!
Then would I have his Harry, and he mine:
90 But let him from my thoughts. What think y
    coz,
Of this young Percy's pride? The prisoners
Which he in this adventure hath surpris'd
To his own use he keeps, and sends me word
I shall have none but Mordake, Earl of Fife.

Westmoreland
95 This is his uncle's teaching, this is Worcester,
Malevolent to you in all aspects,
Which makes him prune himself and bristle u
The crest of youth against your dignity.

King
But I have sent for him to answer this;
100 And for this cause awhile we must neglect
Our holy purpose to Jerusalem.
Cousin, on Wednesday next our Council we
Will hold at Windsor, so inform the lords:
But come yourself with speed to us again,
105 For more is to be said and to be done
Than out of anger can be uttered.

Westmoreland
I will, my liege.   [Exe

Act 1 Scene 2

Whilst his father worries about the safety of the country, Prince Hal amuses himself by teasing his friend, Sir John Falstaff. They are joined by another friend, Poins, who tells them he is planning a robbery. When he is alone, Prince Hal offers an explanation for his conduct.

fat-witted: stupid, slow-minded.

sack: Spanish white wine.

unbuttoning thee: loosening your clothes (because he has eaten so much).

5   *that . . . know*: that you have forgotten how to ask properly for what you really want to know.

12   Hal observes that Falstaff is interested only in food, drink, and women.

capons: chickens.

leaping-houses: brothels.

hot: lustful.

taffeta: prostitutes were recognized by their taffeta (stiff silk) petticoats.

superfluous: unnecessary (also 'self-indulgent').

Scene 2 *London: an Apartment of the Prince's in the Royal Palace*

Enter Prince of Wales *and* Sir John Falstaff

Falstaff

Now, Hal, what time of day is it, lad?

Prince

Thou art so fat-witted with drinking of old sack, and unbuttoning thee after supper, and sleep-ing upon benches after noon, that thou hast
5 forgotten to demand that truly which thou wouldst truly know. What a devil has thou to do with the time of the day? Unless hours were cups of sack, and minutes capons, and clocks the tongues of bawds, and dials the signs of leaping-houses, and
10 the blessed sun himself a fair hot wench in flame-coloured taffeta, I see no reason why thou shouldst be so superfluous to demand the time of the day.

13   *you . . . me*: you've hit the mark
(you show that you understand me).

14   *take purses*: are thieves.
     go by the moon: walk by the light
of the moon (i.e. work at night); and
'tell the time by the moon' (not the
sun).
     the seven stars: the stars that form
the constellation Pleiades.

15   *Phœbus . . . fair*: Falstaff is
probably quoting the words of a
popular song: Phœbus Apollo was the
Greek god of the sun.

16   *prithee*: pray you.
     wag: fool, joker.

17   *grace*: Falstaff plays with three
senses of the word: he addresses Hal
properly as 'Your Highness'; refers to
his lack of spiritual grace; and (in line
20) puns on 'grace' as a prayer before a
meal.

20   *troth*: truth, faith.

21   *egg and butter*: a light meal
(Falstaff implies that this needs only a
short grace).

22   *Come, roundly*: come to the point
(explain what you mean).

23   *Marry*: by (the Virgin) Mary (a
very mild oath).

23–5   'Don't let those of us who work
by night be called thieves in the
daytime'. A nobleman's personal
attendants were called 'squires of the
body'; Falstaff makes a pun here with
'night' and 'knight'—also with 'beauty'
and 'booty'.

25   *Diana's foresters*: hunters who
serve Diana—who was goddess of
hunting and of the moon.

26   *gentlemen*: servants of the royal
household were often called
'Gentlemen'.

27   *good government*: *both* 'serving a
good ruler'; *and* 'law-abiding'.

29   *under whose countenance*: *both* 'by
the light of the moon'; *and* 'with the
approval of'.

30   *steal*: walk secretly; *and* thieve.

Falstaff

Indeed, you come near me now, Hal, for we th
take purses go by the moon and the seven star
15 and not 'by Phœbus, he that wand'ring knight
fair'. And I prithee sweet wag, when thou art kin
as God save thy Grace—Majesty, I should say, f
grace thou wilt have none—

Prince

What, none?

Falstaff

20 No, by my troth, not so much as will serve to
prologue to an egg and butter.

Prince

Well, how then? Come, roundly, roundly.

Falstaff

Marry then sweet wag, when thou art king, let n
us that are squires of the night's body be calle
25 thieves of the day's beauty: let us be Diana
foresters, gentlemen of the shade, minions of th
moon; and let men say we be men of goo
government, being governed as the sea is, by o
noble and chaste mistress the moon, under who
30 countenance we steal.

it holds well: it is a good
comparison (i.e. Falstaff's comparison
of robbers and the sea: Hal now
explains the similarities).

proof: demonstration.

Lay by: the demand of
highwaymen that the travellers should
drop their weapons.

Bring in: the order that they
should be served with food and drink in
the inn.

the ladder: the condemned thief
had to climb a ladder in order to be
hanged (death by hanging was the
punishment for theft).

Hybla: a mountain in Sicily
where the best-quality honey was
made.

old lad of the castle: rioter. It is
possible that, in an early version of this
play, Falstaff was called Sir John
Oldcastle.

a buff . . . durance: Hal refers
obliquely to the possibility of arrest.
The Elizabethan constable wore a
leather ('buff') jerkin, and Hal is able
to make a pun on the two senses of
'durance'—'hard-wearing'; *and*
imprisonment'.

7   *What . . . quiddities*: 'You are full
of jokes and quibbles'.

9   Both the plague (bubonic) and
the pox (venereal disease) provided the
Elizabethans with mild oaths (a modern
equivalent might be 'What the devil').

called . . . reckoning; asked her to
give an account of herself; *and* asked
her for the bill.

7   Hal has paid the bills whenever
he had money; and on other occasions
he has been able to obtain goods 'on
credit' (i.e. with a promise to pay later).

9   *were it . . . apparent*: Falstaff
begins to make an old joke which
depends upon the similarity in sound
between 'here' and 'heir'.

resolution: boldness.

fubbed: restrained.

old father Antic: that old fool (see
also p. viii).

Prince
Thou sayest well, and it holds well too: for the
fortune of us that are the moon's men doth ebb
and flow like the sea, being governed as the sea is,
by the moon—as for proof now, a purse of gold
35 most resolutely snatched on Monday night, and
most dissolutely spent on Tuesday morning; got
with swearing 'Lay by!', and spent with crying
'Bring in!'; now in as low an ebb as the foot of the
ladder, and by and by in as high a flow as the ridge
40 of the gallows.

Falstaff
By the Lord thou say'st true, lad; and is not my
hostess of the tavern a most sweet wench?

Prince
As the honey of Hybla, my old lad of the castle;
and is not a buff jerkin a most sweet robe of
45 durance?

Falstaff
How now, how now, mad wag? What, in thy quips
and thy quiddities? What a plague have I to do
with a buff jerkin?

Prince
Why, what a pox have I to do with my hostess of
50 the tavern?

Falstaff
Well, thou hast called her to a reckoning many a
time and oft.

Prince
Did I ever call for thee to pay thy part?

Falstaff
No. I'll give thee thy due, thou hast paid all there.

Prince
55 Yea, and elsewhere, so far as my coin would
stretch; and where it would not I have used my
credit.

Falstaff
Yea, and so used it that were it not here apparent
that thou art heir apparent—But I prithee sweet
60 wag, shall there be gallows standing in England
when thou art king? And resolution thus fubbed as
it is with the rusty curb of old father Antic the

66   *rare*: splendid.
       brave: fine.
70   *in some sort*: in a way.
70–1 *jumps . . . humour*: suits my
      nature.
73   *suits*: Hal speaks of 'suits' with
      reference to legal petitions (in a court of
      law) or requests for preferment (in the
      royal court). But Falstaff speaks of the
      clothes worn by a hanged man; these
      were always given to the executioner.
75   *lean*: thin.
      'Sblood: an oath (by God's
blood).
76   *gib cat*: tomcat.
      lugged: baited; in the Elizabethan
      sport of bear-baiting, the bear was
      fastened to a post and tormented by
      dogs.
78   *drone . . . bagpipe*: a continuous
      low note on the bagpipes, which were
      as popular in England as they now are
      in Scotland.

79   *hare*: this animal was
proverbially melancholy.
80   *Moorditch*: one of the main open
sewers in London.
82   *comparative*: rich in
comparisons.
      rascalliest: the biggest rascal.

law? Do not thou, when thou art king, hang
thief.
Prince
65 No; thou shalt.
Falstaff
Shall I? O rare! By the Lord, I'll be a brave judg
Prince
Thou judgest false already. I mean—thou sh
have the hanging of the thieves, and so becom
rare hangman.
Falstaff
70 Well, Hal, well; and in some sort it jumps with r
humour as well as waiting in the court, I can t
you.
Prince
For obtaining of suits?
Falstaff
Yea, for obtaining of suits, whereof the hangm
75 hath no lean wardrobe. 'Sblood, I am as mela
choly as a gib cat, or a lugged bear.
Prince
Or an old lion, or a lover's lute.
Falstaff
Yea, or the drone of a Lincolnshire bagpipe.
Prince
What sayest thou to a hare, or the melancholy
80 Moorditch?
Falstaff
Thou hast the most unsavoury similes, and a
indeed the most comparative, rascalliest, sw
young prince. But Hal, I prithee trouble me
more with vanity. I would to God thou and I kn
85 where a commodity of good names were to
bought: an old lord of the Council rated me t
other day in the street about you, sir, but I mark
him not; and yet he talked very wisely, but
regarded him not; and yet he talked wisely, a
90 in the street too.
Prince
Thou didst well, for wisdom cries out in the stre
and no man regards it.

99 Falstaff begins to speak
(comically) in the style of the
Puritans—a religious sect (particularly
opposed to the pleasures of the flesh)
whose speech was modelled on the
Bible. Hal follows his example.
commodity: supply.
rated: reproached.
marked him not: paid no attention
to him.
regarded him not: took no notice
of him.
wisdom . . . it: Hal's words are
quoted from the Bible (*Book of
Proverbs*, 1:20, 24).
iteration: habit of quoting.
upon me: to me.
and: if.
take: steal.
'Zounds: by God's wounds.
make one: join the gang [of
thieves].
an: if.
baffle me: hang me upside down
(Falstaff refers to the treatment given
to a knight who had dishonoured
himself).
-10 *set a match*: planned a robbery.
saved: i.e. from eternal
damnation.
by merit: by their deeds.
(Theologians argue about whether a
man is saved by his good works, or by
his faith in God.
omnipotent: Hal speaks
humorously, using the word to mean
'unequalled'.
true: honest.
Sack-and-Sugar: sugar was
sometimes used to sweeten the wine
(sack); in *Act 2*, Scene 4 (line 23) Hal
speaks of a gift of sugar.
Good Friday: the day on which
Christ was crucified; a strict fast was
kept on this day in the sixteenth
century.
stands to: keeps.
The expression 'Give the devil
his due' usually means 'Give even the
worst person the praise he deserves'.

Falstaff

O, thou hast damnable iteration, and art indeed
able to corrupt a saint! Thou hast done much
95 harm upon me, Hal—God forgive thee for it!
Before I knew thee, Hal, I knew nothing; and now
am I, if a man should speak truly, little better than
one of the wicked. I must give over this life, and I
will give it over: by the Lord, and I do not I am a
100 villain! I'll be damned for never a king's son in
Christendom.

Prince

Where shall we take a purse tomorrow, Jack?

Falstaff

'Zounds, where thou wilt, lad, I'll make one—an I
do not, call me villain and baffle me.

Prince

105 I see a good amendment of life in thee—from
praying to purse-taking.

Falstaff

Why, Hal, 'tis my vocation, Hal; 'tis no sin for a
man to labour in his vocation.

Enter Poins

Poins!—Now shall we know if Gadshill have set a
110 match. O, if men were to be saved by merit, what
hole in hell were hot enough for him? This is the
most omnipotent villain that ever cried 'Stand!' to
a true man.

Prince

Good morrow, Ned.

Poins

115 Good morrow, sweet Hal. What says Monsieur
Remorse? What says Sir John Sack-and-Sugar?
Jack, how agrees the devil and thee about thy soul,
that thou soldest him on Good Friday last for a
cup of Madeira and a cold capon's leg?

Prince

120 Sir John stands to his word, the devil shall have his
bargain; for he was never yet a breaker of proverbs: he will give the devil his due.

Poins

Then art thou damned for keeping thy word with
the devil.

125   *Else*: otherwise.
  cozening: cheating.
127   *Gad's Hill*: on the road between
  London and Canterbury, Gad's Hill
  (near Rochester) is about 30 miles from
  London.
127–8   *pilgrims . . . offerings*: the
  pilgrims (like those of Chaucer's
  Canterbury Tales) were going to visit
  the shrine of St. Thomas à Becket.
130   *vizards*: masks.
131   *Gadshill*: the character in the
  play takes his name from the place
  which is the scene of his crimes.
    lies: stays at the inn.
    bespoke: ordered.
132   *Eastcheap*: a district of London.
134   *tarry*: stay.
136   *Yedward*: a form of 'Edward'.

138   *chops*: fat cheeks, 'fat-face'.

139   *make one*: come with us, join the
  party.

142–3   *cam'st . . . royal*: are not of
  royal birth. Falstaff now makes a pun
  on 'royal' (= a coin worth 50p).
143   *stand for*: fight for; *and* be worth.
144   *once in my days*: for once in my
  life.

146   *come what will*: whatever
  happens.

151   *lay him down*: present him with.

153–5   Falstaff again speaks in the
  manner of a Puritan.

Prince

125 Else he had been damned for cozening the dev

  Poins

  But my lads, my lads, tomorrow morning, by fo
  o'clock early at Gad's Hill, there are pilgrir
  going to Canterbury with rich offerings, a
  traders riding to London with fat purses. I ha

130 vizards for you all; you have horses for yourselv
  Gadshill lies tonight in Rochester. I have bespo
  supper tomorrow night in Eastcheap. We may
  it as secure as sleep. If you will go, I will stuff yo
  purses full of crowns: if you will not, tarry at hor

135 and be hanged.

  Falstaff

  Hear ye, Yedward, if I tarry at home and go n
  I'll hang you for going.

  Poins

  You will, chops?

  Falstaff

  Hal, wilt thou make one?

  Prince

140 Who, I rob? I a thief? Not I, by my faith.

  Falstaff

  There's neither honesty, manhood, nor good f
  lowship in thee, nor thou cam'st not of the blo
  royal, if thou darest not stand for ten shillings.

  Prince

  Well then, once in my days I'll be a madcap.

  Falstaff

145 Why, that's well said.

  Prince

  Well, come what will, I'll tarry at home.

  Falstaff

  By the Lord, I'll be a traitor then, when thou
  king.

  Prince

  I care not.

  Poins

150 Sir John, I prithee leave the Prince and me alor
  I will lay him down such reasons for this adve
  ture that he shall go.

  Falstaff

  Well, God give thee the spirit of persuasion, a

4   *ears of profiting*: the ability to learn (profit) from what he hears.

5   *recreation*: amusement.

7   *poor abuses*: petty crimes.
     want countenance: need protection.

0   *latter spring*: second-late-spring; Hal seems to be implying that Falstaff is in his second childhood.
     All-hallown summer: England sometimes enjoys a period of late summer weather in autumn; the feast of All Saints (hallows) is celebrated on 1 November.

3   *execute*: perform.

6   *waylaid*: ambushed, set a trap for.

9   *part with*: get away from.

1–2 *wherein ... fail*: and we can choose not to appear.

5   *'tis like*: it is likely, probably.

6   *habits*: clothes.
     appointment: pieces of equipment (such as swords).

9   *vizards*: masks.

0   *sirrah*: sir.
     cases of buckram: suits of rough cloth.

1   *nonce*: purpose.
     inmask: conceal.
     noted: well-known.

3   *I doubt*: I'm afraid that.
     hard: strong.

5   *turned back*: ran away.

7   *forswear arms*: stop carrying (and using) weapons.
     virtue: force.
     incomprehensible: endless, beyond all comprehension.

him the ears of profiting, that what thou speakest
155 may move, and what he hears may be believed,
that the true prince may (for recreation sake) prove
a false thief, for the poor abuses of the time want
countenance. Farewell, you shall find me in
Eastcheap.

Prince
160 Farewell, the latter spring! Farewell, All-hallown
summer!   [*Exit* Falstaff

Poins
Now, my good sweet honey lord, ride with us
tomorrow. I have a jest to execute that I cannot
manage alone. Falstaff, Bardolph, Peto, and
165 Gadshill shall rob those men that we have already
waylaid—yourself and I will not be there: and
when they have the booty, if you and I do not rob
them, cut this head off from my shoulders.

Prince
How shall we part with them in setting forth?

Poins
170 Why, we will set forth before or after them, and
appoint them a place of meeting, wherein it is at
our pleasure to fail; and then will they adventure
upon the exploit themselves, which they shall have
no sooner achieved but we'll set upon them.

Prince
175 Yea, but 'tis like that they will know us by our
horses, by our habits, and by every other appoint-
ment, to be ourselves.

Poins
Tut, our horses they shall not see—I'll tie them in
the wood; our vizards we will change after we
180 leave them; and sirrah, I have cases of buckram for
the nonce, to immask our noted outward
garments.

Prince
Yea, but I doubt they will be too hard for us.

Poins
Well, for two of them, I know them to be as true-
185 bred cowards as ever turned back; and for the
third, if he fight longer than he sees reason, I'll
forswear arms. The virtue of this jest will be the
incomprehensible lies that this same fat rogue will

190   *wards*: fighting positions (a technical term in fencing).

191   *extremities*: sufferings.
    reproof: disproof (they will make Falstaff confess that he is lying).

194   *tomorrow night*: either Shakespeare or Hal has forgotten that the robbery at God's Hill is to take place *before* the supper in Eastcheap.

197   *know*: understand.
    awhile: for a time.
    uphold: agree with, share.

198   *unyok'd*: unrestrained.
    humour: mood, nature.

199   *the sun*: this was traditionally a symbol of kingship.

200   *contagious clouds*: the Elizabethans believed that infectious diseases were bred in the clouds.

202   *that . . . himself*: when the sun chooses to shine again.

205   *vapours*: fogs.
    strangle: eclipse.

207   *to sport*: to be on holiday.

208   'When holidays are rare, they are more welcome'.

209   *rare accidents*: unusual events.
    loose behaviour: wild conduct.

210   *pay the debt*: fulfil the obligations.

211   *never promised*: showed no signs of paying.

213   *falsify*: prove wrong.
    hopes: expectations (fears as well as hopes).

214   *sullen ground*: dull background.

216   *goodly*: precious.

218   *Redeeming time*: making up for lost time.

---

tell us when we meet at supper: how thirty at lea
190 he fought with; what wards, what blows, wh
extremities he endured; and in the reproof of th
lives the jest.

Prince
Well, I'll go with thee. Provide us all thin
necessary, and meet me tomorrow night
195 Eastcheap; there I'll sup. Farewell.

Poins
Farewell, my lord.   [*E*

Prince
I know you all, and will awhile uphold
The unyok'd humour of your idleness.
Yet herein will I imitate the sun,
200 Who doth permit the base contagious clouds
To smother up his beauty from the world,
That, when he please again to be himself,
Being wanted he may be more wonder'd at
By breaking through the foul and ugly mists
205 Of vapours that did seem to strangle him.
If all the year were playing holidays,
To sport would be as tedious as to work;
But when they seldom come, they wish'd-f
come,
And nothing pleaseth but rare accidents:
210 So when this loose behaviour I throw off,
And pay the debt I never promised,
By how much better than my word I am,
By so much shall I falsify men's hopes;
And like bright metal on a sullen ground,
215 My reformation, glitt'ring o'er my fault,
Shall show more goodly, and attract more eyes
Than that which hath no foil to set it off.
I'll so offend, to make offence a skill,
Redeeming time when men think least I will.
                              [*E*

Act 1 Scene 3

King Henry confronts the rebels. He argues chiefly with his nephew, Henry Percy (Hotspur), who has refused to surrender his prisoners to the King. Hotspur explains the reason for his refusal: he will give up his prisoners if King Henry will pay the ransom money for Mortimer, whom Henry hates. After the King, in great anger, has left the stage, we are told why he hates Mortimer so much: Mortimer has a stronger claim than Henry to be King of England. Now Hotspur is angry; he urges his father and his uncle to revolt, reminding them of King Henry's ingratitude. The scene ends with a decision to fight against the King.

blood: nature.
'Unwilling to be excited about these insults'.

found me: realized this.

tread upon: take advantage of.

be myself: be the King I am.

condition: natural disposition.

down: the small feathers on a bird.

title of respect: claim to be respected.

house: family (the Percy family, who were Henry's first supporters).

scourge: whip (i.e. Henry's threat to show his power).

holp: helped.

portly: powerful.

presence: appearance.

peremptory: insolent.

majesty: a king (he means himself).

moody: bad-tempered.

frontier: forehead.

servant brow: the frown of a subject.

good leave: permission.

use and counsel: help and advice.

took: captured.

deny'd: refused.

deliver'd: reported.

misprision: misunderstanding.

Scene 3 *Windsor: the Council Chamber*

Enter the King, Northumberland, Worcester, Hotspur, Sir Walter Blunt, *with others*

King
My blood hath been too cold and temperate,
Unapt to stir at these indignities,
And you have found me—for accordingly
You tread upon my patience: but be sure
5 I will from henceforth rather be myself,
Mighty and to be fear'd, than my condition,
Which hath been smooth as oil, soft as young down,
And therefore lost that title of respect
Which the proud soul ne'er pays but to the proud.

Worcester
10 Our house, my sovereign liege, little deserves
The scourge of greatness to be us'd on it—
And that same greatness too which our own hands
Have holp to make so portly.

Northumberland   My lord—

King
Worcester, get thee gone, for I do see
15 Danger and disobedience in thine eye:
O sir, your presence is too bold and peremptory,
And majesty might never yet endure
The moody frontier of a servant brow.
You have good leave to leave us; when we need
20 Your use and counsel we shall send for you.

[*Exit* Worcester
[*To* Northumberland] You were about to speak.

Northumberland   Yea, my good lord.
Those prisoners in your Highness' name demanded,
Which Harry Percy here at Holmedon took,
Were, as he says, not with such strength deny'd
25 As is deliver'd to your Majesty.
Either envy, therefore, or misprision,
Is guilty of this fault, and not my son.

Hotspur
My liege, I did deny no prisoners.
But I remember, when the fight was done,

<table>
<tr><td>

30   *dry*: thirsty.

33   *his chin new reap'd*: his freshly-trimmed beard.

34   'Looked like a corn-field after the corn has been harvested'.

35   *milliner*: the goods sold by milliners (e.g. gloves) were always highly scented.

36   *'twixt*: between.

37   *pouncet-box*: snuff-box—a small box containing perfumed powder.
    ever and anon: from time to time.

39   *Who*: i.e. the lord's nose; the perfumed snuff was intended to take away the smell of the dead bodies on the battlefield.

40   *Took it in snuff*: sniffed it up; the phrase 'to take in snuff' also meant 'to be angry'.
    still: always.

43   *corse*: corpse.

44   *his nobility*: his noble self (Hotspur is ironic).

45   'Using a lot of fancy, lady-like language'.

46   *amongst the rest*: among other things.

</td><td>

30 When I was dry with rage and extreme toil,
Breathless and faint, leaning upon my sword,
Came there a certain lord, neat and trimly dress'd
Fresh as a bridegroom, and his chin new reap'd
Show'd like a stubble-land at harvest-home.
35 He was perfumed like a milliner,
And 'twixt his finger and his thumb he held
A pouncet-box, which ever and anon
He gave his nose, and took't away again—
Who therewith angry, when it next came there,
40 Took it in snuff—and still he smil'd and talk'd;
And as the soldiers bore dead bodies by,
He call'd them untaught knaves, unmannerly,
To bring a slovenly unhandsome corse
Betwixt the wind and his nobility.
45 With many holiday and lady terms
He question'd me, amongst the rest demanded
My prisoners in your Majesty's behalf.
I then, all smarting with my wounds being cold,
To be so pester'd with a popinjay,
50 Out of my grief and my impatience
Answer'd neglectingly, I know not what—
He should, or he should not; for he made me mad

</td></tr>
</table>

all . . . cold: very sore because my wounds were feeling cold.

popinjay: parrot.

grief: pain.

neglectingly: without thinking, carelessly.

shine so brisk: look so smart.

waiting-gentlewoman: lady-in-waiting (a lady of noble birth attending one of even higher rank).

God . . . mark: God preserve us (an exclamation of contempt).

sovereignest thing: most healing medicine.

parmacity: an ointment or liniment.

58–62   Hotspur tries to imitate the lord's effeminate speech.

saltpetre: a mineral used for making gunpowder.

tall: brave.

bald unjointed: empty and disconnected.

indirectly: without thinking.

Come current for: be accepted as money.

retold: recounted.

die: be forgotten.

wrong: harm.

impeach . . . said: prove that he was disloyal in what he said.

so: provided that.

unsay: contradict.

yet: still.

with . . . exception: on condition.

charge: expense.

straight: immediately.

his brother-in-law: see p. 126.

on my soul: an oath.

magician: Glendower's belief in his magic powers is described in *Act 3*, *Scene 1*.

coffers: treasury.

indent with: make a bargain with.

fears: cowards *and* causes for fear.

'When they (the cowards) have given themselves up'.

hold: consider.

To see him shine so brisk, and smell so sweet,
And talk so like a waiting-gentlewoman
55 Of guns, and drums, and wounds, God save the
mark!
And telling me the sovereignest thing on earth
Was parmacity for an inward bruise;
And that it was great pity, so it was,
This villainous saltpetre should be digg'd
60 Out of the bowels of the harmless earth,
Which many a good tall fellow had destroy'd
So cowardly; and but for these vile guns
He would himself have been a soldier.
This bald unjointed chat of his, my lord,
65 I answer'd indirectly, as I said,
And I beseech you, let not his report
Come current for an accusation
Betwixt my love and your high Majesty.

Blunt

The circumstance consider'd, good my lord,
70 Whate'er Lord Harry Percy then had said
To such a person, and in such a place,
At such a time, with all the rest retold,
May reasonably die, and never rise
To do him wrong, or any way impeach
75 What then he said, so he unsay it now.

King

Why, yet he doth deny his prisoners,
But with proviso and exception
That we at our own charge shall ransom straight
His brother-in-law, the foolish Mortimer—
80 Who, on my soul, hath wilfully betray'd
The lives of those that he did lead to fight
Against that great magician, damn'd Glendower
(Whose daughter, as we hear, the Earl of March
Hath lately marry'd). Shall our coffers then
85 Be empty'd to redeem a traitor home?
Shall we buy treason, and indent with fears,
When they have lost and forfeited themselves?
No, on the barren mountains let him starve;
For I shall never hold that man my friend
90 Whose tongue shall ask me for one penny cost
To ransom home revolted Mortimer.

93   *fall off*: lose his allegiance to the King.

95   *no more but one*: only.

96   *mouthed wounds*: wounds which speak for him.
      took: received.

97   *sedgy*: grassy (sedge is a small, grass-like plant).

98   Only these two men were fighting, at close quarters.

99   *confound . . . hour*: spend almost an hour.

100   *changing hardiment*: matching strength.

101   *breath'd*: paused for breath.

101–2 *three . . . flood*: they agreed to drink three times from the river.

102   *flood*: waters.

103   *Who*: i.e. the river.
      affrighted: frightened.

105   *crisp*: rippled (with small waves).

107   *bare*: miserable.

108   *Colour*: justify, make excuses for (*also* stain).

111   *with revolt*: with the accusation of rebellion.

112   *belie*: tell lies about.

113   *encounter with*: fight.

114   *durst*: dare.

118   *with the speediest means*: as quickly as possible.

119   *kind*: way

121   *license*: permit.

123   *And if*: even if.

124   *will*: will follow.
      straight: at once.

125   *ease my heart*: set my heart at rest (by expressing his feelings).

126   'Although I risk having my head cut off'.

Hotspur
Revolted Mortimer!
He never did fall off, my sovereign liege,
But by the chance of war: to prove that true
95 Needs no more but one tongue for all thos
      wounds,
Those mouthed wounds, which valiantly he tool
When on the gentle Severn's sedgy bank,
In single opposition hand to hand,
He did confound the best part of an hour
100 In changing hardiment with great Glendower.
      Three times they breath'd, and three times di
      they drink
Upon agreement of swift Severn's flood;
Who then affrighted with their bloody looks
Ran fearfully among the trembling reeds,
105 And hid his crisp head in the hollow bank,
Bloodstained with these valiant combatants.
Never did bare and rotten policy
Colour her working with such deadly wounds,
Nor never could the noble Mortimer
110 Receive so many, and all willingly.
Then let not him be slander'd with revolt.
      King
Thou dost belie him, Percy, thou dost belie him
He never did encounter with Glendower.
I tell thee, he durst as well have met the devil alon
115 As Owen Glendower for an enemy.
Art thou not asham'd? But sirrah, henceforth
Let me not hear you speak of Mortimer.
Send me your prisoners with the speediest means
Or you shall hear in such a kind from me
120 As will displease you. My Lord Northumberland
We license your departure with your son.
Send us your prisoners, or you will hear of it.
                  [*Exit* King, *with* Blunt *and other lord.*
      Hotspur
And if the devil come and roar for them
I will not send them. I will after straight
125 And tell him so, for I will ease my heart,
Albeit I make a hazard of my head.

Northumberland
What, drunk with choler? Stay, and pause awhile.
Here comes your uncle.

Enter Worcester

Hotspur   Speak of Mortimer?
'Zounds, I will speak of him, and let my soul
130 Want mercy if I do not join with him:
Yea, on his part I'll empty all these veins,
And shed my dear blood drop by drop in the dust,
But I will lift the down-trod Mortimer
As high in the air as this unthankful king,
135 As this ingrate and canker'd Bolingbroke.
Northumberland
Brother, the King hath made your nephew mad.
Worcester
Who struck this heat up after I was gone?
Hotspur
He will forsooth have all my prisoners.
And when I urg'd the ransom once again
140 Of my wife's brother, then his cheek look'd pale,
And on my face he turn'd an eye of death,
Trembling even at the name of Mortimer.
Worcester
I cannot blame him: was not he proclaim'd,
By Richard that dead is, the next of blood?
Northumberland
145 He was, I heard the proclamation.
And then it was, when the unhappy king
(Whose wrong in us God pardon!) did set forth
Upon his Irish expedition;
From whence he, intercepted, did return
150 To be depos'd, and shortly murdered.
Worcester
And for whose death we in the world's wide mouth
Live scandaliz'd and foully spoken of.
Hotspur
But soft, I pray you! Did King Richard then
Proclaim my brother, Edmund Mortimer,
155 Heir to the crown?
Northumberland He did, myself did hear it.
Hotspur
Nay, then I cannot blame his cousin king,

---

7   *choler*: anger.

129–30   *let . . . mercy*: damn me.

131   *on his part*: for his sake.

133   *down-trod*: dejected.

135   *ingrate*: ungrateful.
canker'd: thoroughly rotten.

137   *struck . . . up*: excited this
passion.

138   *forsooth*: indeed.

139   *urg'd*: argued for.

141   *an eye of death*: a look which
threatened death; *or* a look which
showed the king in fear of death.

144   *that dead is*: who is dead.
the next of blood: i.e. the heir to
the throne; see p. 126.

147   *Whose . . . pardon*: may God
forgive the wrong we did to Richard.
148   *his Irish expedition*: see p. v.
149   *intercepted*: interrupted.

151–2   *in . . . spoken of*: throughout the
whole wide world we are abused and
slandered.

153   *soft*: wait a minute.

159   *forgetful*: Hotspur accuses the
   King of having forgotten how he was
   supported by the Percy family.
160   *wear . . . subornation*: suffer the
   terrible disgrace of having aided and
   abetted murder.
163   *base second means*: inferior
   instruments.
165–6   Hotspur asks pardon for
   speaking so plainly when he told
   Worcester and Northumberland that
   they had been only the instruments
   used in murder—they are of the same
   rank and category ('the line and the
   predicament') as the ropes ('cords') and
   ladder needed to hang a man.
167   *range*: rank.
   subtle: cunning.
168   *in these days*: at the present time.
169   'Be written in the history books
   ('chronicles') of the future'.
171   *gage them both*: pawn both the
   nobility and their power.
   behalf: cause.

173   *rose*: Richard II belonged to the
   house of Lancaster, whose emblem was
   a red rose.
174   *canker*: wild rose (or even
   'canker-worm', the disease which kills
   roses).
175   *in more shame*: to your even
   greater shame.
   be further spoken: be said in
   addition.
176   *fool'd*: deceived.
178   *time serves*: there is time.
180   *thoughts*: opinions.
181   *disdain'd*: disdainful.
183   *To answer*: how he can repay.

That wish'd him on the barren mountains starve
But shall it be that you, that set the crown
Upon the head of this forgetful man,
160 And for his sake wear the detested blot
Of murderous subornation—shall it be
That you a world of curses undergo,
Being the agents, or base second means,
The cords, the ladder, or the hangman rather?
165 O, pardon me, that I descend so low,
To show the line and the predicament
Wherein you range under this subtle king!
Shall it for shame be spoken in these days,
Or fill up chronicles in time to come,
170 That men of your nobility and power
Did gage them both in an unjust behalf
(As both of you, God pardon it, have done)
To put down Richard, that sweet lovely rose,
And plant this thorn, this canker Bolingbroke?
175 And shall it in more shame be further spoken,
That you are fool'd, discarded, and shook off
By him for whom these shames ye underwent?
No, yet time serves wherein you may redeem
Your banish'd honours, and restore yourselves
180 Into the good thoughts of the world again:
Revenge the jeering and disdain'd contempt
Of this proud king, who studies day and night
To answer all the debt he owes to you
Even with the bloody payment of your deaths.
185 Therefore I say—
   Worcester   Peace, cousin, say no more.
And now I will unclasp a secret book,
And to your quick-conceiving discontents

Peace: be quiet.

unclasp: unfasten, open (some very precious books were kept shut with locks and keys).

quick-conceiving discontents: discontented minds, which are quick to understand).

-91 Worcester's example of a dangerous exploit is taken from medieval tales where a knight had to cross ('o'er-walk') a river ('current'), using a spear for a bridge.

unsteadfast: insecure.

'If he falls in the river, that is the end—whether he sinks or swims'. Even if he can swim, the man has failed the trial.

So: provided that.

-6 'It is more exciting ('the blood more stirs') to begin a lion-hunt than to chase a hare'. Hotspur uses the correct hunting terms—'rouse' and 'start'—for the different animals.

methinks: I think.

were: would be.

deep: ocean.

fathom-line: a line which sailors dropped into the sea to find how deep it was.

locks: hair; Hotspur now imagines 'honour' in the person of a woman.

redeem: rescue.

corrival: partner.

dignities: trophies.

'But I have no patience ('out upon') with this practice of sharing honour'.

-8 Worcester comments that Hotspur has a rich imagination but he will not pay attention to the real business.

apprehends: catches (imaginatively).

a world: a great many.

figures: fancies, rhetorical devices of speech.

form: substance.

I cry you mercy: I am sorry.

I'll read you matter deep and dangerous,
As full of peril and adventurous spirit
190 As to o'er-walk a current roaring loud
On the unsteadfast footing of a spear.

Hotspur
If he fall in, good night—or sink, or swim!
Send danger from the east unto the west,
So honour cross it from the north to south,
195 And let them grapple: O, the blood more stirs
To rouse a lion than to start a hare!
Northumberland
Imagination of some great exploit
Drives him beyond the bounds of patience.
Hotspur
By heaven, methinks it were an easy leap
200 To pluck bright honour from the pale-fac'd moon,
Or dive into the bottom of the deep,
Where fathom-line could never touch the ground,
And pluck up drowned honour by the locks,
So he that doth redeem her thence might wear
205 Without corrival all her dignities.
But out upon this half-fac'd fellowship!
Worcester
He apprehends a world of figures here,
But not the form of what he should attend.
Good cousin, give me audience for a while.
Hotspur
210 I cry you mercy.

212 *a Scot*: Hotspur makes a pun with 'scot' = a very small payment.

214 *start*: jump.

215 *lend . . . purposes*: do not listen to my plans.

216 *that's flat*: that is certain.

220 *holla*: shout.

221 *starling*: many Elizabethan texts refer to starlings (wild brown birds) which had been taught to speak.

223 *still in motion*: always alive.

225 *defy*: reject.

226 *gall and pinch*: irritate (as a tight saddle rubs and pinches a horse).

227 *sword-and-buckler*: swashbuckling, playboy.

229 *mischance*: accident.

232 *better temper'd*: more controlled.

233 *wasp-stung*: irritable (as though stung by a wasp).

234 *to break . . . mood*: to burst into these feminine tantrums.

235 *Tying thine ear*: listening.

237 *pismires*: ants.

238 *politician*: scheming villain.

241 *kept*: lived.

242 *bow'd my knee*: affirmed my loyalty.

Worcester　　　　　Those same noble Sco
That are your prisoners—
　　Hotspur　　　　　I'll keep them a
By God he shall not have a Scot of them!
No, if a Scot would save his soul he shall not.
I'll keep them, by this hand!
　　Worcester　　　　　You start awa
215 And lend no ear unto my purposes.
Those prisoners you shall keep—
　　Hotspur　　　　Nay, I will: that's fla
He said he would not ransom Mortimer,
Forbade my tongue to speak of Mortimer;
But I will find him when he lies asleep,
220 And in his ear I'll holla 'Mortimer!'
Nay, I'll have a starling shall be taught to spea
Nothing but 'Mortimer', and give it him
To keep his anger still in motion.
　　Worcester
Hear you, cousin, a word—
　　Hotspur
225 All studies here I solemnly defy,
Save how to gall and pinch this Bolingbroke.
And that same sword-and-buckler Prince
　　Wales—
But that I think his father loves him not,
And would be glad he met with some mischance
230 I would have him poison'd with a pot of ale!
　　Worcester
Farewell, kinsman: I'll talk to you
When you are better temper'd to attend.
　　Northumberland
Why, what a wasp-stung and impatient fool
Art thou to break into this woman's mood,
235 Tying thine ear to no tongue but thine own!
　　Hotspur
Why, look you, I am whipp'd and scourg'd wi
　　rods,
Nettled, and stung with pismires, when I hear
Of this vile politician Bolingbroke.
In Richard's time—what do you call the place?
240 A plague upon it, it is in Gloucestershire—
'Twas where the mad-cap duke his uncle kept,
His uncle York—where I first bow'd my knee

Unto this king of smiles, this Bolingbroke—
'Sblood! when you and he came back from
    Ravenspurgh.

Northumberland

245 At Berkeley castle.

Hotspur

You say true.
Why, what a candy deal of courtesy
This fawning greyhound then did proffer me!
'Look when his infant fortune came to age',

250 And 'gentle Harry Percy', and 'kind cousin':
O, the devil take such cozeners!—God forgive me!
Good uncle, tell your tale; I have done.

Worcester

Nay, if you have not, to it again,
We will stay your leisure.

Hotspur   I have done, i'faith.

Worcester

255 Then once more to your Scottish prisoners:
Deliver them up without their ransom straight,
And make the Douglas' son your only mean
For powers in Scotland—which, for divers reasons
Which I shall send you written, be assur'd

260 Will easily be granted. [*To* Northumberland] You,
    my lord,
Your son in Scotland being thus employ'd,
Shall secretly into the bosom creep
Of that same noble prelate well-belov'd,
The Archbishop.

Hotspur   Of York, is it not?

Worcester   True, who bears hard

265 His brother's death at Bristow, the Lord Scroop.
I speak not this in estimation,
As what I think might be, but what I know
Is ruminated, plotted, and set down,
And only stays but to behold the face

270 Of that occasion that shall bring it on.

Hotspur

I smell it. Upon my life it will do well!

'*Sblood*: an oath (by God's blood).

Ravenspurgh: in Yorkshire, where Bolingbroke landed when he returned from exile in 1399.

candy deal: sugary load.

proffer: hold out (as though offering sweets to a child).

Look when: as soon as.

his infant fortune: Bolingbroke's kingship was newly-born.

came to age: matured.

cozeners: cheats (with a pun on 'cousin').

to it again: go on with it.

stay: wait.

once more: let us return to the subject of.

Deliver them up: let them go free.

straight: at once.

the Douglas' son: the son of the Earl of Douglas. It is correct to speak of the head of a Scottish family by using the definite article; Shakespeare is, however, mistaken about the parentage of Mordake, who is the prisoner referred to (see *1*, *1*, *94*).

7-8 *your ... Scotland*: your only way of raising an army ('powers') in Scotland.

divers: various.

bosom: confidence.

prelate: important man in the church hierarchy.

69-70 'And only waits to see an opportunity for action'.

I smell it: 'I can guess what you are talking about'.

272 'You always ('still') release the hounds ('let'st slip') before the hare ('game') is running ('afoot').
273 *choose but be*: be anything other than.

276 *aim'd*: directed, planned.

277 *'tis . . . reason*: i.e. it is a very good reason.
     speed: hurry.
278 'To save our own lives ('heads') by calling up an army ('head')'.
279 'However well we behave ('bear ourselves')'.

284 *strangers to*: unfamiliar with.

288 *ripe*: ready.
289 *steal*: go secretly.
     suddenly: very soon.

291 *fashion*: arrange.
     happily: with luck.
292–3 They will themselves have control over what happens to them (their 'fortunes') instead of being insecure ('at much uncertainty') because they are dependent on the King.
294 *thrive*: do well.
296 *sport*: performance on the battlefield.

Northumberland
Before the game is afoot thou still let'st slip.
　　Hotspur
Why, it cannot choose but be a noble plot;
And then the power of Scotland and of York,
275 To join with Mortimer, ha?
　　Worcester　　　　　　　　And so they shal
　　Hotspur
In faith it is exceedingly well aim'd.
　　Worcester
And 'tis no little reason bids us speed
To save our heads by raising of a head;
For, bear ourselves as even as we can,
280 The King will always think him in our debt,
And think we think ourselves unsatisfy'd,
Till he hath found a time to pay us home:
And see already how he doth begin
To make us strangers to his looks of love.
　　Hotspur
285 He does, he does! We'll be reveng'd on him.
　　Worcester
Cousin, farewell. No further go in this
Than I by letters shall direct your course.
When time is ripe, which will be suddenly,
I'll steal to Glendower and Lord Mortimer,
290 Where you, and Douglas, and our powers ¦
　　　once—
As I will fashion it—shall happily meet,
To bear our fortunes in our own strong arms,
Which now we hold at much uncertainty.
　　Northumberland
Farewell, good brother; we shall thrive, I trust.
　　Hotspur
295 Uncle, adieu: O, let the hours be short
Till fields, and blows, and groans applaud ou
　　sport!
　　　　　　　　　　　　　　　　　[*Exeun*

Act 2

Act 2 Scene 1
t is early morning at Rochester, and
he Carriers are preparing to start their
ourney. The robber Gadshill is also
awake, and when the Carriers have
departed we see how the thief and the
Chamberlain are working together to
plot the robbery.

by the day: in the morning.
Charles' wain: the Plough, or
Great Bear: a constellation in the
northern sky (the Carrier can tell the
time by the position of the stars).
packed: loaded.
ostler: inn-servant in charge of
the stables.
Anon: at once (the usual reply of
an inn-servant).
beat Cut's saddle: i.e. to soften it.
'Cut' was a common name for a
working-horse.
a few flocks: some stuffing.
point: pommel (the front of a
saddle).
poor jade: the absence of the
definite article indicates the rustic,
uneducated, speech idiom; a 'jade' is a
poor quality horse.
wrung in the withers: rubbed on
the shoulders.
out of all cess: excessively.
Peas . . . bots: the Carriers are
complaining that the food provided for
the horses is damp ('dank'), and will
cause worms in the animals.
next: quickest.
11 *This . . . died*: this inn has been
completely disorganized since the death
of the stableman, Robin.
never joyed: he was never happy.

Scene 1 *Rochester: an Inn Yard*

Enter a Carrier *with a lantern in his hand*

First Carrier

Heigh-ho! An it be not four by the day I'll be
hanged; Charles' wain is over the new chimney,
and yet our horse not packed. What, ostler!

Ostler

[*Within*] Anon, anon.

First Carrier

5 I prithee, Tom, beat Cut's saddle, put a few flocks
in the point; poor jade is wrung in the withers out
of all cess.

Enter another Carrier

Second Carrier

Peas and beans are as dank here as a dog, and that
is the next way to give poor jades the bots. This
10 house is turned upside down since Robin Ostler
died.

First Carrier

Poor fellow never joyed since the price of oats
rose; it was the death of him.

14–15   'There must be more fleas here than at any other inn ('house') on the road to London'.

15   *stung*: bitten.
      tench: a fish whose speckled markings look like flea-bites.

16   *By the mass*: an old-fashioned oath.
      a king christen: a Christian king. Kings have the best (and most) of everything, and the Carrier assumes that they must therefore have more and better flea-bites.

Second Carrier

I think this be the most villainous house in
15 London road for fleas; I am stung like a tench

First Carrier

Like a tench! By the mass, there is ne'er a ki
christen could be better bit than I have been sir
the first cock.

Second Carrier

Why, they will allow us ne'er a jordan, and then
20 we leak in your chimney, and your chamber-lye
breeds fleas like a loach.

First Carrier

What, ostler! Come away, and be hanged! Come
away!

Second Carrier

I have a gammon of bacon and two razes of ginger,
25 to be delivered as far as Charing Cross.

First Carrier

God's body! The turkeys in my pannier are quite
starved. What, ostler! A plague on thee, hast thou
never an eye in thy head? Canst not hear? And
'twere not as good deed as drink to break the pate
30 on thee, I am a very villain. Come, and be hanged!
Hast no faith in thee?

Enter Gadshill

Gadshill

Good morrow, carriers, what's o'clock?

First Carrier

I think it be two o'clock.

Gadshill

I prithee lend me thy lantern, to see my gelding in
35 the stable.

First Carrier

Nay, by God, soft! I know a trick worth two of
that, i'faith.

Gadshill

I pray thee lend me thine.

Second Carrier

Ay, when? Canst tell? Lend me thy lantern, quoth
40 he! Marry, I'll see thee hanged first.

---

the first cock: midnight (it was generally agreed that the first cock-crow—marking the beginning of a new day—should be at midnight.)

allow . . . jordan: they won't even give us chamber-pot, and so we urinate ('leak') in the fireplace ('chimney'), and urine encourages the fleas to breed.

loach: a small fish reputed to breed fleas.

Come away: hurry up.

gammon: almost half a pig (the best portion).

razes: roots (ginger was imported from the East, and this would be a valuable commodity).

Charing Cross: a village on the opposite side of London.

pannier: the large basket holding the Carrier's merchandise.

hast . . . head: can't you see what needs to be done (i.e. the turkeys should have been fed).

as . . . drink: a proverbial saying. The Carrier seems to be saying that it is necessary to hit the ostler over his head ('break the pate on thee') in order to make him do anything.

Hast . . . thee: can you not be trusted.

Good morrow: Good morning.

what's o'clock: what time is it.

gelding: horse (the castrated male, used for most working purposes).

I know . . . that: I'm not such a fool—you can't catch me that way.

Ay . . . tell: words uttered to deride, or refuse, a request.

quoth he: says he (the speaker mocks Gadshill).

41 *mean*: intend.
43 *Time enough*: with plenty of time.
to go . . . candle: to go to bed with a candle (the Carriers are refusing to give information to Gadshill).
44 *call up*: rouse, awaken.
45 *will along*: want to go along with us.
46 *great charge*: a lot to look after.
48 *At hand . . . pickpurse*: I'm here, says the thief; the Chamberlain speaks a common catchphrase.
49 *fair*: true.
50–51 Telling people to steal is just as bad as the actual theft.
52 *thou . . . how*: you say how it (the robbery) is to be done.
53 *holds current*: is still true.
54 *franklin*: a land-owning farmer.
55 *Wild*: Weald: a rich part of the county of Kent.
marks: gold coins.
57 *auditor*: an official of the Royal Exchequer.
58 *abundance of charge*: a lot to look after.
59 *eggs and butter*: i.e. for breakfast.
60 *will away*: will leave.
presently: immediately.
61 *Saint Nicholas' clerks*: highwaymen, robbers; St Nicholas was the patron saint of travellers—and therefore of highwaymen.
62 *give . . . neck*: be hanged.
63 *I'll . . . it*: I don't want it.
67 *fat . . . gallows*: there will be a fat (or 'rich') pair of us on the gallows.
69 *starveling*: thin, starved creature.
Troyans: mates, companions (the Trojans were great heroes who fought against the Greeks in classical mythology). Gadshill is referring to Prince Hal—but he dare not name him.
70 *the which*: who.
for sport sake: for their own amusement.
71 *to do . . . grace*: to honour the profession (of robbers).
71–3 'Who, if any questions are asked, would make everything all right for the sake of their own reputations ('credit')'.

Gadshill
Sirrah carrier, what time do you mean to co
to London?
Second Carrier
Time enough to go to bed with a candle, I warr
thee. Come, neighbour Mugs, we'll call up
45 gentlemen; they will along with company, for th
have great charge.   [*Exeunt* Carri
Gadshill
What ho! Chamberlain!

Enter Chamberlain

Chamberlain
'At hand, quoth pick-purse.'
Gadshill
That's even as fair as 'At hand, quoth
50 chamberlain': for thou variest no more fr
picking of purses than giving direction doth fr
labouring—thou layest the plot how.
Chamberlain
Good morrow, master Gadshill. It holds curr
that I told you yesternight: there's a franklin in
55 Wild of Kent hath brought three hundred ma
with him in gold; I heard him tell it to one of
company last night at supper—a kind of audit
one that hath abundance of charge too, God kno
what. They are up already, and call for eggs a
60 butter—they will away presently.
Gadshill
Sirrah, if they meet not with Saint Nichol
clerks, I'll give thee this neck.
Chamberlain
No, I'll none of it; I pray thee keep that for
hangman, for I know thou worshippest Sa
65 Nicholas as truly as a man of falsehood may.
Gadshill
What talkest thou to me of the hangman? I
hang, I'll make a fat pair of gallows: for if I ha
old Sir John hangs with me, and thou knowest
is no starveling. Tut, there are other Troyans t
70 thou dream'st not of, the which for sport sake
content to do the profession some grace; t
would (if matters should be looked into) for th

joined with: accompanied by.

foot-landrakers: robbers wandering around on foot.

long . . . strikers: thieves who used long poles to knock the riders from their horses in order to steal mounts which were often paltry (worth no more than sixpence).

mad . . . maltworms: crazy drunken revellers with their whiskers and purple faces. The 'mustachio' (moustache) was thought by such men to be a sign of virility; their faces were red as a result of heavy drinking of strong liquor (brewed from 'malt').

nobility: noble men (both 'men of high rank' and 'men of good character').

tranquillity: peaceful men (in contrast to the riotous 'maltworms').

burgomasters: important men in the town.

great oneyers: great men; the noun seems to be Gadshill's own invention.

can hold in: are self-disciplined (they can keep secrets; stay together; and concentrate on the job they are doing).

will strike . . . pray: they will hit a man (or rob him) before they speak to him; and challenge ('speak'—calling 'stay by') rather than drink; and drink rather than pray.

commonwealth: the state (and also 'wealth', which the thieves believe to be common'—free for all).

boots: spoil, booty.

Will the boots keep you dry in muddy roads; *and* Will the state protect you in a time of trouble.

justice . . . her: Those who operate the laws have been given bribes.

as in a castle: with complete safety.

cocksure: confidently.

receipt of: recipe for.

fernseed: fernseed was believed to appear only on 23 June (Midsummer Eve); any man who wore it became invisible.

own credit sake make all whole. I am joined with
no   foot-landrakers,   no   long-staff   sixpenny
75 strikers, none of these mad mustachio purple-
hued maltworms, but with nobility and tranquillity, burgomasters and great oneyers, such as can
hold in, such as will strike sooner than speak, and
speak sooner than drink, and drink sooner than
80 pray—and yet, 'zounds, I lie, for they pray con-
tinually to their saint the commonwealth—or
rather not pray to her, but prey on her, for they
ride up and down on her and make her their boots.

Chamberlain

What, the commonwealth their boots? Will she
85 hold out water in foul way?

Gadshill

She will, she will; justice hath liquored her. We
steal as in a castle, cock-sure: we have the receipt
of fern-seed, we walk invisible.

89   *more beholding to*: owe more to.

Chamberlain
Nay, by my faith, I think you are more behold
90 to the night than to fern-seed for your walk
invisible.
Gadshill
Give me thy hand. Thou shalt have a share in
purchase, as I am a true man.
Chamberlain
Nay, rather let me have it, as you are a false th
Gadshill
95 Go to, 'homo' is a common name to all men.
the ostler bring my gelding out of the sta
Farewell, you muddy knave.   [*Exe*

93   *purchase*: the goods we steal.
true: honest.
95   *Go to ... men*: Gadshill resents
being called thief and argues that he has
a right to be called a man. He quotes
from a Latin text-book which explains
the difference between 'proper' and
'common' nouns with the example that
homo is the common noun for 'man'.

97   *muddy*: stupid.

Act 2 Scene 2
The thieves are assembling at their
meeting-place, ready to waylay the
travellers on the road to London.
Prince Hal, Poins and Peto have played
a trick on Falstaff by hiding his horse,
so that the fat knight has to walk. The
Prince and Poins hide (as they had
planned to do in *Act 1*, Scene 2). After
the robbery, Hal and Poins return (in
disguise) and attack the robbers.
2   *frets*: is irritated, worries.
a gummed velvet: velvet was
treated with gum to make it shine, but
the gum irritated the wearer's skin and
was said to 'fret' or chafe.
3   *Stand close*: hide.
5   *fat-kidneyed*: the kidneys are
always enclosed in fat, but Falstaff's
must have more fat than normal
kidneys.
6   'What a terrible noise you are
making'.
8   *is walked*: has walked.
12–13   *If I ... afoot*: If I go another
four feet on foot ('afoot'); a 'squier' is a
measuring-rod.
13   *break my wind*: burst my lungs.
13–14   *I doubt ... this*: I am sure I shall
die a good Christian death as a result of
all this suffering.

Scene 2 *Gad's Hill : the Highway*

Enter Prince, Poins, *and* Peto

Poins
Come, shelter, shelter! I have removed Falsta
horse, and he frets like a gummed velvet.
Prince
Stand close!   [*They hide themse*

Enter Falstaff

Falstaff
Poins! Poins, and be hanged! Poins!
Prince
5   [*Comes forward*] Peace, ye fat-kidneyed ras
What a brawling dost thou keep!
Falstaff
Where's Poins, Hal?
Prince
He is walked up to the top of the hill; I'll go s
him.   [*
Falstaff
10 I am accursed to rob in that thief's company!
rascal hath removed my horse and tied him I kr
not where. If I travel but four foot by the squ
further afoot, I shall break my wind. Well, I do
not but to die a fair death for all this, if I sc

scape hanging: avoid being hanged.

forsworn his company: sworn not to be in his company.

hourly . . . years: every hour for the past 22 years.

medicines: love-potions.

else: otherwise (there is no other explanation).

starve: die.

rob . . . further: do any more robbing (especially on foot).

and: if.

3   *as good . . . man*: as sensible to become honest as it is to drink.

veriest varlet: biggest villain.

6   *eight . . . with me*: to walk eight yards over uneven ground is worse for me than for other men to go 70 miles.

15 hanging for killing that rogue. I have forsworn his company hourly any time this two and twenty years, and yet I am bewitched with the rogue's company. If the rascal have not given me medicines to make me love him, I'll be hanged. It could

20 not be else: I have drunk medicines. Poins! Hal! A plague upon you both! Bardolph! Peto! I'll starve ere I'll rob a foot further—and 'twere not as good a deed as drink to turn true man and to leave these rogues, I am the veriest varlet that ever chewed

25 with a tooth. Eight yards of uneven ground is threescore and ten miles afoot with me, and the stony-hearted villains know it well enough. A plague upon it when thieves cannot be true one to another! [*They whistle*] Whew! A plague upon you

30 all! Give me my horse, you rogues, give me my horse and be hanged!

33   *list*: listen.

35   *being down*: when I am lying down.

36–7   *bear . . . afoot*: carry my own body on foot.

37   *coin*: money.

38   *colt*: trick.

39   *uncolted*: unhorsed; the Prince makes a pun on 'colt' = to trick, and 'colt' = a young horse.

42   The Prince pretends to think that Falstaff is speaking to him as though he were a stableboy.

43   'Hang yourself in your own garters' was a popular expression; Falstaff adapts it slightly, playing on the fact that as heir apparent to the throne the Prince is a member of the Order of the Garter.

44   *ta'en*: taken, caught.
        peach: impeach, inform on you.
        and I have not: if I do not have.

45   *ballads*: songs (to be sung to well-known tunes) which were printed on sheets of paper and sold in the streets. They were the equivalent of newspapers, describing current events; and they could also be used (as Falstaff now threatens) to ridicule enemies.
        on: about.
        filthy tunes: tunes associated with unpleasant songs (so that the ballads would be even more hurtful).

46   *let . . . poison*: let me be poisoned with a glass of wine.

46–7   *is so forward*: goes so far (is taken to such extremes).

Prince

[*Comes forward*] Peace, ye fat guts! Lie down; thine ear close to the ground, and list if thou ca hear the tread of travellers.

Falstaff

35 Have you any levers to lift me up again, bei down? 'Sblood, I'll not bear my own flesh so afoot again for all the coin in thy father's e chequer. What a plague mean ye to colt me th

Prince

40 Thou liest: thou art not colted, thou art uncolt

Falstaff

I prithee good Prince Hal, help me to my hor good king's son.

Prince

Out, ye rogue, shall I be your ostler?

Falstaff

Hang thyself in thine own heir-apparent garte If I be ta'en, I'll peach for this. And I have n
45 ballads made on you all, and sung to filthy tun let a cup of sack be my poison—when a jest is forward, and afoot too! I hate it.

Enter Gadshill *and* Bardolph

Gadshill

Stand!

Falstaff

So I do, against my will.

Poins

50 O, 'tis our setter; I know his voice. [*Con forward with* Peto] Bardolph, what news?

Bardolph

Case ye, case ye, on with your vizards! Ther money of the King's coming down the hill; going to the King's exchequer.

Falstaff

55 You lie, ye rogue, 'tis going to the King's taver

Gadshill

There's enough to make us all.

Falstaff

To be hanged.

setter: a word used by thieves, meaning 'informant'.
Case ye: disguise yourselves.
vizards: masks.
make us all: make all our fortunes.
front: confront.
scape: escape.
light on: meet.
be: are.
Some: about.

Paunch: the Prince speaks playfully of Falstaff's belly.

John of Gaunt: Hal's grandfather took his name from the town of Gaunt (now Ghent); he was a brave soldier—and he was also thin.
to the proof: to be tested.

fast: firm (do not run away).

hard by: near by.
stand close: hide.

happy . . . dole: good luck, everybody ('dole' = fortune).
'Let everyone do his job'.

Prince
Sirs, you four shall front them in the narrow lane:
Ned Poins and I will walk lower—if they scape
60 from your encounter, then they light on us.
Peto
How many be there of them?
Gadshill
Some eight or ten.
Falstaff
'Zounds, will they not rob us?
Prince
What, a coward, Sir John Paunch?
Falstaff
65 Indeed, I am not John of Gaunt your grandfather,
but yet no coward, Hal.
Prince
Well, we leave that to the proof.
Poins
Sirrah Jack, thy horse stands behind the hedge;
when thou need'st him, there thou shalt find him.
70 Farewell, and stand fast.
Falstaff
Now cannot I strike him, if I should be hanged.
Prince
[*to* Poins] Ned, where are our disguises?
Poins
Here, hard by, stand close.
                              [*Exeunt* Prince *and* Poins
Falstaff
Now, my masters, happy man be his dole, say I.
75 Every man to his business.

Enter the Travellers

First Traveller
Come, neighbour, the boy shall lead our horses
down the hill; we'll walk afoot awhile and ease our
legs.
Thieves
Stand!
Second Traveller
80 Jesus bless us!
Falstaff
Strike! Down with them! Cut the villains' throats!

82   *whoreson caterpillars*: idle parasites.
          bacon-fed: well-fed.
83   *us youth*: us young men.
          fleece them: rob them.
85   *undone*: ruined.
          ours: our families.
86   *gorbellied*: fat-bellied.
87   *chuffs*: misers.
          your store: all you possess.
89   *grandjurors*: great jurymen (only the rich could serve on a grand jury).
          jure: the word has no special meaning; Falstaff is uttering vague threats such as 'We'll show you'.

91–2   *could . . . rob*: if you and I could rob.
93   *argument*: something to talk about.
          laughter: something to laugh at.

Ah, whoreson caterpillars! Bacon-fed knave
They hate us youth! Down with them, flee
them!

First Traveller

85 O, we are undone, both we and ours for ever!

Falstaff

Hang ye, gorbellied knaves, are ye undone? No,
fat chuffs; I would your store were here! (
bacons, on! What, ye knaves! Young men mu
live. You are grandjurors, are ye? We'll jure y
90 faith.

[*They rob them and bind them. Exeu*

Enter the Prince *and* Poins, *disguised*

Prince

The thieves have bound the true men. Now cou
thou and I rob the thieves and go merrily
London, it would be argument for a week, laug
ter for a month, and a good jest for ever.

Poins

95 Stand close, I hear them coming

[*They stand ba*

Enter Falstaff, Gadshill, Bardolph *and*
Peto

Falstaff

Come, my masters, let us share, and then to horse
before day. And the Prince and Poins be not two
arrant cowards there's no equity stirring; there's
no more valour in that Poins than in a wild duck.

[*As they are sharing, the* Prince
and Poins *attack them*

Prince

100 Your money!

Poins

Villains!

[*They all run away, and* Falstaff *after a blow or two
runs away too, leaving the booty behind them*

Prince

Got with much ease. Now merrily to horse!
The thieves are all scatter'd and possess'd with
fear so strongly that they dare not meet each other:
105 each takes his fellow for an officer! Away, good
Ned—Falstaff sweats to death, and lards the lean
earth as he walks along. Were't not for laughing I
should pity him.

Poins

How the fat rogue roared.   [*Exeunt*

---

share: i.e. what they have stolen.
to horse . . . day: ride away before
it is light.
And: if.
arrant: total.
no . . . stirring: no judgement
alive.

Each one thinks that the other is
an officer of the law (they cannot
recognize each other in the dark).
lards: drips fat (as a cook bastes a
lean joint of meat).
Were't . . . laughing: if I were not
laughing so much.

Scene 3 *Warkworth Castle*

Enter Hotspur *reading a letter*

Hotspur

'*But, for mine own part, my lord, I could be well
contented to be there, in respect of the love I bear your
house.*' He could be contented: why is he not then?
In respect of the love he bears our house! He
5 shows in this, he loves his own barn better than he
loves our house. Let me see some more. '*The
purpose you undertake is dangerous*'—Why, that's
certain; 'tis dangerous to take a cold, to sleep, to
drink; but I tell you, my lord fool, out of this
10 nettle, danger, we pluck this flower, safety. '*The*

Act 2 Scene 3
Hotspur is reading a letter. The writer
(we never learn his identity) is unable
to join the rebellion, and he warns
Hotspur not to go ahead with his plans.
The warnings, however, only make
Hotspur more determined. Kate,
Hotspur's wife, tries to find out what is
worrying her husband, but he refuses
to tell his secrets. He calls for his horse,
and prepares to ride away.
for mine own part: to speak for
myself.
there: i.e. with Hotspur and the
rebels, fighting against the King.
in respect of: because of.

4	*house*: family; in line 6 Hotspur deliberately misunderstands, making word-play with the sense of 'house' = a building.
8	*take a cold*: catch a cold.
9	*my lord fool*: my foolish lord.
	nettle : a wild plant whose leaves sting when touched.
12	*uncertain*: unreliable.
	unsorted: badly chosen.
13	*light*: weak.
	for . . . of : to be balanced against.
15	*hind*: peasant.
16	*lack-brain*: idiot.
19	*expectation*: hope.
20	*frosty-spirited*: faint-hearted, cowardly.
21	*my Lord of York*: i.e. the Archbishop of York.
22	*course of the action*: plan of campaign.
	Zounds: by God's wounds.
23	*by*: near.
	brain: knock out his brains.
28	*to meet me*: promising to meet me.
	in arms: ready to fight.
29	*set forward*: started.
30	*pagan*: unbelieving (he does not believe that Hotspur will succeed).
	infidel: faithless.
31–2	*in very . . . heart*: perfect honesty caused by fear and cowardice.
32	*will he*: he will go.
	lay open: reveal.
33	*proceedings*: plans.
33–4	*I could . . . buffets*: I wish I could split myself in two and let the two parts fight each other.
34	*moving*: persuading.
	dish . . . milk: weakling (Hotspur compares the writer to milk which has lost its cream).
36	*set forward*: start out.

purpose you undertake is dangerous, the friends y
have named uncertain, the time itself unsorted, a
your whole plot too light, for the counterpoise of
great an opposition.' Say you so, say you so? I s
15 unto you again, you are a shallow cowardly hin
and you lie. What a lack-brain is this! By the Lor
our plot is a good plot, as ever was laid, our frien
true and constant: a good plot, good friends, ar
full of expectation; an excellent plot, very go
20 friends. What a frosty-spirited rogue is this! Wh
my Lord of York commends the plot, and th
general course of the action. 'Zounds, and I we
now by this rascal, I could brain him with h
lady's fan. Is there not my father, my uncle, ar
25 myself? Lord Edmund Mortimer, my Lord
York, and Owen Glendower? Is there n
besides, the Douglas? Have I not all their letters
meet me in arms by the ninth of the next mont
and are they not some of them set forward alread
30 What a pagan rascal is this, an infidel! Ha! Yo
shall see now—in very sincerity of fear and co
heart will he to the King, and lay open all o
proceedings! O, I could divide myself, and go
buffets, for moving such a dish of skim milk wi
35 so honourable an action! Hang him, let him tell t
King! We are prepared. I will set forward tonig

Enter Lady Percy

How now, Kate? I must leave you within the
two hours.

Lady Percy
O my good lord, why are you thus alone?
40 For what offence have I this fortnight been

stomach: appetite.

bend . . . earth: stare at the ground.

start: stir (as though startled).

Why . . . cheeks: why are you so pale.

3 *given . . . melancholy*: exchanged my pleasure and marital rights for dull-eyed thoughtfulness and miserable depression.

faint slumbers: disturbed sleep.

watch'd: been awake.

Speak . . . manage: use the language of horsemanship.

sallies and retires: advances and retreats.

palisadoes: defences made with pointed iron stakes in the ground.

frontiers, parapets: fortifications.

basilisks . . . cannon . . . culverin: different kinds of cannon.

currents: movements.

heady: violent.

at war: distressed.

bestirr'd: disturbed.

late-disturbed: recently disturbed.

motions: movements.

hest: command.

what . . . these: what do these things mean.

heavy: important.

else: otherwise (i.e. if he does not tell me).

packet: parcel of letters.

A banish'd woman from my Harry's bed?
Tell me, sweet lord, what is't that takes from thee
Thy stomach, pleasure, and thy golden sleep?
Why dost thou bend thine eyes upon the earth,
45 And start so often when thou sit'st alone?
Why hast thou lost the fresh blood in thy cheeks,
And given my treasures and my rights of thee
To thick-ey'd musing and curst melancholy?
In thy faint slumbers I by thee have watch'd,
50 And heard thee murmur tales of iron wars,
Speak terms of manage to thy bounding steed,
Cry 'Courage! To the field!' And thou hast talk'd
Of sallies and retires, of trenches, tents,
Of palisadoes, frontiers, parapets,
55 Of basilisks, of cannon, culverin,
Of prisoners' ransom, and of soldiers slain,
And all the currents of a heady fight.
Thy spirit within thee hath been so at war,
And thus hath so bestirr'd thee in thy sleep,
60 That beads of sweat have stood upon thy brow
Like bubbles in a late-disturbed stream;
And in thy face strange motions have appear'd,
Such as we see when men restrain their breath
On some great sudden hest. O, what portents are
65   these?
Some heavy business hath my lord in hand,
And I must know it, else he loves me not.
   Hotspur
What ho!

Enter a Servant

Is Gilliams with the packet gone?
   Servant
He is, my lord, an hour ago.

72   *even now*: just now.
73   *a roan, a crop-ear*: in a 'roan' horse the main colour (perhaps chestnut) is mixed with grey or white; horses' ears were sometimes cut (cropped) to make the animal look more alert.
75   *back him*: mount him.
      straight: immediately.
      Esperance: hope; the Percy family motto was 'Esperance ma comforte'.
77   *hear you*: listen.
79   'What is the business that takes you away from home'.
80   Hotspur wilfully misunderstands his wife.
82-3 *A weasel ... toss'd with*: a weasel has not such an excitable temper as you are troubled with. Weasels are very savage, reddish-brown little animals, sometimes used to kill rabbits. The Elizabethans believed that the spleen was the source of irritable emotions.

85   *stir*: make trouble.
86   *About his title*: see p. 128.
87   *line*: strengthen (as the lining strengthens a coat).
88   *afoot*: on foot.
89   *paraquito*: talking parrot.
89-90 *answer me directly*: give me a straight answer.
91   *little finger*: only lovers would twist each other's little fingers (as Kate and Hotspur seem to be doing here).
      And if: if.
96   *mammets*: dolls (feminine things).
      tilt with lips: fight with lips—i.e. kiss.
97   *crowns*: skulls; in the next line Hotspur speaks of 'crowns' as coins.

Hotspur
70 Hath Butler brought those horses from t
sheriff?
Servant
One horse, my lord, he brought even now.
Hotspur
What horse? A roan, a crop-ear, is it not?
Servant
It is, my lord.
Hotspur   That roan shall be my thro
75 Well, I will back him straight: O Esperance!
Bid Butler lead him forth into the park.
                              [*Exit* Serva

Lady Percy
But hear you, my lord.
Hotspur
What say'st thou, my lady?
Lady Percy
What is it carries you away?
Hotspur
80 Why, my horse, my love, my horse.
Lady Percy
Out, you mad-headed ape!
A weasel hath not such a deal of spleen
As you are toss'd with. In faith,
I'll know your business, Harry, that I will!
85 I fear my brother Mortimer doth stir
About his title, and hath sent for you
To line his enterprise. But if you go—
Hotspur
So far afoot I shall be weary, love.
Lady Percy
Come, come, you paraquito, answer me direc
90 unto this question that I ask; in faith, I'll break
little finger, Harry, and if thou wilt not tell me
things true.
Hotspur
Away,
Away, you trifler! Love! I love thee not;
95 I care not for thee, Kate. This is no world
To play with mammets, and to tilt with lips;
We must have bloody noses, and crack'd crow

pass them current: exchange them as though they were good (cracked coins were not acceptable currency).

God's me: God save me (an exclamation of impatience).

What . . . me: what do you want from me.

'Tell me if you are joking or not'.

a-horseback: mounted on my horse.

reason whereabout: wonder where I am (*or* what I am doing).

I must: I must go.

no farther wise: no more wise.

constant: faithful.

closer: more able to keep secrets.
'You will not talk about what you do not know'.

so far: i.e. not at all (he has told her nothing).

of force: of necessity.

And pass them current too. God's me, my horse!
What say'st thou, Kate? What wouldst thou have
  with me?
    Lady Percy
100 Do you not love me? Do you not indeed?
Well, do not then; for since you love me not
I will not love myself. Do you not love me?
Nay, tell me if you speak in jest or no.
    Hotspur
Come, wilt thou see me ride?
105 And when I am a-horseback, I will swear
I love thee infinitely. But hark you, Kate,
I must not have you henceforth question me
Whither I go, nor reason whereabout:
Whither I must, I must; and, to conclude,
110 This evening must I leave you, gentle Kate.
I know you wise, but yet no farther wise
Than Harry Percy's wife; constant you are,
But yet a woman; and for secrecy,
No lady closer, for I well believe
115 Thou wilt not utter what thou dost not know;
And so far will I trust thee, gentle Kate.
    Lady Percy
How? So far?
    Hotspur
Not an inch further. But hark you, Kate:
Whither I go, thither shall you go too;
120 Today will I set forth, tomorrow you.
Will this content you, Kate?
    Lady Percy   It must, of force.   [*Exeunt*

Act 2 Scene 4
At the Boar's Head Tavern in Eastcheap, Prince Hal and Poins are waiting for Falstaff. To amuse themselves, they play a trick on Francis, one of the Drawers in the tavern. Falstaff and the other thieves arrive. Falstaff gives an account of what happened at Gad's Hill, telling enormous lies until the Prince

Scene 4 *Eastcheap: the Boar's Head Tavern*

Enter Prince *and* Poins

    Prince
Ned, prithee come out of that fat room, and lend
me thy hand to laugh a little.
    Poins
Where hast been, Hal?

interrupts and confronts Falstaff with the truth. A message arrives for Prince Hal: he is commanded to go to the royal palace for an interview with his father. The friends then hold two 'rehearsals' for the interview: in the first, Falstaff plays the part of King Henry IV; in the second 'rehearsal' Prince Hal speaks for his father. The laughter ceases when the Sheriff comes to arrest Falstaff. Hal protects his friend.

1   *fat*: stuffy.

4   *loggerheads*: thickheads, fools.

5   *hogsheads*: large barrels; the Prince has been in the cellars of the tavern (inn-servants invited favourite customers to drink there).

sounded . . . string: reached the very lowest level (the base-string plays the lowest notes on a stringed instrument).

6   *I am . . . brother*: I have promised to be a brother (according to the rules of chivalry).

7   *leash*: set of three (especially hounds).

drawers: waiters, tapsters.

8   *christen*: Christian (christened).

9   *take . . . salvation*: are already prepared to swear by their hopes of eternal salvation.

10   *king of courtesy*: the most courteous (polite) man (in this respect Hal is a king, although in fact he is only a prince).

11   *flatly*: without hesitation.
Jack: fellow.

12   *a Corinthian*: a wild fellow (Corinth was famous for riotous living).
a good boy: one of us.

15   *the good lads*: i.e. their mates, the other drawers.
drinking deep: drinking heavily, emptying the cup.

16   *dyeing scarlet*: because heavy drinkers usually have red faces.
breathe . . . watering: pause for breath whilst drinking.

17   *Play it off*: get on with it.

18   *proficient*: expert.

Prince
With three or four loggerheads, amongst three
5 fourscore hogsheads. I have sounded the very bas
string of humility. Sirrah, I am sworn broth
to a leash of drawers, and can call them all t
their christen names, as Tom, Dick, and Franc
They take it already upon their salvation, th
10 though I be but Prince of Wales, yet I am the kir
of courtesy, and tell me flatly I am no proud Jac
like Falstaff, but a Corinthian, a lad of mettle,
good boy (by the Lord, so they call me!), and whe
I am King of England I shall command all th
15 good lads in Eastcheap. They call drinking dee
'dyeing scarlet'; and when you breathe in you
watering, they cry 'Hem!' and bid you 'Play it off
To conclude, I am so good a proficient in on
quarter of an hour that I can drink with any tink
20 in his own language during my life. I tell the
Ned, thou hast lost much honour that thou we
not with me in this action. But, sweet Ned—
sweeten which name of Ned I give thee th
pennyworth of sugar, clapped even now into m
25 hand by an underskinker, one that never spak
other English in his life than 'Eight shillings an
sixpence', and 'You are welcome', with this shri
addition, 'Anon, anon, sir! Score a pint of bastar
in the Half-moon', or so. But Ned, to drive awa
30 the time till Falstaff come—I prithee do tho
stand in some by-room, while I question my pun
drawer to what end he gave me the sugar, and d

9 'For the rest of my life I shall be able to drink with tinkers (notoriously heavy drinkers) and use their own language (which he has just learned)'.

The Prince speaks of his meeting with the drawers as though it were a military battle ('action').

sugar: this was sold in taverns to sweeten the sack.

even now: just now.

clapped: thrust.

underskinker: under-tapster, tapster's assistant.

The Prince comments that the tapster's vocabulary is limited to the words he uses in his job.

Anon: at once, I'm coming.

Score: note the price of; as the tapster served the drinks, he called to the tavern-keeper who made out the bills.

bastard: sweet Spanish wine.

29 *the Half-moon*: names were given to the different inn-rooms.

or so: or something like that.

drive away: pass.

31 *by-room*: side room, leading out of a larger one.

puny: young, inexperienced.

32 *to what end*: for what purpose, why.

32–3 *do thou never leave*: don't ever stop.

thou never leave calling 'Francis!', that his tal[e]
me may be nothing but 'Anon'. Step aside, and [I'll]
35 show thee a precedent.   [*Exit Po[ins*]

Poins
[*Within*] Francis!

Prince
Thou art perfect.

Poins
[*Within*] Francis!

Enter Francis, *a Drawer*

Francis
Anon, anon, sir. Look down into the Pomgar[net,]
40 Ralph.

Prince
Come hither, Francis.

Francis
My lord?

Prince
How long hast thou to serve, Francis?

Francis
Forsooth, five years, and as much as to—

Poins
45 [*Within*] Francis!

Francis
Anon, anon, sir.

Prince
Five year! By'r lady, a long lease for the clinkin[g of]
pewter. But Francis, darest thou be so valiant a[s to]
play the coward with thy indenture, and show [a]
50 fair pair of heels, and run from it?

Francis
O lord, sir, I'll be sworn upon all the books [in]
England, I could find in my heart—

Poins
[*Within*] Francis!

Francis
Anon, sir.

Prince
55 How old art thou, Francis?

Francis
Let me see, about Michaelmas next I shall be—

33–4   'So that all he answers to my questions is "I'm coming"'.
35   *show . . . precedent*: show you what I mean.
39   *Pomgarnet*: Pomegranate (another of the inn-rooms).
43   *to serve*: i.e. as an apprentice; an apprenticeship was for seven years.

47   *By'r lady*: by Our Lady.
47–8   *long . . . .pewter*: a long time to spend clashing pewter mugs (cheap drinking vessels were made of pewter).
49   *indenture*: apprentice's contract.
51   *books*: Bibles (anyone making a formal oath must place his right hand on a Bible).
52   *I could . . . heart*: I would like to.
56   *Michaelmas*: Michaelmas (St Michael's) Day is 29 September.

would: wish.
a-Thursday: on Thursday.
73 The Prince describes the inn-
keeper.
    leathern-jerkin: leather tunic.
    crystal-button: glass buttoned.
    not-pated: short-haired (a
gentleman's hair was long).
    agate-ring: signet-ring with an
agate stone.
    puke-stocking: 'puke' was a dark
woollen material.
    caddis-garter: 'caddis' was a
coarse material used for garters.
    smooth-tongue: fast talking.
    Spanish pouch: the innkeeper
wore on his belt a purse of soft Spanish
leather.

77 The Prince now seems to be
talking complete nonsense; he perhaps
means to imply that Francis should not
think about changing his trade.
    brown bastard: very sweet wine.
    your only: the best.
    look you: be careful.
    your white . . . sully: your apron
will get dirty.

Poins
[*Within*] Francis!
    Francis
Anon, sir—pray stay a little, my lord.
    Prince
Nay—but hark you, Francis; for the sugar thou
60 gavest me—'twas a pennyworth, was't not?
    Francis
O Lord! I would it had been two!
    Prince
I will give thee for it a thousand pound—ask me
when thou wilt, and thou shalt have it.
    Poins
[*Within*] Francis!
    Francis
65 Anon, anon.
    Prince
Anon, Francis? No, Francis, but tomorrow,
Francis; or, Francis, a-Thursday; or indeed,
Francis, when thou wilt. But Francis!
    Francis
My lord?
    Prince
70 Wilt thou rob this leathern-jerkin, crystal-button,
not-pated, agate-ring, puke-stocking, caddis-
garter, smooth-tongue Spanish pouch?
    Francis
O Lord, sir, who do you mean?
    Prince
Why then your brown bastard is your only drink:
75 for look you, Francis, your white canvas doublet
will sully. In Barbary, sir, it cannot come to so
much.
    Francis
What, sir?
    Poins
[*Within*] Francis!
    Prince
80 Away, you rogue, dost thou not hear them call?
    [*Here they both call him; the* Drawer *stands
    amazed, not knowing which way to go*

    Enter Vintner

82   *Look to*: attend to.

90   *merry as crickets*: the comparison
      is proverbial; crickets are little insects
      which make a continuous chirping
      sound.
90–92 *what . . . drawer*: what clever
      trick have you been playing with this
      joke on the drawer.
92   *what's the issue*: what is
      happening.
93–6 The Prince is ready for anything:
      humours: moods.
      showed themselves: been
      recognized.
      goodman Adam: old Father Adam
      (the first human being).
      pupil age: youth.

99   *That ever*: how odd.

101–102 *His industry . . . down stairs*: all
      his work is running up and down stairs.
102   *his eloquence . . . reckoning*: all his
      conversation consists of the parts of a
      bill.
103   *of Percy's mind*: like Percy (i.e.
      Hotspur).
105   *at a breakfast*: for a beginning.
106   *Fie upon*: I'm bored with.
      work: something to do.
108   *drench*: dose of medicine.
109   *Some*: about.
110   *a trifle*: nothing much.
111   *brawn*: fat pig.

Vintner
What, stand'st thou still and hear'st such a callin
Look to the guests within. [*Exit* Francis] My lor
old Sir John with half-a-dozen more are at t
door—shall I let them in?

Prince
85 Let them alone awhile, and then open the do
[*Exit* Vintner] Poins!

Enter Poins

Poins
Anon, anon, sir.

Prince
Sirrah, Falstaff and the rest of the thieves are at t
door; shall we be merry?

Poins
90 As merry as crickets, my lad; but hark ye, wl
cunning match have you made with this jest of t
drawer: come, what's the issue?

Prince
I am now of all humours that have show
95 themselves humours since the old days of goo
man Adam to the pupil age of this present twel
o'clock at midnight.

Enter Francis

What's o'clock, Francis?

Francis
Anon, anon, sir.   [*E.*

Prince
That ever this fellow should have fewer wor
100 than a parrot, and yet the son of a woman! H
industry is up-stairs and down-stairs, h
eloquence the parcel of a reckoning. I am not yet
Percy's mind, the Hotspur of the north—he th
kills me some six or seven dozen of Scots at
105 breakfast, washes his hands, and says to his wi
'Fie upon this quiet life, I want work'. 'O r
sweet Harry', says she, 'how many hast thou kill
today?' 'Give my roan horse a drench', says h
and answers, 'Some fourteen', an hour after,
110 trifle, a trifle'. I prithee call in Falstaff; I'll pl
Percy, and that damned brawn shall play Dai

Rivo: a (meaningless) word used by drinkers: a modern equivalent is 'Cheers'.

Tallow: dripping (the fat melted from roasted meat).

7   *nether-stocks*: stockings.
8   *foot them*: put feet in the stockings.

9   *virtue*: courage.
    extant: living.

1–4   The exact sense of these lines is not clear. Falstaff's red face is bent over the cup of sack, and the Prince is reminded of a hot sun ('Titan' was a name for the sun-god) shining on and melting a dish of butter.

4   *compound*: combination (Falstaff and the wine).

5   *lime*: lime was used to make poor quality sack seem more sparkling and dry.

1   *shotten herring*: a common simile for extreme thinness: after the herring (a fish) has shot its roe (released its eggs) it is very thin.

    lives: a singular verb with plural subject is quite common at this time.

2   *one of them*: Falstaff means himself.

3   *God . . . while*: God help these times.

4   *I would*: I wish.
    weaver . . . psalms: weavers were often Puritans, and the songs they sang as they worked were the religious psalms.

6   *wool-sack*: Falstaff is as fat and shapeless as a sack of wool.

8   *dagger of lath*: a wooden dagger; see p. xxviii.

39   *afore*: before.

40   *hair on my face*: a beard.

42   *whoreson*: disgusting.

Mortimer his wife. 'Rivo!' says the drunkard. Call in Ribs, call in Tallow.

Enter Falstaff, Gadshill, Bardolph, *and* Peto; *followed by* Francis, *with wine*

Poins
Welcome, Jack; where hast thou been?

Falstaff
115 A plague of all cowards, I say, and a vengeance too, marry and amen! Give me a cup of sack, boy. Ere I lead this life long. I'll sew nether-stocks, and mend them and foot them too. A plague of all cowards! Give me a cup of sack, rogue; is there no
120 virtue extant?   [*He drinks*

Prince
Didst thou never see Titan kiss a dish of butter (pitiful-hearted Titan!), that melted at the sweet tale of the sun's? If thou didst, then behold that compound.

Falstaff
125 You rogue, here's lime in this sack too! There is nothing but roguery to be found in villainous man, yet a coward is worse than a cup of sack with lime in it. A villainous coward! Go thy ways, old Jack, die when thou wilt—if manhood, good manhood,
130 be not forgot upon the face of the earth, then am I a shotten herring: there lives not three good men unhanged in England, and one of them is fat, and grows old. God help the while! A bad world, I say. I would I were a weaver; I could sing psalms, or
135 anything. A plague of all cowards, I say still.

Prince
How now, wool-sack, what mutter you?

Falstaff
A king's son! If I do not beat thee out of thy kingdom with a dagger of lath, and drive all thy subjects afore thee like a flock of wild geese, I'll
140 never wear hair on my face more. You, Prince of Wales!

Prince
Why, you whoreson round man, what's the matter?

146   *and*: if.

151–2   *sees your back*: i.e. as you run
         away.
152   *call ... backing*: is that what you
         call supporting (the pun is on 'back').
158   *All ... that*: that doesn't matter.
165   *poor*: merely.
167   *at half-sword*: fighting very
         closely—only the length of half a sword
         from his opponents.
170   *buckler*: shield.
172   *ecce signum*: behold the sign
         (Falstaff displays his battered sword).
         dealt: fought.
173   *all ... do*: it was not enough (to
         save the money they had stolen).

Falstaff

Are not you a coward? Answer me to that—an
145 Poins there?

Poins

'Zounds, ye fat paunch. And ye call me coward, b
the Lord I'll stab thee.

Falstaff

I call thee coward? I'll see thee damned ere I ca
thee coward; but I would give a thousand pound
150 could run as fast as thou canst. You are straigh
enough in the shoulders, you care not who see
your back: call you that backing of your friends?
plague upon such backing, give me them that wi
face me! Give me a cup of sack: I am a rogue if
155 drunk today.

Prince

O villain! Thy lips are scarce wiped since tho
drunk'st last.

Falstaff

All is one for that. [*He drinks*] A plague of a
cowards, still say I.

Prince

160 What's the matter?

Falstaff

What's the matter? There be four of us here hav
ta'en a thousand pound this day morning.

Prince

Where is it, Jack, where is it?

Falstaff

Where is it? Taken from us it is. A hundred upo
165 poor four of us.

Prince

What, a hundred, man?

Falstaff

I am a rogue if I were not at half-sword with
dozen of them two hours together. I have scape
by miracle. I am eight times thrust through th
170 doublet, four through the hose, my buckler cu
through and through, my sword hacked like
handsaw—*ecce signum*! I never dealt better since
was a man: all would not do. A plague of a
cowards! Let them speak—if they speak more o

sons of darkness: damned (the phrase is from the Bible).
set upon: attacked.

an Ebrew Jew: a Hebrew (Jewish) Jew.

sharing: i.e. the stolen goods.
fresh: different.

other: others (the men they had first attacked).
radish: thin root vegetables.

no two-legged creature: not a man.
that's . . . for: it is too late to pray for that.
peppered: killed.
paid: finished.
buckram suits: the 'cases of buckram' (disguises made of coarse fabric) that Poins promised to obtain in *Act 1*, Scene 2.
old ward: usual fighting position.
here . . . point: this is how I placed myself, and this is how I held my sword.
let drive: thrust their swords.
Thou . . . now: just now you said there were only two of them.

175 less than truth, they are villains, and the sons of darkness.

Prince
Speak, sirs, how was it?

Gadshill
We four set upon some dozen—

Falstaff
Sixteen at least, my lord.

Gadshill
180 And bound them.

Peto
No, no, they were not bound.

Falstaff
You rogue, they were bound, every man of them, or I am a Jew else: an Ebrew Jew.

Gadshill
As we were sharing, some six or seven fresh men
185 set upon us—

Falstaff
And unbound the rest, and then come in the other.

Prince
What, fought you with them all?

Falstaff
All? I know not what you call all, but if I fought not with fifty of them I am a bunch of radish: if
190 there were not two or three and fifty upon poor old Jack, then am I no two-legged creature.

Prince
Pray God you have not murdered some of them.

Falstaff
Nay, that's past praying for: I have peppered two of them. Two I am sure I have paid, two rogues in
195 buckram suits. I tell thee what, Hal, if I tell thee a lie, spit in my face, call me horse. Thou knowest my old ward—here I lay, and thus I bore my point. Four rogues in buckram let drive at me—

Prince
What, four? Thou saidst but two even now.

Falstaff
200 Four, Hal; I told thee four.

Poins
Ay, ay, he said four.

202 *afront*: abreast.
     mainly: violently.
203 *I . . . ado*: I myself made no more
     fuss.
203–4 *took . . . target*: received all seven
     sword-points in my shield.
208 *hilts*: the handle of his sword (in
     the form of a cross—see illustration).

209 *let him alone*: don't argue with
     him.
212 *mark*: pay attention to.
216–17 Falstaff speaks of the points of
     the swords; but Poins pretends to
     understand 'points' as the laces which
     fastened doublet and hose together.

218 *give me ground*: give way (yield)
     to me.
     followed me close: quickly seized
     my advantage.
219 *came . . . hand*: advanced, with
     my feet and my sword.
     with a thought: quick as a
     thought.
220 *paid*: killed.

Falstaff
These four came all afront, and mainly thrust
me; I made me no more ado, but took all the
seven points in my target, thus!
    Prince
205 Seven? Why, there were but four even now.
    Falstaff
In buckram?
    Poins
Ay, four, in buckram suits.
    Falstaff
Seven, by these hilts, or I am a villain else.
    Prince
[*To* Poins] Prithee let him alone; we shall ha
210 more anon.
    Falstaff
Dost thou hear me, Hal?
    Prince
Ay, and mark thee too, Jack.
    Falstaff
Do so, for it is worth the listening to. These ni
in buckram that I told thee of—
    Prince
215 So, two more already.
    Falstaff
Their points being broken—
    Poins
Down fell their hose.
    Falstaff
Began to give me ground; but I followed me clo
came in, foot and hand—and, with a though
220 seven of the eleven I paid..

Prince

O monstrous! Eleven buckram men grown out of two!

Falstaff

But as the devil would have it, three misbegotten knaves in Kendal green came at my back and let
225 drive at me; for it was so dark, Hal, that thou couldst not see thy hand.

Prince

These lies are like their father that begets them: gross as a mountain, open, palpable. Why, thou clay-brained guts, thou knotty-pated fool, thou
230 whoreson obscene greasy tallow-catch,—

Falstaff

What, art thou mad? Art thou mad? Is not the truth the truth?

Prince

Why, how couldst thou know these men in Kendal green when it was so dark thou couldst not see thy
235 hand? Come, tell us your reason. What sayest thou to this?

Poins

Come, your reason, Jack, your reason.

Falstaff

What, upon compulsion? 'Zounds, and I were at the strappado, or all the racks in the world, I
240 would not tell you on compulsion. Give you a reason on compulsion? If reasons were as plentiful as blackberries, I would give no man a reason upon compulsion, I.

Prince

I'll be no longer guilty of this sin. This sanguine
245 coward, this bed-presser, this horse-back-breaker, this huge hill of flesh,—

Falstaff

'Sblood, you starveling, you eel-skin, you dried neat's-tongue, you bull's pizzle, you stock-fish—O for breath to utter what is like thee!—you tailor's-
250 yard, you sheath, you bow-case, you vile standing tuck!

Prince

Well, breathe awhile, and then to it again, and

---

23   *misbegotten*: cursed.
      Kendal green: coarse green cloth, worn by peasants.
29   *knotty-pated*: block-headed.
30   *whoreson*: bastardly.
      tallow-catch: lump of fat.
38   *and*: if.
39   *strappado*: a form of torture (which pulled the victim's joints apart).
      racks: this torture stretched the man's body until he died (or confessed).
41   *reasons*: the pronunciation of this word allows Falstaff to make a pun with 'raisins'—which had to be imported into England, unlike the 'blackberries', which grow wild.
44   *this sin*: i.e. of appearing to believe Falstaff's story.
      sanguine: ruddy-faced (cowards are usually pale).
47   *starveling*: skinny creature.
      eel-skin: eels are long, snakelike fishes.
48   *neat's-tongue*: cow's tongue.
      bull's-pizzle: bull's penis (when dried, it was used as a whip).
      stock-fish: dried cod-fish (stored in long strips to be eaten in winter).
50   *yard*: measuring-stick (it was one yard long).
      sheath: in which the sword was kept.
      bow-case: the long, narrow cover for an archer's bow.
51-2 *standing tuck*: rapier (a long thin sword) standing on its end.
52   *breathe awhile*: stop for a moment to get your breath back.
      to it again: continue to insult me.

253   'When you are tired of making
these wretched comparisons'.
254   'Let me say just this'.
255   *Mark*: take notice.
257   *were . . . of*: took possession.
258   *put you down*: beat you.
259   *with a word*: quite simply.
        outfaced: defeated.
264   *slave*: wretch.
267   *starting-hole*: hiding-place.
268   *apparent*: obvious.
269   *trick*: excuse.
270   *he . . . ye*: i.e. God.
272   *turn upon*: attack.
274   *Hercules*: the super-man of
classical mythology.
        beware: take notice of.
274-5   *the lion . . . prince*: this was a very
old belief.

276-7   *think the better*: have a higher
opinion.
277   *during my life*: for as long as I
live.
280   *clap to*: shut.
        Watch: stay awake. The Bible
instructs Christians to 'watch and pray;
but Falstaff separates the two activities.
281   *Gallants*: gentlemen.

when thou hast tired thyself in base comparison
hear me speak but this.

Poins

255 Mark, Jack.

Prince

We two saw you four set on four, and bound ther
and were masters of their wealth—mark now ho
a plain tale shall put you down. Then did we tw
set on you four, and, with a word, out-faced yo
260 from your prize, and have it; yea, and can show
you here in the house. And, Falstaff, you carrie
your guts away as nimbly, with as quick dexterit
and roared for mercy, and still run and roared, a
ever I heard bull-calf. What a slave art thou t
265 hack thy sword as thou hast done, and then say
was in fight! What trick, what device, wha
starting-hole canst thou now find out, to hide the
from this open and apparent shame?

Poins

Come, let's hear, Jack, what trick hast thou now

Falstaff

270 By the Lord, I knew ye as well as he that made ye
Why, hear you, my masters, was it for me to ki
the heir-apparent? Should I turn upon the tru
prince? Why, thou knowest I am as valiant a
Hercules: but beware instinct—the lion will no
275 touch the true prince; instinct is a great matter.
was now a coward on instinct: I shall think th
better of myself, and thee, during my life—I for
valiant lion, and thou for a true prince. But by th
Lord, lads, I am glad you have the money
280 Hostess, clap to the doors! Watch tonight, pra
tomorrow!—Gallants, lads, boys, hearts of gold
all the titles of good fellowship come to you
What, shall we be merry, shall we have a pla
extempore?

Prince

285 Content, and the argument shall be thy running
away.

Falstaff

Ah, no more of that, Hal, and thou lovest me.

Enter Hostess

283   *shall . . . extempore*: shall we improvise a play. This was a popular form of entertainment in Elizabethan taverns; the Prince has already suggested such amusement (line 110).
285   *argument*: subject.

292   *would speak*: who wishes to speak.

294   *a royal man*: it was a favourite joke amongst the Elizabethans to make puns on 'noble' and 'royal'—the names of two coins.
296   *manner*: kind.

298   'What is an old man doing out of bed at midnight'.

301   *send . . . packing*: make him go away very quickly.

302   *fair*: well.

307   *in earnest*: seriously.

310   *swear . . . England*: swear until truth has been driven out of England.

313   *spear-grass*: grass with very sharp edges.
314   *beslubber*: smear.
316–17   *I did . . . before*: I did something that I haven't done for seven years.

Hostess

O Jesu, my lord the Prince!

Prince

How now, my lady the hostess, what say'st thou to
290   me?

Hostess

Marry, my lord, there is a nobleman of the court at door would speak with you: he says he comes from your father.

Prince

Give him as much as will make him a royal man,
295   and send him back again to my mother.

Falstaff

What manner of man is he?

Hostess

An old man.

Falstaff

What doth gravity out of his bed at midnight?
Shall I give him his answer?

Prince

300   Prithee do, Jack.

Falstaff

Faith, and I'll send him packing.   [*Exit*

Prince

Now, sirs: by'r Lady, you fought fair; so did you,
Peto, so did you, Bardolph; you are lions too, you
ran away upon instinct, you will not touch the true
305   prince; no, fie!

Bardolph

Faith; I ran when I saw others run.

Prince

Faith, tell me now in earnest, how came Falstaff's
sword so hacked?

Peto

Why, he hacked it with his dagger, and said he
310   would swear truth out of England but he would
make you believe it was done in fight, and
persuaded us to do the like.

Bardolph

Yea, and to tickle our noses with spear-grass, to
make them bleed, and then to beslubber our
315   garments with it, and swear it was the blood of
true men. I did that I did not this seven year

317   *devices*: schemes.
319   *taken . . . manner*: caught in the act (i.e. as he was stealing).
320   *extempore*: without any special cause (Bardolph has a very red face—like Falstaff, he is a heavy drinker).
321   *fire*: i.e. Bardolph's fiery red face.
322   *What instinct*: the Prince is still joking about the excuse that Falstaff offered for his running away (line 275).
323–4   *meteors . . . exhalations*: Bardolph refers to the spots and bumps on his face as though they were astrological phenomena (which would have some special meaning).
326   *portend*: signify.
327   Bardolph's red, spotty face must be caused by an overheated liver, the result of too much drinking; and the drinking has also caused his 'cold' (empty) purse.
328   *Choler*: quick-temper; the word is pronounced like 'collar', which suggests a pun with 'halter'.
       rightly taken: properly understood ('taken').
329   If you are arrested ('taken') as you deserve to be, you will be hanged; the 'halter' is the hangman's noose.
331   *bombast*: stuffing.
334   *thy years*: your age.
335   My waist was not as round as an eagle's claw.

336   *alderman's thumb-ring*: rich citizens wore rings on their thumbs (which could be used for sealing documents).

before—I blushed to hear his monstrous device:

Prince
O villain, thou stolest a cup of sack eighteen year
ago, and wert taken with the manner, and eve
320 since thou hast blushed extempore. Thou had:
fire and sword on thy side, and yet thou ran':
away—what instinct hadst thou for it?

Bardolph
My lord, do you see these meteors? Do you behol
these exhalations?

Prince
325 I do.

Bardolph
What think you they portend?

Prince
Hot livers and cold purses.

Bardolph
Choler, my lord, if rightly taken.

Prince
No, if rightly taken, halter.

Enter Falstaff

330 Here comes lean Jack, here comes bare-bon
How now, my sweet creature of bombast? Hov
long is't ago, Jack, since thou sawest thine ow
knee?

Falstaff
My own knee? When I was about thy years, Hal,
335 was not an eagle's talon in the waist; I could hav
crept into any alderman's thumb-ring. A plague o

abroad: about, discussed publicly.
-9 *here ... father*: Sir John Bracy was sent here by your father.
must: must go.
he of Wales: that chap from Wales.
Amamon: the name of a devil.
bastinado: a beating on the soles of the feet.
made Lucifer cuckold: seduced Lucifer's wife; Lucifer was the name of the chief devil. It was popularly believed that a man whose wife had been seduced would grow horns on his head (the devil is often portrayed with horns).
liegeman: subject.
the cross ... hook: the Welsh fought with long-handled axes (which did not, in fact, have cross-pieces).
Scot of Scots: most famous of all Scotsmen.
runs a-horseback: gallops on his horse.
a hill perpendicular: i.e. a hill so steep that it seems to stand at a right angle to the level ground.
hit it: got it right.
'Well, he never hit the sparrow.'
-9 In these lines Falstaff and the Prince play with the different meanings of their words.
'He (Hotspur) is a rogue ('rascal'), but he is brave ('hath good mettle in him') and will not run away'.
rascal is a deer that will not be hunted ('run').
mettle makes a pun with 'metal': good metal does not melt ('run').
cuckoo: a small brown bird which utters only two notes.
budge: give way.

sighing and grief, it blows a man up like a bladder. There's villainous news abroad: here was Sir John Bracy from your father; you must to the court in 340 the morning. That same mad fellow of the north, Percy, and he of Wales that gave Amamon the bastinado, and made Lucifer cuckold, and swore the devil his true liegeman upon the cross of a Welsh hook—what a plague call you him?

Poins

345 O, Glendower.

Falstaff

Owen, Owen, the same; and his son-in-law Mortimer, and old Northumberland, and that sprightly Scot of Scots, Douglas, that runs a-horseback up a hill perpendicular—

Prince

350 He that rides at high speed, and with his pistol kills a sparrow flying.

Falstaff

You have hit it.

Prince

So did he never the sparrow.

Falstaff

Well, that rascal hath good mettle in him; he will 355 not run.

Prince

Why, what a rascal art thou then, to praise him so for running!

Falstaff

A-horseback, ye cuckoo! But afoot he will not budge a foot.

360   *on instinct*: the Prince returns
      again to Falstaff's own words (line
      274).
361   *I grant ye*: I admit that.
      is there: with the rebels.
362   *one*: a certain.
      blue-caps: Scottish soldiers wore
      blue caps.
363   *stolen away*: gone away secretly
      (to join the rebels).
365   When civil war was threatened,
      many landlords tried to sell their
      property, preferring to take a low price
      rather than risk losing everything if the
      country was captured by the rebels.
366   *it is like*: probably.
      come . . . June: if we have a hot
      summer.
367   *this . . . hold*: these civil wars
      continue.
367–8 It will be as easy to get a woman
      as it is to buy nails for mending boots
      (hob-nails): they will be selling
      themselves in hundreds.
371   *horrible afeard*: dreadfully
      frightened.
371–2 You are the heir to the throne,
      and you could not have three such
      terrible enemies anywhere in the world.
373   *spirit*: devil.
375   *thrill*: shiver with cold fear.
376   *Not a whit*: not in the least.
377   *chid*: scolded.
378   *if you love me*: for my sake.
378–9 *practise an answer*: prepare what
      you are going to say.
380   *Do . . . for*: you play the part of.
      examine: question.
381   *particulars*: details.
382   *state*: throne.
385   *is taken for*: is seen to be.
      joint-stool: a stool made by a
      joiner.
386   *leaden dagger*: cheap dagger
      made of lead (see p. xxviii).
387   *bald crown*: i.e. the crown of
      Falstaff's head.
388   *and . . . thee*: if you have any
      conscience (or shame) left in you.
389   *moved*: affected, made to feel
      ashamed.

Prince

360 Yes, Jack, upon instinct.

Falstaff

I grant ye, upon instinct. Well, he is there too, a
one Mordake, and a thousand blue-caps mo
Worcester is stolen away tonight; thy fathe
beard is turned white with the news; you may b

365 land now as cheap as stinking mackerel.

Prince

Why then, it is like, if there come a hot June, a
this civil buffeting hold, we shall buy maidenhea
as they buy hob-nails, by the hundreds.

Falstaff

By the mass, lad, thou sayest true; it is like we sh

370 have good trading that way. But tell me, Hal,
not thou horrible afeard? Thou being heir a
parent, could the world pick thee out three su
enemies again, as that fiend Douglas, that spi
Percy, and that devil Glendower? Art thou

375 horribly afraid? Doth not thy blood thrill at it

Prince

Not a whit, i'faith. I lack some of thy instinct.

Falstaff

Well, thou wilt be horribly chid tomorrow wh
thou comest to thy father; if thou love me pract
an answer.

Prince

380 Do thou stand for my father and examine me up
the particulars of my life.

Falstaff

Shall I? Content! This chair shall be my sta
this dagger my sceptre, and this cushion
crown.

Prince

385 Thy state is taken for a joint-stool, thy gold
sceptre for a leaden dagger, and thy precious r
crown for a pitiful bald crown.

Falstaff

Well, and the fire of grace be not quite out of th
now shalt thou be moved. Give me a cup of sack

391   *in passion*: with powerful emotion.
392   *in . . . vein*: in the manner of *King Cambyses*—a play written more than 20 years before *Henry IV Part 1*; in lines 396 and 399–400 Shakespeare parodies the style of such old-fashioned plays.
393   *leg*: bow.
394   *nobility*: Falstaff speaks to the crowd of thieves and drinkers as though they were the king's courtiers.
397   *vain*: useless.
398   *holds his countenance*: keeps a straight (solemn) face.
399   *convey*: remove.
       tristful: unhappy.
400   'Her eyes are over-flowing with tears'.
401   *as like . . . players*: just like one of those ridiculous actors.
403   *Peace*: be quiet.
       pint-pot: one of the mugs in which the hostess would serve ale.
       tickle-brain: strong drink, alcohol.
405   *how . . . accompanied*: what sort of friends you have.
406–7   In these lines Shakespeare parodies a popular style of writing called *euphuism* (it was first used in the novel *Euphues* by John Lyly).
       camomile: a strong little herb, used on lawns, which gives a pleasant scent and grows faster when it is trodden on.
407   *wasted*: spent in riotous living.
408   *wears*: is ruined.
408–9   *have . . . word*: partly because your mother says so.
410–11 *chiefly . . . lip*: mainly because you have a certain look about your eyes, and the naughty way you pout your lower lip.
411   *warrant me*: assure me, resemble me.
413   *pointed at*: scoffed at.
414   *micher*: truant (as schoolboys played truant from school to pick blackberries).

390 make my eyes look red, that it may be though have wept, for I must speak in passion; and I w do it in King Cambyses' vein.

Prince
Well, here is my leg.

Falstaff
And here is my speech. Stand aside, nobility.

Hostess
395 O Jesu, this is excellent sport, i'faith.

Falstaff
Weep not, sweet Queen, for trickling tears a vain.

Hostess
O the Father. How he holds his countenance!

Falstaff
For God's sake, lords, convey my tristful Quee
400 For tears do stop the floodgates of her eyes.

Hostess
O Jesu, he doth it as like one of these harlot players as ever I see!

Falstaff
Peace, good pint-pot, peace, good tickle-brain. Harry, I do not only marvel where thou spend
405 thy time, but also how thou art accompanied. F though the camomile, the more it is trodden on t faster it grows, yet youth, the more it is wasted t sooner it wears. That thou art my son I have par thy mother's word, partly my own opinion, b
410 chiefly a villainous trick of thine eye, and a fooli hanging of thy nether lip, that doth warrant me. then thou be son to me, here lies the point—wl being son to me, art thou so pointed at? Shall t blessed sun of heaven prove a micher, and e
415 blackberries? A question not to be asked. Shall t son of England prove a thief, and take purses? question to be asked. There is a thing, Harr which thou hast often heard of, and it is known many in our land by the name of pitch. This pit
420 (as ancient writers do report) doth defile; so do the company thou keepest. For, Harry, now I not speak to thee in drink, but in tears; not pleasure, but in passion; not in words only, but woes also. And yet there is a virtuous man whom

son of England: i.e. of the King of
England.

take: steal.

-21 Falstaff's speech is rich with
biblical overtones.

pitch: a dark, sticky substance
made from tar—which stained anyone
who touched it (see *Ecclesiasticus*,
13:1).

'I am speaking with such
emotion because I am weeping, not
because I am drunk ('in drink')'.

passion: anger.

noted: observed.

manner: kind.

goodly portly: very dignified.

a corpulent: with a good figure.

carriage: behaviour.

inclining to threescore:
approaching sixty.

lewdly given: living a wicked life.

-5 *if the tree . . . the fruit*: if the true
character (i.e. the tree) can be judged
from the outward appearance (the
fruit'); Falstaff is quoting from *St
Matthew*, 12:33.

peremptorily . . . it: I say with
complete conviction.

him keep with: keep him as your
friend.

naughty varlet: wicked lad.

this month: all this month.

stand for me: act my part.

half so gravely: with half as much
dignity.

word: i.e. a choice of words.

matter: meaning.

rabbit-sucker: young rabbit.

poulter's hare: hare hung by its
hind legs in a poulterer's shop.

425 have often noted in thy company, but I know not
his name.

Prince

What manner of man, and it like your Majesty?

Falstaff

A goodly portly man, i'faith, and a corpulent; of a
cheerful look, a pleasing eye, and a most noble
430 carriage; and, as I think, his age some fifty, or—
by'r Lady—inclining to threescore; and now I
remember me, his name is Falstaff. If that man
should be lewdly given, he deceiveth me; for,
Harry, I see virtue in his looks. If then the tree
435 may be known by the fruit, as the fruit by the tree,
then peremptorily I speak it, there is virtue in that
Falstaff; him keep with, the rest banish. And tell
me now, thou naughty varlet, tell me where hast
thou been this month?

Prince

440 Dost thou speak like a king? Do thou stand for me,
and I'll play my father.

Falstaff

Depose me? If thou dost it half so gravely, so
majestically, both in word and matter, hang me up
by the heels for a rabbit-sucker, or a poulter's
445 hare.

446   *set*: in position.
447   *Judge*: i.e. judge which is the
   better actor.
451   *'Sblood*: by God's blood.
451–2 *I'll . . . prince*: I'll make you
   laugh when I play the young prince.
453   *ungracious*: wicked, profane.
454   *violently*: dreadfully.
455   *haunts thee*: is always with you.
       likeness: appearance.
456   *tun*: barrel.
457   *converse*: keep company with.
       trunk of humours: body full of
   corruptions.
458   *bolting-hutch*: rubbish-bin (the
   'bolting-hutch' was the box where the
   coarse flour remained after the better
   quality had been sifted off).
459   *dropsies*: dropsy is a disease in
   which the body is swollen with fluid.
       bombard: leather vessel for wine.

460   *cloak-bag*: portmanteau (an extra
   large suitcase).
460–61 *roasted . . . belly*: an ox roasted
   whole, stuffed with a mixture of meat
   and herbs (the 'pudding') was part of
   the entertainment at village fairs and
   festivals. Manningtree is in Essex—
   perhaps famous for fat oxen.

Prince
Well, here I am set.
   Falstaff
And here I stand. Judge, my masters.
   Prince
Now, Harry, whence come you?
   Falstaff
My noble lord, from Eastcheap.
   Prince
450 The complaints I hear of thee are grievous.
   Falstaff
'Sblood, my lord, they are false! (Nay, I'll tickle
for a young prince, i'faith.)
   Prince
Swearest thou, ungracious boy? Henceforth ne'
look on me. Thou art violently carried away fro
455 grace. There is a devil haunts thee in the liken
of an old fat man; a tun of man is thy companio
Why dost thou converse with that trunk
humours, that bolting-hutch of beastliness, th
swollen parcel of dropsies, that huge bombard
460 sack, that stuffed cloak-bag of guts, that roast
Manningtree ox with the pudding in his belly, th
reverend vice, that grey iniquity, that fath
ruffian, that vanity in years? Wherein is he goo
but to taste sack and drink it? Wherein neat a
465 cleanly, but to carve a capon and eat it? Where
cunning, but in craft? Wherein crafty, but
villainy? Wherein villainous, but in all thing
Wherein worthy, but in nothing?
   Falstaff
I would your Grace would take me with yo
470 whom means your Grace?
   Prince
That villainous abominable misleader of yout
Falstaff, that old white-bearded Satan.
   Falstaff
My lord, the man I know.
   Prince
I know thou dost.
   Falstaff
475 But to say I know more harm in him than in mys
were to say more than I know. That he is old, t

The following string of epithets
ntrasts Falstaff's age with his
nduct.

reverend: respected.
vice: see p. xxviii.
grey: grey-haired.
vanity: worthlessness.
in years: aged.
Wherein is he good: what is he
od for.
but: except.
Wherein . . . cleanly: what can he
well and properly.
capon: chicken.
cunning: knowledgeable.
craft: wickedness.
crafty: skilful.
I would: I wish.
take me with you: explain what
u mean.
misleader of youth: see p. xxx.
the man I know: I know the man.
witness it: give evidence for it.
saving your reverence: with all
spect (a phrase used before any
pleasant or impolite expression).
a whoremaster: one who earns his
ving immorally.
host: innkeeper.
Pharaoh's lean kine: the lean
ws ('kine') were a sign that times of
arvation were approaching; they were
erefore to be hated, not loved.
*(*Genesis, 41:19–21).
banish not him: do not banish
m.
90   *banish . . . world*: if you banish fat
ck, you will banish the whole world.
monstrous watch: large company
guards.
Play out: finish.
the devil . . . stick: you are
aking the devil of a fuss.
are come: have come.
3   *Never . . . seeming so*: don't
istake the real thing for imitation—
u yourself are truly royal ('essentially
ade'), although you do not behave in
royal manner.

more the pity: his white hairs do witness it. But
that he is, saving your reverence, a whoremaster,
that I utterly deny. If sack and sugar be a fault,
480 God help the wicked! If to be old and merry be a
sin, then many an old host that I know is damned.
If to be fat be to be hated, then Pharaoh's lean kine
are to be loved. No, my good lord; banish Peto,
banish Bardolph, banish Poins—but for sweet
485 Jack Falstaff, kind Jack Falstaff, true Jack Falstaff,
valiant Jack Falstaff, and therefore more valiant,
being as he is old Jack Falstaff, banish not him thy
Harry's company, banish not him thy Harry's
company. Banish plump Jack, and banish all the
490 world.

Prince
I do, I will. [*A knocking is heard. Exeunt* Hostess,
Francis, *and* Bardolph

Enter Bardolph, *running*

Bardolph
O my lord, my lord, the sheriff with a most
monstrous watch is at the door!

Falstaff
Out, ye rogue! Play out the play! I have much to
495 say in the behalf of that Falstaff.

Enter the Hostess

Hostess
O Jesu, my lord, my lord!

Prince
Heigh, heigh, the devil rides upon a fiddle-stick!
What's the matter?

Hostess
The sheriff and all the watch are at the door; they
500 are come to search the house. Shall I let them in?

Falstaff
Dost thou hear, Hal? Never call a true piece of
gold a counterfeit: thou art essentially made without seeming so.

504   *without instinct*: i.e. without the 'instinct' which Falstaff boasted in line 275 (at last the Prince accuses Falstaff of lying and cowardice).

505   *your major*: the main part of your argument ('major' is a technical term used in logic).

        so: good.

506–7   *If I . . . man*: if I do not look as fine as any man in the cart (that takes thieves to the gallows for execution).

507   *bringing up*: education.

508   *I shall . . . another*: the hangman's noose will strangle me faster than anyone else (because of his weight).

510   *arras*: in houses (and taverns) the arras was a curtain on a wooden frame between the wall and the main part of the room; in the theatre it would be the curtain concealing the acting area at the back of the stage.

511   *above*: i.e. they could stand on the stage balcony and watch the Prince and the Sheriff from there.

        true face: serious expression.

513   *their . . . out*: I have lost them (their lease has expired).

517   *hue and cry*: crowd of people chasing a thief.

523–4   He is doing something for me at this moment.

525   *engage . . . thee*: promise you.

527   *charg'd withal*: accused of.

Prince
And thou a natural coward without instinct.

Falstaff
505 I deny your major. If you will deny the sheriff, if not, let him enter. If I become not a cart as w as another man, a plague on my bringing up hope I shall as soon be strangled with a halter another.

Prince
510 Go hide thee behind the arras, the rest walk above. Now, my masters, for a true face, and g conscience.

Falstaff
Both which I have had, but their date is out, a therefore I'll hide me.

            [*Exeunt all but the* Prince *and P*

Prince
515 Call in the sheriff.

            Enter Sheriff *and the* Carrier

Now, master sheriff, what is your will with m

Sheriff
First, pardon me, my lord. A hue and cry h follow'd certain men unto this house.

Prince
What men?

Sheriff
520 One of them is well known, my gracious lord— a gross fat man—

Carrier
As fat as butter.

Prince
The man I do assure you is not here, for I mys at this time have employ'd him. And sheriff, I v
525 engage my word to thee, that I will by tomorr dinner-time send him to answer thee, or any m for anything he shall be charg'd withal. And so me entreat you leave the house.

Sheriff
I will, my lord: there are two gentlemen have
530 this robbery lost three hundred marks.

answerable: made to repay the sum.

morrow: morning.

oily: fat.
Paul's: St Paul's Cathedral—a famous London landmark.

fetches: draws.
ob: half a penny (obolus).

Prince
It may be so: if he have robb'd these men he shall be answerable. And so, farewell.
Sheriff
Good night, my noble lord.
Prince
I think it is good morrow, is it not?
Sheriff
535 Indeed, my lord, I think it be two o'clock.
[*Exit, with* Carrier
Prince
This oily rascal is known as well as Paul's. Go call him forth.
Peto
Falstaff! Fast asleep behind the arras, and snorting like a horse.
Prince
540 Hark how hard he fetches breath. Search his pockets. What has thou found?
[Peto *searches* Falstaff's *pockets and finds some papers*
Peto
Nothing but papers, my lord.
Prince
Let's see what they be. Read them.
Peto [*Reads*]
Item, a Capon   .   .   .   .   .   2s. 2d.
545 Item, Sauce .   .   .   . 4d.
Item, Sack two gallons .   .   .   . 5s. 8d.
Item, Anchovies and sack after supper   2s. 6d.
Item, Bread .   .   .   . ob.

550 *intolerable deal*: incredible
amount.
551 *keep close*: hide.
at more advantage: when there is
more time.
552 *I'll to*: I will go to.
553 *must all to*: must all go to.
thy place: the Prince will make
sure that Peto gets a commission in the
army.
555 *a charge of foot*: a whole company
of infantry (foot-soldiers).
555–6 *his death . . . score*: it will kill him
to walk two hundred and forty steps.
556 *The money*: i.e. that which
Falstaff and the thieves had stolen.
557 *advantage*: interest; he will give
the travellers some extra money (as
compensation for their trouble).
betimes: early.

Prince

O monstrous! But one halfpennyworth of bread
550 this intolerable deal of sack! What there is el
keep close; we'll read it at more advantage. The
let him sleep till day. I'll to the court in t
morning. We must all to the wars, and thy pla
shall be honourable. I'll procure this fat rogue
555 charge of foot, and I know his death will be
march of twelve score. The money shall be pa
back again with advantage. Be with me betimes
the morning; and so, good morrow, Peto.

Peto

Good morrow, good my lord.   [*Exeu*

Act 3

Act 3 Scene 1
The rebels have now moved south;
they are meeting in Wales, at the castle
of Owen Glendower. Hotspur teases
Glendower, refusing to believe the
Welshman's claims to have magic
powers. But there are serious
arguments, too: they cannot agree on
the division of the kingdom which they
hope to win when they have fought
King Henry's forces. The men are
joined by their wives, and the scene
ends peacefully.
   promises: i.e. of support from
those who sympathize with the rebels.
   parties: supporters.
   sure: to be trusted.
   induction: the way things have
started.
   prosperous hope: hope that we
shall do well (prosper).
   Glendower first speaks formally
('Percy'), and then uses the more
familiar nickname ('Hotspur').
   Lancaster: i.e. King Henry IV.
   in heaven: i.e. dead.
   nativity: birth.
   front: face (the sky).
   cressets: torches.

17   There would have been the same
phenomena at that time whether or not
Glendower was born.

   was . . . mind: did not share my
opinion.

Scene 1 *A Castle in Wales*

Enter Hotspur, Worcester, Lord Mortimer, Owen Glendower

Mortimer
These promises are fair, the parties sure,
And our induction full of prosperous hope.
Hotspur
Lord Mortimer, and cousin Glendower, will you sit down?
And uncle Worcester. A plague upon it!
5 I have forgot the map.
Glendower   No, here it is:
Sit, cousin Percy, sit, good cousin Hotspur;
For by that name as oft as Lancaster doth speak of you
His cheek looks pale, and with a rising sigh
He wisheth you in heaven.
Hotspur   And you in hell,
10 As oft as he hears Owen Glendower spoke of.
Glendower
I cannot blame him; at my nativity
The front of heaven was full of fiery shapes,
Of burning cressets, and at my birth
The frame and huge foundation of the earth
15 Shak'd like a coward.
Hotspur
Why, so it would have done at the same season if your mother's cat had but kitten'd, though yourself had never been born.
Glendower
I say the earth did shake when I was born.
Hotspur
20 And I say the earth was not of my mind,

as fearing you: because it was
afraid of you.

oft: often.
teeming: fruitful.

enlargement: freedom.
beldam: old woman.

grandam: grandmother.
distemp'rature: disorder.
passion: suffering.
of many . . . crossings: I do not
tolerate such contradictions from many
men.

mark'd me: shown that I am.
courses: events.
in the roll: on the list.
clipp'd in with: confined by.
chides the banks: restrains the
shores.

read to me: taught me.
And show me any human being.
trace me: follow me.
tedious: difficult.
art: magic.
hold me pace: keep up with me.
deep: profound, mysterious.
I'll to: I will go to.

call: Glendower means 'conjure',
'raise up'; but Hotspur wilfully
misunderstands him.
vasty deep: ocean.

If you suppose as fearing you it shook.
Glendower
The heavens were all on fire, the earth did
   tremble—
   Hotspur
O, then the earth shook to see the heavens on fire,
And not in fear of your nativity.
25 Diseased nature oftentimes breaks forth
In strange eruptions; oft the teeming earth
Is with a kind of colic pinch'd and vex'd
By the imprisoning of unruly wind
Within her womb, which for enlargement striving
30 Shakes the old beldam earth, and topples down
Steeples and moss-grown towers. At your birth
Our grandam earth, having this distemp'rature,
In passion shook.
   Glendower   Cousin, of many men
I do not bear these crossings; give me leave
35 To tell you once again that at my birth
The front of heaven was full of fiery shapes,
The goats ran from the mountains, and the herds
Were strangely clamorous to the frighted fields.
These signs have mark'd me extraordinary,
40 And all the courses of my life do show
I am not in the roll of common men.
Where is he living, clipp'd in with the sea
That chides the banks of England, Scotland,
   Wales,
Which calls me pupil or hath read to me?
45 And bring him out that is but woman's son
Can trace me in the tedious ways of art,
And hold me pace in deep experiments.
   Hotspur
I think there's no man speaks better Welsh: I'll to
dinner.
   Mortimer
50 Peace, cousin Percy; you will make him mad.
   Glendower
I can call spirits from the vasty deep.
   Hotspur
Why, so can I, or so can any man;
But will they come when you do call for them?

56   *coz*: an abbreviation (used in familiarity) of 'cousin'.
57   *telling truth*: Hotspur implies that Glendower is lying.
      tell . . . devil: a proverb.
58-9 If you have the ability to bring the devil here, I am sure that I am able to make him so ashamed that he will go away.
60   *while you live*: always.
61   *unprofitable*: useless.
62-3 *made . . . power*: attacked my forces.
65   *Bootless*: unsuccessful; Hotspur makes the obvious pun.
      weather-beaten: the history books describe the unusually severe weather on each of the three defeats.
67   *How . . . agues*: how does he manage not to catch a bad cold.
68-9 *divide . . . ta'en*: divide the country so that each of the three rebel leaders gets his proper share ('right').
69   *threefold order*: triple division.
      ta'en: taken, already decided.
70   *The Archdeacon*: historically, the division of the kingdom was planned in the house of the Archdeacon of Bangor.
71   *limits*: regions; see map.
73   *to . . . assign'd*: allotted to my share.
75   *bound*: boundary.
77   The rest of England lying north of the river Trent.
78   Our contracts have been written in tripartite form; this legal expression meant that the three contracts were all written on a single piece of parchment (see illustration). The separate contracts were then cut off *with a jagged cut*—so that only the original three contracts could be fitted together, and any attempt at forgery could be detected.

Glendower
Why, I can teach you, cousin, to command th
55 devil.
      Hotspur
And I can teach thee, coz, to shame the devil,
By telling truth; tell truth, and shame the devil
If thou have power to raise him, bring him hithe
And I'll be sworn I have power to shame hi
      hence:
60 O, while you live, tell truth, and shame the devi
      Mortimer
Come, come, no more of this unprofitable chat.
      Glendower
Three times hath Henry Bolingbroke made hea
Against my power; thrice from the banks of W:
And sandy-bottom'd Severn have I sent him
65 Bootless home, and weather-beaten back.
      Hotspur
Home without boots, and in foul weather too!
How scapes he agues, in the devil's name?
      Glendower
Come, here is the map; shall we divide our rig]
According to our threefold order ta'en?
      Mortimer
70 The Archdeacon hath divided it
Into three limits very equally:
England, from Trent and Severn hitherto,
By south and east is to my part assign'd;

All westward, Wales beyond the Severn shore,
75 And all the fertile land within that bound,
To Owen Glendower; and, dear coz, to you
The remnant northward lying off from Trent.
And our indentures tripartite are drawn,
Which being sealed interchangeably,
80 (A business that this night may execute)
Tomorrow, cousin Percy, you and I
And my good Lord of Worcester will set forth
To meet your father and the Scottish power,
As is appointed us, at Shrewsbury.
85 My father Glendower is not ready yet,
Nor shall we need his help these fourteen days.
[*To* Glendower] Within that space you may have
      drawn together
Your tenants, friends, and neighbouring
      gentlemen.
Glendower
A shorter time shall send me to you, lords,
90 And in my conduct shall your ladies come,
From whom you now must steal and take no leave,
For there will be a world of water shed
Upon the parting of your wives and you.
Hotspur
Methinks my moiety, north from Burton here,
95 In quantity equals not one of yours:
See how this river comes me cranking in,
And cuts me from the best of all my land
A huge half-moon, a monstrous cantle out.
I'll have the current in this place damm'd up,
100 And here the smug and silver Trent shall run
In a new channel fair and evenly;

sealed interchangeably: each of the three contracts carried three wax seals; each of the three men signing the contracts would impress his own mark (often a device worn on a ring) on the wax of all three copies.

that . . . execute: that we can perform tonight.

power: army.

As . . . us: as it has been arranged for us.

these fourteen days: for another two weeks.

space: time.

in my conduct: under my protection.

steal: go secretly.

take no leave: not say goodbye.

world of water: flood of tears.

Methinks: in my opinion.

moiety: share (of the country). Is not as big as either of your shares.

comes . . . in: comes winding in here.

8   And cuts an enormous corner ('cantle'), in the shape of a half-moon, out of the best part of my territory.

in this place: at this point Hotspur indicates on the map how he will change the course of the river).

smug: smooth.

102   *indent*: curve.
103   *so . . . bottom*: such a fertile
    valley.
106   *mark*: notice.
    bears his course: continues.
    runs me up: flows into my
    territory.
107   Giving you exactly the same
    advantage on the opposite side.
108   *Gelding*: cutting away from.
    continent: bank.
110   *charge*: i.e. of explosives.
    trench him: dig a channel for him
    (the river).
115   *say me nay*: stop me.
120   *train'd up*: educated.
121   *framed*: fitted, set to music.
123   Added beauty to the voice (with
    the music of the harp).

124   *A virtue*: an accomplishment.
126   *had rather*: would rather.
127   *same . . . mongers*: singers of
    rubbishy ballads.
128   *brazen . . . turn'd*: brass
    candlesticks ('cansticks') were polished
    by being turned on a lathe, so that
    metal grated on metal.
129   *dry*: without oil.
    axle-tree: the rod on which a
    wheel turns.

It shall not wind with such a deep indent,
To rob me of so rich a bottom here.
>   **Glendower**
Not wind? It shall, it must—you see it doth.
>   **Mortimer**
105 Yea,
But mark how he bears his course, and runs me u
With like advantage on the other side,
Gelding the opposed continent as much
As on the other side it takes from you.
>   **Worcester**
110 Yea, but a little charge will trench him here,
And on this north side win this cape of land,
And then he runs straight and even.
>   **Hotspur**
I'll have it so, a little charge will do it.
>   **Glendower**
I'll not have it alter'd.
>   **Hotspur**   Will not you
>   **Glendower**
115 No, nor you shall not.
>   **Hotspur**   Who shall say me nay
>   **Glendower**
Why, that will I.
>   **Hotspur**
Let me not understand you then, speak it i
Welsh.
>   **Glendower**
I can speak English, lord, as well as you,
120 For I was train'd up in the English court,
Where, being but young, I framed to the harp
Many an English ditty lovely well,
And gave the tongue a helpful ornament—
A virtue that was never seen in you.
>   **Hotspur**
125 Marry, and I am glad of it with all my heart!
I had rather be a kitten and cry 'mew'
Than one of these same metre ballad-mongers;
I had rather hear a brazen canstick turn'd,
Or a dry wheel grate on the axle-tree,

-31 Those noises would not make me lench my teeth so much as the sound f jogging poetry.

mincing: walking in an unnatural manner.

It is as though an old horse ('nag') which can only walk with difficulty (shuffle) were compelled ('forc'd') to move at some uncomfortable pace ('gait').

turn'd: diverted.

in ... bargain: when I am making a bargain.

mark ye me: take notice.

I'll argue over the smallest details.

Are ... drawn: are the contracts all written out?

Shall ... gone: isn't it time we went?

may away: can get away (i.e. they can travel by the light of the moon).

haste: hurry.

withal: at the same time.

Break with: inform.

cross: annoy.

I ... choose: I can't help it.

sometime: sometimes.

angers: infuriates.

moldwarp: mole.

Merlin: the Welsh magician and prophet at the court of King Arthur.

griffin: a legendary beast with a lion's body and the beak of an eagle; its wings were those of an eagle, but they were clipped so that it could not fly.

moulten: moulted, shed its old feathers.

couching: a heraldic term (*couchant*) which indicated that the animal was lying down.

ramping: another heraldic term (*rampant*); the animal was rearing.

130 And that would set my teeth nothing on edge,
Nothing so much as mincing poetry:
'Tis like the forc'd gait of a shuffling nag.
  Glendower
Come, you shall have Trent turn'd.
  Hotspur
I do not care, I'll give thrice so much land
135 To any well-deserving friend:
But in the way of bargain, mark ye me,
I'll cavil on the ninth part of a hair.
Are the indentures drawn? Shall we be gone?
  Glendower
The moon shines fair; you may away by night.
140 I'll haste the writer, and withal
Break with your wives of your departure hence.
I am afraid my daughter will run mad,
So much she doteth on her Mortimer.   [*Exit*
  Mortimer
Fie, cousin Percy, how you cross my father!
  Hotspur
145 I cannot choose. Sometime he angers me
With telling me of the moldwarp and the ant,
Of the dreamer Merlin and his prophecies,
And of a dragon and a finless fish,
A clip-wing'd griffin and a moulten raven,
150 A couching lion and a ramping cat,

151   *skimble-skamble*: rubbish; the word is Hotspur's own invention.

152   *puts . . . faith*: makes me lose my own (Christian) faith. Glendower expects Hotspur to believe so much that he finishes by believing nothing.

153   *held me*: made me listen.

154   *several*: different.

155   *lackeys*: servants.
    Well, go to: well, really.

156   *mark'd . . . word*: did not believe a word he said.

157   *railing*: nagging.

159   *cheese and garlic*: very poor food.
    windmill: i.e. with the constant noise of grinding machinery.
    far: far (much) rather.

160   *cates*: luxury foods, delicacies.

161   *summer house*: a house in the country, built so that the owner could spend summer away from London.
    Christendom: Christ's kingdom—i.e. all those parts of the world converted to Christianity.

163   *profited*: skilled.

164   *concealments*: mysteries, magic arts.

166   *mines of India*: Elizabethans were very impressed by the rich gold and jewels to be found in the newly-discovered eastern mines.

167   *temper*: character.

168   *curbs*: restrains.
    natural scope: usual mood.

169   *come 'cross*: oppose.

170   *that . . . alive*: there is no man living.

171   *tempted him*: i.e. to show his violent nature.

172   *taste*: threat.
    reproof: disgrace.

173   *Do . . . oft*: do not take too much advantage of Glendower's respect for you.

174   *wilful-blame*: wrong to be so obstinate.

176   To make him lose all patience.

177   *You . . . learn*: you really must learn.

And such a deal of skimble-skamble stuff
As puts me from my faith. I tell you what—
He held me last night at least nine hours
In reckoning up the several devils' names
155 That were his lackeys. I cried 'Hum', and 'We go to!'
But mark'd him not a word. O, he is as tedious
As a tired horse, a railing wife;
Worse than a smoky house. I had rather live
With cheese and garlic in a windmill, far,
160 Than feed on cates and have him talk to me
In any summer house in Christendom.

Mortimer
In faith, he is a worthy gentleman,
Exceedingly well read, and profited
In strange concealments, valiant as a lion,
165 And wondrous affable, and as bountiful
As mines of India. Shall I tell you, cousin?
He holds your temper in a high respect
And curbs himself even of his natural scope
When you come 'cross his humour—faith he doe
170 I warrant you that man is not alive
Might so have tempted him as you have done
Without the taste of danger and reproof.
But do not use it oft, let me entreat you.

Worcester
In faith, my lord, you are too wilful-blame,
175 And since your coming hither have done enoug
To put him quite besides his patience;
You must needs learn, lord, to amend this faul
Though sometimes it show greatness, courag blood—
And that's the dearest grace it renders you—
180 Yet oftentimes it doth present harsh rage,
Defect of manners, want of government,
Pride, haughtiness, opinion, and disdain,
The least of which haunting a nobleman
Loseth men's hearts, and leaves behind a stain
185 Upon the beauty of all parts besides,
Beguiling them of commendation.

Hotspur
Well, I am school'd—good manners be yo speed!

it: i.e. the determined obstinacy
referred to in line 174.
    blood: spirit.
    dearest grace: finest quality.
    want of government: lack of self-
control.
    opinion: conceit.
    haunting: affecting.
    Making them lose the respect
('commendation') of other men.
    am school'd: have been taught my
lesson.
    good . . . speed: I hope your good
manners will be successful.
    spite: irritation.
    she'll not: she does not want to.
    she'll to: she wants to go to.
    in your conduct: under your
protection.
    harlotry: silly little girl (no sexual
insult is intended).
    do good upon: have any effect on.
    that pretty Welsh: that lovely
language (i.e. her tears).
    swelling heavens: i.e. her eyes,
swollen with crying.
    I . . . in: I understand too well.
    but for shame: if I were not
ashamed.
    parley: speech.

    feeling disputation: discussion in
emotions (instead of words).
    be a truant: stop my lessons (as a
child stays away from school).
    tongue: speech.
    ditties . . . penn'd: beautifully
written songs.
    To the accompaniment of
enchanting notes on her lute.
    melt: show signs of weakness (i.e.
shed tears).

    wanton: luxuriant, comfortable.
    rushes: soft green plants were
used as floor-covering.
    'And send you to sleep'; in
classical mythology the god of sleep
was Morpheus.

Here come our wives, and let us take our leave.

Enter Glendower *with* Lady Percy *and*
Lady Mortimer

Mortimer
This is the deadly spite that angers me,
190 My wife can speak no English, I no Welsh.
Glendower
My daughter weeps; she'll not part with you,
She'll be a soldier too, she'll to the wars.
Mortimer
Good father, tell her that she and my aunt Percy
shall follow in your conduct speedily.
[Glendower *speaks in Welsh to* Lady Mortimer;
and she answers him in the same language
Glendower
195 She is desperate here, a peevish, self-willed
harlotry, one that no persuasion can do good upon.
            [Lady Mortimer *speaks in Welsh*
Mortimer
I understand thy looks. That pretty Welsh
Which thou pourest down from these swelling
    heavens
I am too perfect in, and, but for shame,
200 In such a parley should I answer thee.
            [Lady Mortimer *speaks again in Welsh*
I understand thy kisses, and thou mine,
And that's a feeling disputation;
But I will never be a truant, love,
Till I have learnt thy language, for thy tongue
205 Makes Welsh as sweet as ditties highly penn'd,
Sung by a fair queen in a summer's bow'r
With ravishing division to her lute.
Glendower
Nay, if you melt, then will she run mad.
            [Lady Mortimer *speaks again in Welsh*
Mortimer
O, I am ignorance itself in this!
Glendower
210 She bids you on the wanton rushes lay you down,
And rest your gentle head upon her lap,
And she will sing the song that pleaseth you,
And on your eyelids crown the god of sleep,

214   *blood*: spirits.
         heaviness: drowsiness.
215   *wake and sleep*: being awake and
         being asleep.
217   *the ... team*: the sun, in classical
         mythology, was often portrayed as a
         god (Phœbus Apollo) driving a team of
         horses across the sky.
218   *progress*: royal journey.
220   *our ... drawn*: our agreement
         (about the division of the kingdom) will
         be written out.
221-3 Glendower boasts that with his
         magic powers he can bring musicians
         from a great distance.
221   *and*: if.
222   *Hang in the air*: in the
         Elizabethan theatres, musicians were
         usually placed above the stage.
         leagues: a 'league' was a measure
         of distance—about 3 miles.

223   *straight*: immediately.
224   *perfect in*: very good at.
227   Because he hears the music,
         Hotspur pretends to believe
         Glendower's boast about being able to
         command the devil.
228   *humorous*: temperamental.
230-31 Then you should be very musical
         yourself, since you are completely
         dominated by your different moods.
233   *brach*: hound bitch.
         Irish: this may refer to the sound
         of the Irish language; or perhaps
         'Lady' was an Irish wolf-hound.

Charming your blood with pleasing heaviness,
215 Making such difference 'twixt wake and sleep
As is the difference betwixt day and night,
The hour before the heavenly-harness'd team
Begins his golden progress in the east.
      Mortimer
With all my heart I'll sit and hear her sing,
220 By that time will our book, I think, be drawn.
      Glendower
Do so, and those musicians that shall play to yo
Hang in the air a thousand leagues from hence,
And straight they shall be here: sit, and attend.
      Hotspur
Come, Kate, thou art perfect in lying down:
225 Come, quick, quick, that I may lay my head in th
      lap.
      Lady Percy
Go, ye giddy goose.   [*The music play*
      Hotspur
Now I perceive the devil understands Welsh,
And 'tis no marvel he is so humorous.
By'r Lady, he is a good musician.
      Lady Percy
230 Then should you be nothing but musical,
For you are altogether govern'd by humours.
Lie still, ye thief, and hear the lady sing in Welsh
      Hotspur
I had rather hear Lady my brach howl in Irish.
      Lady Percy
Wouldst thou have thy head broken?
      Hotspur
235 No.
      Lady Percy
Then be still.
      Hotspur
Neither, 'tis a woman's fault.
      Lady Percy
Now God help thee!
      Hotspur
To the Welsh lady's bed.
      Lady Percy
240 What's that?

Do you want me to smack your head?

still: quiet.
Neither: I won't do that, either.
a woman's fault: Hotspur must be ironic; silence is not (traditionally) a female quality.
in good sooth: indeed (a very mild expression).
comfit-maker: confectioner.
sarcanet surety: flimsy assurance ('sarcanet' was a thin silk).
Finsbury: London citizens used to walk in Finsbury Fields—a very respectable kind of public park.
lady: noblewoman (not a middle-class citizen's wife).
mouth-filling: robust.
protest: oaths, protestations.
pepper-gingerbread: a light, easily swallowed, cake.
velvet-guards: clothes trimmed with velvet, which would be worn by the respectable citizens as their best ('Sunday') clothes.

Hotspur
Peace she sings.

    [*Here* Lady Mortimer *sings a Welsh song*
Come, Kate, I'll have your song too.
Lady Percy
Not mine, in good sooth.
Hotspur
Not yours, in good sooth! Heart, you swear like a
245 comfit-maker's wife—'Not you, in good sooth!',
and 'As true as I live!', and 'As God shall mend
me!', and 'As sure as day!'—
And givest such sarcenet surety for thy oaths
As if thou never walk'st further than Finsbury.
250 Swear me, Kate, like a lady as thou art,
A good mouth-filling oath, and leave 'In sooth',
And such protest of pepper-gingerbread,
To velvet-guards, and Sunday citizens.
Come, sing.
Lady Percy
255 I will not sing.

256–7 *'Tis . . . teacher*: singing is the quickest ('next') way to turn yourself into a tailor or a teacher of song-birds.

256 *redbreast*: a small brown bird, with red breast-feathers, which has a very sweet song.

257 *And*: if.

261 *on fire*: keen.

262 *By . . . drawn*: our contracts will be written out by now.
but seal: just sign and seal them.

Hotspur

'Tis the next way to turn tailor, or be redbreas
teacher. And the indentures be drawn, I'll aw
within these two hours; and so come in when
will.   [E:

Glendower

260 Come, come, Lord Mortimer, you are as slow
As hot Lord Percy is on fire to go.
By this our book is drawn—we'll but seal,
And then to horse immediately.

Mortimer   With all my hea
                                                        [*Exeu*

Act 3 Scene 2
King Henry has a serious talk with his son. He first recalls his own conduct when, as Henry Bolingbroke, he competed with King Richard II and won the people's respect: although Richard was the rightful king, Henry was the people's choice. Now the King believes that Prince Hal is behaving in the same way as Richard, whilst Hotspur, by contrast, wins the respect and admiration which may one day help *him* to win the crown. The Prince apologizes to his father; he explains the reason for his conduct, and promises to reform.

1 *give us leave*: please leave us alone.

2 *some private conference*: a talk together.

3 *presently*: very soon.

4 *God . . . so*: it is God's will.

5 *displeasing service*: sin.

6 *doom*: judgement.
out of my blood: from my own family.

7 *scourge*: whip, punishment.

Scene 2 *London: Westminster Palace*

Enter the King, Prince of Wales, a
others

King

Lords, give us leave; the Prince of Wales and I
Must have some private conference: but be near
  hand,
For we shall presently have need of you.
                                        [*Exeunt Lor*
I know not whether God will have it so
5 For some displeasing service I have done,
That, in his secret doom, out of my blood
He'll breed revengement and a scourge for me;

8   *passages*: conduct.
9   *only mark'd*: especially chosen.
11   *mistreadings*: errors,
wrongdoings.
     else: is there any other
explanation.
12   *inordinate*: unworthy.
13   *bare*: wretched.
     lewd: low.
     mean: base.
     attempts: actions.
14   *rude*: rough.
15   *match'd withal*: accompanied by.
     grafted to: attached to.
16   *blood*: birth, rank.
17   *hold . . . with*: be approved by.
18   *So please*: if you please.
     would: wish.
19   *Quit*: clear myself.
     clear excuse: good explanation.
20   *doubtless*: sure.
     purge: clear.
21   *charg'd withal*: accused of now.
22–7 Prince Hal hopes that his father
     will make allowances for the fact that
     there are always rumours surrounding
     someone in his position.
22   *extenuation*: consideration,
allowance.
23   *reproof*: disproving.
     devis'd: made up, invented.
24   Which a great man is often
     forced to hear.
25   *smiling pickthanks*: flatterers—
     who think this is a way to earn the
     King's thanks.
     newsmongers: gossips; the
     modern equivalent would be
     'newspapermen'.
26–8 The Prince hopes that because he
     can prove these rumours to be false, he
     will be forgiven for some real faults
     ('some things true') which he confesses
     to.
     true submission: sincere
confession.
29   *Yet . . . wonder*: but I am still
     very surprised.
30   *affections*: inclinations.

But thou dost in thy passages of life
Make me believe that thou art only mark'd
10 For the hot vengeance and the rod of heaven
To punish my mistreadings. Tell me else,
Could such inordinate and low desires,
Such poor, such bare, such lewd, such me[an]
     attempts,
Such barren pleasures, rude society,
15 As thou art match'd withal, and grafted to,
Accompany the greatness of thy blood,
And hold their level with thy princely heart?
     Prince
So please your Majesty, I would I could
Quit all offences with as clear excuse
20 As well as I am doubtless I can purge
Myself of many I am charg'd withal:
Yet such extenuation let me beg
As, in reproof of many tales devis'd,
Which oft the ear of greatness needs must hear,
25 By smiling pickthanks, and base newsmongers,
I may for some things true, wherein my youth
Hath faulty wander'd and irregular,
Find pardon on my true submission.
     King
God pardon thee! Yet let me wonder, Harry,
30 At thy affections, which do hold a wing
Quite from the flight of all thy ancestors.
Thy place in Council thou hast rudely lost,
Which by thy younger brother is supply'd;
And art almost an alien to the hearts
35 Of all the court and princes of my blood.
The hope and expectation of thy time
Is ruin'd, and the soul of every man
Prophetically do forethink thy fall.
Had I so lavish of my presence been,
40 So common-hackney'd in the eyes of men,
So stale and cheap to vulgar company,
Opinion, that did help me to the crown,
Had still kept loyal to possession,
And left me in reputeless banishment,
45 A fellow of no mark nor likelihood.
By being seldom seen, I could not stir
But like a comet I was wonder'd at,

31 *Hold . . . Quite*: fly in a completely different direction (i.e. are quite unlike).

supply'd: taken.

alien: stranger.

of my blood: i.e. of your own family.

7 The hopes and expectations we had when you were young ('of thy time') have been disappointed.

do: Shakespeare uses a plural form because 'every man' implies a number.

forethink: anticipate, expect.

If I had been seen around so much.

common-hackneyed: ordinary, a thing to be seen every day (like a hackney—a working-horse).

vulgar company: the society of common people.

Opinion: public opinion.

possession: the man who already possessed the crown (i.e. Richard II).

reputeless: without reputation.

fellow: another ordinary man.

of no mark: with no importance.

likelihood: hope.

stole . . . heaven: assumed a heavenly graciousness (by seeming to be 'from heaven', the 'courtesy' might imply that his claim to the throne was divinely approved).

dress'd . . . humility: behaved with such humility.

robe pontifical: the vestments worn only by bishops on great festivals.

state: appearance.

show'd . . . feast: was like a festival (i.e. something very special).

Achieved such dignity because it was so unusual.

skipping: thoughtless (like a playful child).

rash . . . wits: bright young men ('bavin' is a wood that quickly catches fire, and is soon burnt out).

carded his state: lost his dignity (the verb *card* = to mix drinks with water, to weaken).

That men would tell their children, 'This is he!'
Others would say, 'Where, which is Bolingbroke?'
50 And then I stole all courtesy from heaven,
And dress'd myself in such humility
That I did pluck allegiance from men's hearts,
Loud shouts and salutations from their mouths,
Even in the presence of the crowned King.
55 Thus did I keep my person fresh and new;
My presence, like a robe pontifical,
Ne'er seen but wonder'd at; and so my state—
Seldom, but sumptuous—show'd like a feast,
And won by rareness such solemnity.
60 The skipping King, he ambled up and down,
With shallow jesters, and rash bavin wits,
Soon kindled and soon burnt, carded his state;
Mingled his royalty with cap'ring fools,

64   Allowed his royal name to be dishonoured and despised.

65   *gave his countenance*: consented.
      against his name: in a manner that was most unsuitable.

66   *gibing*: insulting.
      stand the push: tolerate the impudence.

67   *beardless*: young.
      comparative: insulting competitor (compare *1, 2, 78*).

68   *Grew . . . to*: i.e. was frequently to be found in.

69   *Enfeoff'd*: was a slave to.

71-2 They were sick of the sight of him, as though they had eaten too much honey (were 'surfeited with honey').

74   *had occasion*: it was necessary.

75   *the cuckoo*: the call of this bird ('cuck-oo') is welcomed in April as a sign that spring has arrived; in June, however, it is tedious.

77   *blunted*: grown dull.
      community: familiarity.

78   Pay no special attention.

79   *bent*: turned.
      sun-like: the sun was the symbol of kingship, because it is brighter than all other stars.

81   *drows'd*: the eyes (referred to in line 76) became sleepy.

82   *face*: presence.
      render'd . . . aspect: stared back at him in such a way.

83   *cloudy*: hostile.

85   *very line*: same class.

87   *With . . . participation*: by keeping such rotten company.

88   *of . . . sight*: with seeing you so often.

89   *Save*: except.

91   *tenderness*: i.e. tears.

92   *thrice*: most.

93   *Be . . . myself*: behave as I ought to do.
      For . . . world: exactly.

94   *to . . . hour*: at this moment.

95   When I returned from France, landing at Ravenspurgh.

Had his great name profaned with their scorns,

65   And gave his countenance against his name
     To laugh at gibing boys, and stand the push
     Of every beardless vain comparative,
     Grew a companion to the common streets,
     Enfeoff'd himself to popularity,

70   That, being daily swallow'd by men's eyes,
     They surfeited with honey, and began
     To loathe the taste of sweetness, whereof a little
     More than a little is by much too much.
     So, when he had occasion to be seen,

75   He was but as the cuckoo is in June,
     Heard, not regarded; seen, but with such eyes
     As, sick and blunted with community,
     Afford no extraordinary gaze,
     Such as is bent on sun-like majesty

80   When it shines seldom in admiring eyes,
     But rather drows'd and hung their eyelids down
     Slept in his face, and render'd such aspect
     As cloudy men use to their adversaries,
     Being with his presence glutted, gorg'd, and full

85   And in that very line, Harry, standest thou,
     For thou hast lost thy princely privilege
     With vile participation. Not an eye
     But is a-weary of thy common sight,

even: exactly.
Percy: i.e. Hotspur.
to boot: as well.
-9   Hotspur's merit (worth) gives
him a better claim ('interest') to the
kingdom than your own, which is
dependent on the vague theory
('shadow') of heredity ('succession').
ɔ   *of no right*: with no just cause.
        nor . . . right: or even the
appearance of a just cause.
ɪ   *fields*: i.e. battlefields.
        harness: armour—i.e. armed
men.
ɟ   *Turns head*: opposes his forces.
        the lion's . . . jaws: i.e. the King's
armed forces; the lion was a symbol of
royalty.
ɟ   *no more . . . years*: no older; see
p. 126.
ɟ   *bruising arms*: hurtful war.
7-11   *whose*: i.e. those of Douglas, who
had the best military reputation in
Christendom until he was beaten by
Hotspur.
        high: brave.
ɟ   *hot incursions*: fierce attacks.
        name in arms: reputation in
battle.
ɟ   *chief majority*: greater eminence.
ɔ   *And . . . capital*: and the chief
military title.
ɟ   *Thrice*: see p. 128.
        Mars: the classical god of war.
        swathling clothes: the wrappings
of a new-born baby.
ɟ   *enterprises*: actions.
ɟ   *Discomfited*: faced in battle.
        ta'en: taken, captured.
ɟ   *Enlarged him*: set him free.
ɟ   To increase ('fill . . . up') the calls
of mighty defiance.
ɔ   *Capitulate*: form an agreement.
        are up: i.e. up in arms—ready to
fight.
ɟ   *dearest*: most loved; *and* worst.
ɟ   *like enough*: quite likely.
        vassal: servile.
ɟ   *Base inclination*: tendency to do
ignoble deeds.
        start of spleen: fit of bad temper.

Save mine, which hath desir'd to see thee more,
90 Which now doth that I would not have it do—
Make blind itself with foolish tenderness.
> **Prince**
I shall hereafter, my thrice gracious lord,
Be more myself.
> **King**   For all the world
As thou art to this hour was Richard then
95 When I from France set foot at Ravenspurgh;
And even as I was then is Percy now.
Now by my sceptre, and my soul to boot,
He hath more worthy interest to the state
Than thou the shadow of succession.
100 For of no right, nor colour like to right,
He doth fill fields with harness in the realm,
Turns head against the lion's armed jaws,
And—being no more in debt to years than thou—
Leads ancient lords and reverend bishops on
105 To bloody battles, and to bruising arms.
What never-dying honour hath he got
Against renowned Douglas—whose high deeds,
Whose hot incursions and great name in arms,
Holds from all soldiers chief majority
110 And military title capital
Through all the kingdoms that acknowledge
    Christ.
Thrice hath this Hotspur, Mars in swathling
    clothes,
This infant warrior, in his enterprises
Discomfited great Douglas, ta'en him once,
115 Enlarged him, and made a friend of him,
To fill the mouth of deep defiance up,
And shake the peace and safety of our throne.
And what say you to this? Percy, Northumberland,
The Archbishop's Grace of York, Douglas,
    Mortimer,
120 Capitulate against us and are up.
But wherefore do I tell these news to thee?
Why, Harry, do I tell thee of my foes,
Which art my nearest and dearest enemy?
Thou that art like enough, through vassal fear,
125 Base inclination, and the start of spleen,

To fight against me under Percy's pay,
To dog his heels, and curtsy at his frowns,
To show how much thou art degenerate.
     Prince
Do not think so, you shall not find it so;
130 And God forgive them that so much have sway
Your Majesty's good thoughts away from me!
I will redeem all this on Percy's head,
And in the closing of some glorious day
Be bold to tell you that I am your son,
135 When I will wear a garment all of blood,
And stain my favours in a bloody mask,
Which, wash'd away, shall scour my shame wi
     it;
And that shall be the day, whene'er it lights,
That this same child of honour and renown,
140 This gallant Hotspur, this all-praised knight,
And your unthought-of Harry chance to meet.
For every honour sitting on his helm,
Would they were multitudes, and on my head
My shames redoubled! For the time will come
145 That I shall make this northern youth exchange
His glorious deeds for my indignities.
Percy is but my factor, good my lord,
To engross up glorious deeds on my behalf;
And I will call him to so strict account
150 That he shall render every glory up,
Yea, even the slightest worship of his time,
Or I will tear the reckoning from his heart.
This in the name of God I promise here,
The which if He be pleas'd I shall perform,
155 I do beseech your Majesty may salve
The long-grown wounds of my intemperance:
If not, the end of life cancels all bands,
And I will die a hundred thousand deaths
Ere break the smallest parcel of this vow.

126   *under Percy's pay*: on Hotspur's
   side, and paid by him (see p. 131).
127   *dog his heels*: follow him (as a dog
   walks at his master's heel).
   curtsy . . . frowns: bow humbly
   when he looks severe.
128   *degenerate*: untrue to your royal
   birth.
130   *sway'd*: turned, influenced.
132   The Prince promises to rescue
   his lost reputation by fighting Hotspur.
133   *day*: battle.
136   *favours*: features.
138   *lights*: happens.
141   *unthought-of*: despised.
142   *helm*: helmet.
143-4   *Would . . . redoubled*: I wish that
   Hotspur had far more honours, and
   that I had even more faults to atone for.
147   *but my factor*: merely my agent;
   the Prince says he is using Hotspur to
   collect ('engross up') great deeds so
   that they will all become Hal's when he
   kills Hotspur.
149   I shall make him give such a
   very good account of himself (i.e. Hal
   will fight so fiercely).
150   *render*: surrender.
151   *the slightest . . . time*: the smallest
   honour he has won in all his life.

4 If it is God's will that I should do all this.

5 *salve*: heal.

6 The hurt that has for so long been caused by my riotous living.

7 *If not*: i.e. if it is not God's will that Prince Hal should beat Hotspur.

bands: bonds, debts.

9 *parcel*: part.

1 *charge*: command.

sovereign trust: the authority of a king.

2 *Thy . . . speed*: you look as though you are in a hurry.

3 *So . . . business*: i.e. the 'business' is also 'full of speed'.

7 *head*: force.

8 If all those who have promised support (to the rebels) keep their promises.

9 *offer'd*: threatened.

2 *advertisement*: information.

6 *by which account*: in which case.

7 *Our . . . valued*: having estimated the time that this will take.

8 *general*: entire.

9 *Our . . . business*: we have a lot to do.

0 The King's speech sounds like a proverb: his meaning is that if they waste time ('delay'), others could benefit (grow 'fat') by taking advantage.

King

160 A hundred thousand rebels die in this!
   Thou shalt have charge and sovereign trust herein.

Enter Blunt

   How now, good Blunt? Thy looks are full of speed.

   Blunt

   So hath the business that I come to speak of.
   Lord Mortimer of Scotland hath sent word
165 That Douglas and the English rebels met
   The eleventh of this month at Shrewsbury.
   A mighty and a fearful head they are,
   If promises be kept on every hand,
   As ever offer'd foul play in a state.

   King

170 The Earl of Westmoreland set forth today,
   With him my son, Lord John of Lancaster;
   For this advertisement is five days old.
   On Wednesday next, Harry, you shall set forward;
   On Thursday we ourselves will march.
175 Our meeting is Bridgnorth; and, Harry, you
   Shall march through Gloucestershire—by which account,
   Our business valued, some twelve days hence
   Our general forces at Bridgnorth shall meet.
   Our hands are full of business; let's away:
180 Advantage feeds him fat while men delay.

   [*Exeunt*

Act 3 Scene 3
Falstaff is in the tavern; he is rather bored and depressed, but he jokes with Bardolph until the Hostess joins them. They begin to quarrel and insult each other: Falstaff is angry because he has been robbed, and the Hostess complains that Falstaff owes money to her. Prince Hal returns from the interview with his father; he listens to their accusations, promises to settle all the difficulties, and finally announces that war has been declared and the fooling must stop.

Scene 3 *Eastcheap: the Boar's Head Tavern*

Enter Falstaff *and* Bardolph

   Falstaff

Bardolph, am I not fallen away vilely since this last action? Do I not bate? Do I not dwindle? Why, my skin hangs about me like an old lady's loose gown. I am withered like an old apple-john. Well,
5 I'll repent, and that suddenly, while I am in some liking; I shall be out of heart shortly, and then I shall have no strength to repent. And I have not forgotten what the inside of a church is made of, I

1   *am . . . vilely*: haven't I lost weight terribly.

2   *action*: i.e. the robbery at Gad's Hill; Falstaff speaks as though it were a military battle.
bate: get thin.

4   *apple-john*: a kind of apple whose skin wrinkles with keeping.

5   *suddenly*: at once.
while . . . liking: while I feel like repenting; *and* while I still have some flesh left.

6   *out of heart*: lost interest; *and* in poor condition.

7   *And*: if.

9   *peppercorn*: small, dried berry.
brewer's horse: brewers were notorious for over-working and under-feeding the horses that pulled their heavy loads of barrels.

10–11   *hath . . . me*: has ruined me.

13   *there is it*: that's it (Falstaff pretends to be resigned).

14   *I was . . . given*: I lived as virtuously.

16   *diced*: gambled (throwing dice).

17   *bawdy-house*: brothel.
a quarter: usually this means 'quarter of a year'; but Falstaff is quick to change the sense.

19   *in good compass*: in good order, within bounds; the pun is inevitable.

24   *thy face*: apparently Bardolph has a big red nose (as well as spots—see 2,4,315); this is now the object of Falstaff's wit. At sea, the ships used to follow the light ('lantern') carried at the back ('in the poop') of the leading ship (the 'admiral'). In the new title for Bardolph, Falstaff parodies a popular fictional character of the time, Amadis, Knight of the Burning Sword.

am a peppercorn, a brewer's horse. The inside of
10 church! Company, villainous company, hath bee
the spoil of me.

Bardolph

Sir John, you are so fretful you cannot live long

Falstaff

Why, there is it. Come, sing me a bawdy son,
make me merry. I was as virtuously given as
15 gentleman need to be—virtuous enough: swo
little; diced not above seven times—a week; we
to a bawdy-house not above once in a quarter—
an hour; paid money that I borrowed—three
four times; lived well, and in good compass. An
20 now I live out of all order, out of all compass.

Bardolph

Why, you are so fat, Sir John, that you must nee
be out of all compass, out of all reasonab
compass, Sir John.

Falstaff

Do thou amend thy face, and I'll amend my lif
25 thou art our admiral, thou bearest the lantern
the poop, but 'tis in the nose of thee: thou art t
Knight of the Burning Lamp.

Bardolph

Why, Sir John, my face does you no harm.

Falstaff

No, I'll be sworn, I make as good use of it as many
30 a man doth of a death's-head or a *memento mori*. I
never see thy face but I think upon hell-fire, and
Dives that lived in purple: for there he is in his
robes, burning, burning. If thou wert any way
given to virtue, I would swear by thy face: my oath
35 should be 'By this fire, that's God's angel!' But
thou art altogether given over; and wert indeed,
but for the light in thy face, the son of utter
darkness. When thou ran'st up Gad's Hill in the
night to catch my horse, if I did not think thou
40 hadst been an *ignis fatuus*, or a ball of wildfire,
there's no purchase in money. O, thou art a
perpetual triumph, an everlasting bonfire-light!
Thou hast saved me a thousand marks in links and
torches, walking with thee in the night betwixt
45 tavern and tavern: but the sack that thou hast
drunk me would have bought me lights as good
cheap at the dearest chandler's in Europe. I have
maintained that salamander of yours with fire any
time this two and thirty years, God reward me for
50 it!

Bardolph

'Sblood, I would my face were in your belly!

Falstaff

God-a-mercy! so should I be sure to be heartburnt.

I'll be sworn: I agree.
a death's-head: a skull—or a ring
with a skull, which was worn as a
memento mori, a reminder of death.
   Dives: the story of Dives, the
man who lived richly ('in purple') and
feasted whilst the beggar Lazarus
starved, is told in St Luke's Gospel
(16:19–31); Dives was condemned to
burn in the fires of hell.
   given to virtue: virtuous.
   God's angel: angels were often
said to appear in fiery flames—so
Bardolph's red nose could be mistaken
for an angel.
   given over: committed to evil,
damned.
   wert: would be.
   but: except.
38 *the son . . . darkness*: i.e. a child of
the devil.
   ignis fatuus: will o' the wisp (a
flickering light caused by gas over
marsh ground).
   ball of wildfire: flaming ball of
gunpowder; *or* a kind of lightning.
   no . . . money: money won't buy
anything.
   triumph: festival (with bright
lights, or a firework display).
   links: flares (burning lights on
sticks to show the way at night).
   drunk me: drunk at my expense.
   good cheap: cheaply.
   dearest chandler's: the most
expensive candle-maker.
   salamander: a kind of lizard that
was supposed to live in fire.
49 *any . . . years*: throughout the
past thirty-two years.
   be heartburnt: have indigestion.

Enter Hostess

54   *dame Partlet*: a traditional name
      for a hen (and so for any fussy woman).

55   *picked my pocket*: stole things
      from my pocket.

How now, dame Partlet the hen, have you er
55 quired yet who picked my pocket?

Hostess

Why, Sir John, what do you think, Sir John? D
you think I keep thieves in my house? I hav
searched, I have inquired, so has my husband
man by man, boy by boy, servant by servant—th

60   *tithe*: tenth part.

60 tithe of a hair was never lost in my house befor

Falstaff

Ye lie, hostess: Bardolph was shaved and los
many a hair, and I'll be sworn my pocket wa
picked. Go to, you are a woman, go.

Hostess

63   *Go to*: don't be silly.
      a woman: Falstaff does not
specify the meaning of his insult.

64   *I defy thee*: I deny it (the Hostess
does not understand what she is being
accused of).

Who, I? No, I defy thee! God's light, I was neve
65 called so in mine own house before.

Falstaff

Go to, I know you well enough.

Hostess

No, Sir John; you do not know me, Sir John:
know you, Sir John. You owe me money, Sir John
and now you pick a quarrel to beguile me of it.

69   *beguile*: cheat.
70   *to your back*: to wear on your
      back.

70 bought you a dozen of shirts to your back.

Falstaff

71   *Dowlas*: cheap, coarse fabric.
72   *bolters*: cloths for sifting flour.

Dowlas, filthy dowlas. I have given them away t
bakers' wives; they have made bolters of them.

Hostess

73   *holland*: the finest lawn.
      of: at a cost of; the price quoted
by the Hostess is exaggerated—about
twice the actual amount.

74   *an ell*: about a metre.
75   *diet*: meals.
      by-drinking: drinks between
meals.

Now, as I am a true woman, holland of eigh
shillings an ell! You owe money here besides, S
75 John, for your diet, and by-drinkings, and mone
lent you, four and twenty pound.

Falstaff

He had his part of it; let him pay.

Hostess

He? Alas, he is poor; he hath nothing.

Falstaff

80   *coin*: turn into money
(Bardolph's face is red and glistening—
like gold).

81   *denier*: a small copper coin—
quite worthless.

82-3 *will . . . me*: do you think I am
some spendthrift novice ('younker').

83   *take . . . inn*: relax where I want
he phrase is proverbial).

84   *but . . . have*: without having.

How? Poor? Look upon his face. What call yo
80 rich? Let them coin his nose, let them coin hi
cheeks. I'll not pay a denier. What, will you make
younker of me? Shall I not take mine ease in min
inn but I shall have my pocket picked? I have los
a seal-ring of my grandfather's worth forty mark

Hostess

85 O Jesu, I have heard the Prince tell him, I know
not how oft, that that ring was copper!

Falstaff

How? The Prince is a jack, a sneak-up. 'Sblood,
and he were here I would cudgel him like a dog
if he would say so.

Enter the Prince *marching, with* Peto,
and Falstaff *meets him, playing upon his
truncheon like a fife*

90 How now, lad? Is the wind in that door, i'faith?
Must we all march?

Bardolph

Yea, two and two, Newgate fashion.

Hostess

My lord, I pray you hear me.

Prince

What say'st thou, Mistress Quickly? How doth
95 thy husband? I love him well, he is an honest man.

Hostess

Good my lord, hear me.

Falstaff

Prithee let her alone, and list to me.

Prince

What say'st thou, Jack?

Falstaff

The other night I fell asleep here, behind the
100 arras, and had my pocket picked: this house is
turned bawdy-house; they pick pockets.

Prince

What didst thou lose, Jack?

Falstaff

Wilt thou believe me, Hal, three or four bonds of
forty pound apiece, and a seal-ring of my
105 grandfather's.

Prince

A trifle, some eightpenny matter.

Hostess

So I told him, my lord, and I said I heard your
Grace say so; and, my lord, he speaks most vilely
of you, like a foul-mouthed man as he is, and said
110 he would cudgel you.

---

jack: low fellow.
sneak-up: coward.
cudgel: beat.
so: i.e. that the ring was made of copper.

Is . . . door: is that the way things are (i.e. is it time for us to be soldiers).

Newgate fashion: convicts were made to walk in pairs—handcuffed together—to Newgate prison.

Please take no notice of her and listen to me.

bonds: papers promising to pay money to the bearer (an early form of cheque).

some . . . matter: a trivial thing.

114-115   *a stewed prune*: a bawd (stewed prunes were sold in brothels).

115   *drawn*: hunted; when 'drawn' out of its lair the fox would be especially cunning.

116-7   *Maid . . . thee*: compared to you, Maid Marian is a respectable woman. 'Maid Marian' was a character in the May Day morris dances; the part was played by a man, and was both grotesque and obscene.

117   *deputy's . . . ward*: wife of the deputy of the ward—the most responsible citizen in a section of the city.

118   *thing*: creature (the abuse is vague).

120   *to . . . on*: to be thankful to God for (once again, the abuse is vague, and the Hostess does not know how to react).

123   *setting . . . aside*: despite the fact that you are a knight (who should not insult a lady).

Prince
What! He did not?

Hostess
There's neither faith, truth, nor womanhood in m else.

Falstaff
There's no more faith in thee than in a stewe
115 prune, nor no more truth in thee than in a draw fox—and for womanhood, Maid Marian may b the deputy's wife of the ward to thee. Go, yo thing, go!

Hostess
Say, what thing, what thing?

Falstaff
120 What thing? Why, a thing to thank God on.

Hostess
I am no thing to thank God on, I would tho shouldst know it! I am an honest man's wife, an setting thy knighthood aside, thou art a knave call me so.

Falstaff
125 Setting thy womanhood aside, thou art a beast say otherwise.

Hostess
Say, what beast, thou knave, thou?

Falstaff
What beast? Why, an otter.

Prince
An otter, Sir John? Why an otter?

Falstaff
130 Why? She's neither fish nor flesh; a man know not where to have her.

Hostess
Thou art an unjust man in saying so. Thou or an man knows where to have me, thou knave, thou

Prince
Thou say'st true, hostess, and he slanders the
135 most grossly.

Hostess
So he doth you, my lord, and said this other da you ought him a thousand pound.

Prince
Sirrah, do I owe you a thousand pound?

an otter: a small furry mammal that eats fish and lives mainly in water; scholars argued about whether it was fish or animal.

where . . . her: how to take her (i.e. understand her; *or* make sexual advances to her).

ought: owed.

jack: fellow (a term of mild abuse).

as good as: keep.

lion: Falstaff himself explains the meaning in his next line: the lion, as king of beasts, was a symbol of royalty.

girdle: belt.

midriff: stomach.

embossed: swollen.

reckonings: bills.

long-winded: sugar was given to fighting-cocks to improve their breathing (Falstaff needs it to help his drinking).

injuries: articles whose loss was an injury.

stand to it: insist that you are telling the truth.

pocket up: endure, tolerate.

–9   *in the . . . fell*: when it was created the world was pure; even then Adam (the first man) committed a sin and lost ('fell' from) the grace of God (*Genesis* chapter 1).

Falstaff

A thousand pound, Hal? A million! Thy love is
140 worth a million; thou owest me thy love.

Hostess

Nay, my lord, he called you jack, and said he
would cudgel you.

Falstaff

Did I, Bardolph?

Bardolph

Indeed, Sir John, you said so.

Falstaff

145 Yea, if he said my ring was copper.

Prince

I say 'tis copper. Darest thou be as good as thy
word now?

Falstaff

Why, Hal, thou knowest as thou art but man I
dare, but as thou art prince, I fear thee as I fear the
150 roaring of the lion's whelp.

Prince

And why not as the lion?

Falstaff

The King himself is to be feared as the lion: dost
thou think I'll fear thee as I fear thy father? Nay,
and I do, I pray God my girdle break.

Prince

155 O, if it should, how would thy guts fall about thy
knees! But sirrah, there's no room for faith, truth,
nor honesty in this bosom of thine; it is all filled up
with guts and midriff. Charge an honest woman
with picking thy pocket? Why, thou whoreson
160 impudent, embossed rascal, if there were anything
in thy pocket but tavern reckonings, memoran-
dums of bawdy-houses, and one poor pennyworth
of sugar-candy to make thee long-winded—if thy
pocket were enriched with any other injuries but
165 these, I am a villain: and yet you still stand to it,
you will not pocket up wrong! Art thou not
ashamed?

Falstaff

Dost thou hear, Hal? Thou knowest in the state of
innocency Adam fell, and what should poor Jack
170 Falstaff do in the days of villany? Thou seest I

171–2   *more flesh . . . frailty*: there was a
proverb, 'Flesh is frail'—meaning that
humankind is (morally) weak and so
must sin.
174   *by the story*: i.e. from the account
Hal has already given of the contents of
Falstaff's pocket.
177   *tractable*: obedient, responsive.
178   *pacified still*: always easily
pacified.
179   *to*: we will turn our attention to.
180   What about the robbery? How
have you explained that?
182   *beef*: ox.
be good angel: be your good angel
(get you out of trouble).
184–5 *'Tis . . . labour*: it makes twice as
much work (the first 'labour' was the
robbery).
188   *exchequer*: government funds.
189   *with unwashed hands*: without
delay (a proverbial expression).
191   *a charge of foot*: the command of
an infantry regiment (foot-soldiers).

192   *I would . . . horse*: I wish it had
been a cavalry regiment.
193   *one*: a man (Falstaff needs a
servant).
194–5 *heinously unprovided*: terribly ill-
equipped.
195–7 Falstaff welcomes the rebellion.
196   *laud*: praise.

have more flesh than another man, and therefo
more frailty. You confess then, you picked n
pocket?

Prince

It appears so by the story.

Falstaff

175 Hostess, I forgive thee! Go make ready breakfa
love thy husband, look to thy servants, cherish t
guests; thou shalt find me tractable to any hono
reason. Thou seest I am pacified still—na
prithee be gone. [*Exit* Hostess] Now, Hal, to t
180 news at court: for the robbery, lad, how is th
answered?

Prince

O my sweet beef, I must still be good angel
thee—the money is paid back again.

Falstaff

O, I do not like that paying back! 'Tis a doub
185 labour.

Prince

I am good friends with my father, and may
anything.

Falstaff

Rob me the exchequer the first thing thou do
and do it with unwashed hands too.

Bardolph

190 Do, my lord.

Prince

I have procured thee, Jack, a charge of foot.

Falstaff

I would it had been of horse. Where shall I fi
one that can steal well? O for a fine thief of the a
of two and twenty or thereabouts: I am heinous
195 unprovided. Well, God be thanked for the
rebels, they offend none but the virtuous; I la
them, I praise them.

Prince

Bardolph!

Bardolph

My lord?

Prince

200 Go bear this letter to Lord John of Lancaster,

the Temple hall: the hall of the
Inner Temple (one of the Inns of Court
in London).

thy charge: your regiment.

order: directions.

furniture: equipment.

The . . . burning: the country is
on fire (= eager) for war.

Percy: the Percy family (i.e. the
rebels); but Hal could also mean,
specifically, Hotspur.

stands on high: has risen up.

drum: the soldiers of a regiment
assembled round the regimental
drum.

my brother John, this to my Lord of West-
moreland.   [*Exit* Bardolph
Go, Peto, to horse, to horse; for thou and I have
thirty miles to ride yet ere dinner-time.
                                                      [*Exit* Peto
205 Jack, meet me tomorrow in the Temple hall at two
o'clock in the afternoon: There shalt thou know
thy charge, and there receive money and order for
their furniture. The land is burning, Percy stands
on high, and either we or they must lower lie.
                                                      [*Exit*

Falstaff

210 Rare words! Brave world! Hostess, my breakfast,
come!
O, I could wish this tavern were my drum. [*Exit*

Act 4

Act 4 Scene 1
In the rebel camp, Hotspur is given the
bad news that his father (the Earl of
Northumberland) is unable to join the
rebellion. At first he is angry, but he is
quickly able to make the best of the
situation, although Worcester is very
depressed. Sir Richard Vernon brings
news that now the King's forces, led by
Prince Hal, are ready for the combat.

2   *fine*: refined (Hotspur is ironic).
3   *attribution*: praise.
      the Douglas: the Earl of Douglas
(Hotspur uses the correct form of
address for the head of a Scottish
family.)
4–5   No soldiers of the present time
should be valued more highly
throughout the world. Hotspur's
metaphor is from coinage.
4   *stamp*: minting.
5   *current*: valued.
6   *defy*: despise.
7   *soothers*: flatterers.
      braver: higher, more exalted.
9   *task . . . word*: put me to my
word—give me a chance to show that I
mean what I say.
      approve: test.
10   *king of honour*: most honourable
of men.
11   *potent*: powerful.
      breathes . . . ground: i.e. is alive.
12   *beard*: confront, face.
13   *I . . . you*: these words are
addressed to the Douglas.
16   *grievous*: seriously.
18   *justling*: unsettled, busy.
      power: army.

Scene 1 *Shrewsbury : the Rebel Camp*

Enter Hotspur, Worcester, *and* Doug

Hotspur
Well said, my noble Scot! If speaking truth
In this fine age were not thought flattery,
Such attribution should the Douglas have
As not a soldier of this season's stamp
5 Should go so general current through the worl
By God, I cannot flatter; I do defy
The tongues of soothers! But a braver place
In my heart's love hath no man than yourself:
Nay, task me to my word, approve me, lord.
Douglas
10 Thou art the king of honour:
No man so potent breathes upon the ground
But I will beard him.
Hotspur   Do so, and 'tis we

Enter a Messenger *with letters*

What letters hast thou there?—I can but tha
you.
Messenger
These letters come from your father.
Hotspur
15 Letters from him? Why comes he not himself?
Messenger
He cannot come, my lord, he is grievous sick.
Hotspur
'Zounds, how has he the leisure to be sick
In such a justling time? Who leads his power?
Under whose government come they along?
Messenger
20 His letters bear his mind, not I, my lord.

does . . . bed: is he confined to
bed?

ere: before.

He: his life (the doctors were
afraid that he would die).

state of time: present situation.

whole: healthy.

visited: afflicted.

better worth: more important.
The infection will spread as far
as the camp.

writes me here: tells me in this
letter.

inward: internal.

friends: supporters.

by deputation: by means of a
deputy (i.e. by someone else).

drawn: gathered together.

meet: right.

dear: important.

trust: responsibility.

any . . . remov'd: anyone not so
closely concerned.

advertisement: advice.

conjunction: combined forces.

should on: should march on.
To see what luck we have.

quailing: hesitating.

possess'd: informed.

purposes: intentions.

maim: wound.

a . . . off: Hotspur continues the
imagery of wounding by saying that the
absence of his father is indeed as
though a limb had been cut off.

His . . . want: the loss of him at
the present time.

Were it good: would it be a good
thing.

set: risk.

exact: total.

states: fortunes.

cast: throw of the dice.

main: store.

nice hazard: evenly balanced
chance; 'hazard' is also the name of a
gambling game played with dice.

hour: occasion.

therein: i.e. on that one occasion.

list: limit.

where: whereas.

Worcester

I prithee tell me, doth he keep his bed?

Messenger

He did, my lord, four days ere I set forth,
And at the time of my departure thence
He was much fear'd by his physicians.

Worcester

25 I would the state of time had first been whole
Ere he by sickness had been visited:
His health was never better worth than now.

Hotspur

Sick now? Droop now? This sickness doth infect
The very life-blood of our enterprise;
30 'Tis catching hither, even to our camp.
He writes me here that inward sickness—
And that his friends by deputation could not
So soon be drawn, nor did he think it meet
To lay so dangerous and dear a trust
35 On any soul remov'd but on his own.
Yet doth he give us bold advertisement
That with our small conjunction we should on,
To see how fortune is dispos'd to us;
For, as he writes, there is no quailing now,
40 Because the King is certainly possess'd
Of all our purposes. What say you to it?

Worcester

Your father's sickness is a maim to us.

Hotspur

A perilous gash, a very limb lopp'd off—
And yet, in faith, it is not! His present want
45 Seems more than we shall find it. Were it good
To set the exact wealth of all our states
All at one cast? To set so rich a main
On the nice hazard of one doubtful hour?
It were not good, for therein should we read
50 The very bottom and the soul of hope,
The very list, the very utmost bound
Of all our fortunes.

Douglas

Faith, and so we should, where now remains

54   *reversion*: inheritance.
54–5   *we may . . . in*: we can freely use
        what we have now, assured that more
        (soldiers) will be coming to our aid.
56   This (the knowledge that
        Northumberland's forces are yet to
        come) is a support we can retreat
        (retire) to.
58   *mischance*: misfortune, bad luck.
        look big: threaten
59   *the maidenhead*: i.e. the
        beginning.
60   *would*: wish.
61   *hair*: nature.
62   *Brooks*: permits.
64   *mere*: pure, absolute.
66   *apprehension*: notion,
        interpretation of the situation.
67   *turn the tide*: change the opinions
        of.
        fearful faction: timid rebellion.
68   *in*: about.
69   *off'ring*: challenging.
70   *keep . . . from*: avoid.
        strict arbitrement: critical
        judgement.
71   *stop*: close.
        loop: loop-hole.
73   *draws*: draws back.
74   *the ignorant*: i.e. those who do
        not know about Northumberland's
        sickness.
75   *strain too far*: exaggerate things.
76   *make this use*: see it this way.
77   *opinion*: prestige.
78   *a larger dare*: greater boldness.
80   *make a head*: form an army, make
        an attack.
82   *topsy-turvy down*: quite upside
        down.
83   *Yet*: at this moment.
        our . . . whole: the different parts
        of our army are united.
84   *As . . . think*: as anyone could
        imagine.

A sweet reversion—we may boldly spend
55 Upon the hope of what is to come in.
A comfort of retirement lives in this.
    Hotspur
A rendezvous, a home to fly unto,
If that the devil and mischance look big
Upon the maidenhead of our affairs.
    Worcester
60 But yet I would your father had been here.
The quality and hair of our attempt
Brooks no division; it will be thought,
By some that know not why he is away,
That wisdom, loyalty, and mere dislike
65 Of our proceedings kept the Earl from hence.
And think how such an apprehension
May turn the tide of fearful faction,
And breed a kind of question in our cause.
For well you know we of the off'ring side
70 Must keep aloof from strict arbitrement,
And stop all sight-holes, every loop from when
The eye of reason may pry in upon us.
This absence of your father's draws a curtain
That shows the ignorant a kind of fear
75 Before not dreamt of.
    Hotspur   You strain too f
I rather of his absence make this use:
It lends a lustre and more great opinion,
A larger dare to our great enterprise,
Than if the Earl were here; for men must thin
80 If we without his help can make a head
To push against a kingdom, with his help
We shall o'erturn it topsy-turvy down.
Yet all goes well, yet all our joints are whole.
    Douglas
As heart can think. There is not such a word
85 Spoke of in Scotland as this term of fear.

Enter Sir Richard Vernon

    Hotspur
My cousin Vernon! Welcome, by my soul!
    Vernon
Pray God my news be worth a welcome, lord.

87   *Pray . . . welcome*: I hope that my
        news is welcome.

seven . . . strong: with an army of seven thousand.

–2 *is . . . speedily*: has already started out, or else intends to march here very soon.

preparation: forces.

daff'd: tossed (i.e. ignored what was happening or being said in the world).

bid it pass: let it [the world] go its own way.

furnish'd: prepared for battle.

–9 They are all wearing plumes like ostriches that beat their wings with the wind, just like eagles which have recently bathed.

0 *images*: statues (which were often gilded).

3 *Wanton*: lively.

4 *beaver*: helmet.

5 *cushes*: armour to protect the thighs.

6 *feather'd Mercury*: the messenger of the classical gods had wings on his sandals and cap.

The Earl of Westmoreland, seven thousand
    strong,
Is marching hitherwards, with him Prince John.
    Hotspur
90 No harm. What more?
    Vernon   And further, I have learn'd,
The King himself in person is set forth,
Or hitherwards intended speedily,
With strong and mighty preparation.
    Hotspur
He shall be welcome too: where is his son,
95 The nimble-footed madcap Prince of Wales,
And his comrades that daff'd the world aside
And bid it pass?
    Vernon   All furnish'd, all in arms;
All plum'd like estridges that with the wind
Bated, like eagles having lately bath'd;
100 Glittering in golden coats like images;

As full of spirit as the month of May,
And gorgeous as the sun at midsummer;
Wanton as youthful goats, wild as young bulls.
I saw young Harry with his beaver on,
105 His cushes on his thighs, gallantly arm'd,
Rise from the ground like feather'd Mercury,
And vaulted with such ease into his seat
As if an angel dropp'd down from the clouds
To turn and wind a fiery Pegasus,
110 And witch the world with noble horsemanship

Hotspur

No more, no more! Worse than the sun in Marc
This praise doth nourish agues. Let them com
They come like sacrifices in their trim,
And to the fire-ey'd maid of smoky war
115 All hot and bleeding will we offer them.
The mailed Mars shall on his altar sit
Up to the ears in blood. I am on fire
To hear this rich reprisal is so nigh,
And yet not ours! Come, let me taste my horse
120 Who is to bear me like a thunderbolt
Against the bosom of the Prince of Wales.
Harry to Harry shall, hot to horse to horse,
Meet and ne'er part till one drop down a corse
O that Glendower were come!

Vernon   There is more new
125 I learn'd in Worcester as I rode along
He cannot draw his power this fourteen days.

Douglas

That's the worst tidings that I hear of yet.

Worcester

Ay, by my faith, that bears a frosty sound.

Hotspur

What may the King's whole battle reach unto?

Vernon

130 To thirty thousand.

Hotspur   Forty let it b
My father and Glendower being both away,
The powers of us may serve so great a day.
Come, let us take a muster speedily.
Doomsday is near; die all, die merrily.

107   Only a very strong and skilful
man could mount a horse easily when
he was wearing full armour.
109   *turn and wind*: technical terms of
horsemanship; 'wind' = wheel about.
      fiery: spirited.
      Pegasus: a winged horse (in the
classical mythology) which no mortal
could ride.
110   *witch*: bewitch.
111–2 *the sun . . . agues*: it was thought
that the early spring sun (in March)
caused ague—whose symptoms were
fever and shivering.
113   *sacrifices . . . trim*: sacrificial
beasts with their decorations.
114   *the fire-ey'd maid*: the goddess of
war—Bellona.
116   *the mailed Mars*: Mars (the
classical god of war) in armour (mail).
118   *reprisal*: prize.
      nigh: near.
119   *taste*: try, get the feel of.
122–3 *Harry . . . Meet*: one Harry
(himself) will meet another (Prince
Hal), with one eager horse against
another.
123   *drop . . . corse*: fall lifeless.
126   *draw his power*: gather his army.
      this . . . days: for another
fortnight.
127   *tidings*: news.
128   *bears . . . sound*: sounds bad.
129   How big is the King's army, as a
whole?
130   *Forty . . . be*: even if it were forty
(thousand).
132   *The . . . us*: our own soldiers.
      may serve: will be enough for.
133   *muster*: roll-call.
134   *Doomsday*: the Day of
Judgement.
      die all, die merrily: if we all die,
we shall die happily.

I am . . . fear: I have not been
~~r~~aid.

Of death . . . hand: of dying, or of
~~th~~e way in which I die.

for . . . year: for the past six
~~m~~onths.

~~A~~ct 4 **Scene 2**

~~F~~alstaff and his soldiers are marching
~~to~~ join the King's forces. But Falstaff
~~ha~~s recruited only poor men: those who
~~co~~uld afford the bribe have been left at
~~ho~~me (and Falstaff has taken their
~~m~~oney for himself).

get thee before: you go on ahead.

we'll to: we will march to.

Sutton Co'fil': Sutton Coldfield,
~~1~~0 miles from Coventry (although not
~~in~~ the right direction for Shrewsbury—
~~se~~e map p. xxxiv).

lay out: use your own money
~~in~~stead of the official expenses).

makes: brings the amount up to.

an angel: a gold coin bearing the
~~im~~age of the archangel Michael.

And . . . do: if it does.

take . . . labour: Falstaff pretends
~~to~~ take the literal meaning of
~~B~~ardolph's words (i.e. that the bottle is
~~m~~aking a coin), and offers the money as
~~a~~ tip.

answer: be responsible for
~~co~~ining money was illegal).

town's end: outside the town.

soused: pickled; a *gurnet* was a
~~sm~~all fish.

the King's press: officers were
~~gi~~ven a commission from the King to
~~co~~nscript ('press') men into their
~~re~~giments.

of: for.

and odd: and a few more.

press . . . but: force into service
~~on~~ly.

good: wealthy.

~~2~~5 *yeomen's sons*: the sons of farmers
~~w~~ho owned their small farms.

Douglas

135 Talk not of dying, I am out of fear
Of death or death's hand for this one half year.

[*Exeunt*

Scene 2   *A Road near Coventry*

Enter Falstaff *and* Bardolph

Falstaff

Bardolph, get thee before to Coventry; fill me a
bottle of sack. Our soldiers shall march through;
we'll to Sutton Co'fil' tonight.

Bardolph

Will you give me money, captain?

Falstaff

5 Lay out, lay out.

Bardolph

This bottle makes an angel.

Falstaff

And if it do, take if for thy labour—and if it make
twenty, take them all; I'll answer the coinage. Bid
my lieutenant Peto meet me at town's end.

Bardolph

10 I will, captain: farewell.   [*Exit*

Falstaff

If I be not ashamed of my soldiers, I am a soused
gurnet; I have misused the King's press damnably. I have got, in exchange of a hundred and
fifty soldiers, three hundred and odd pounds. I
15 press me none but good householders, yeomen's
sons; inquire me out contracted bachelors, such as
had been asked twice on the banns—such a
commodity of warm slaves as had as lief hear the
devil as a drum, such as fear the report of a caliver
20 worse than a struck fowl or a hurt wild duck. I
pressed me none but such toasts-and-butter, with
hearts in their bellies no bigger than pins' heads,
and they have bought out their services; and now
my whole charge consists of ancients, corporals,
25 lieutenants, gentlemen of companies—slaves as
ragged as Lazarus in the painted cloth, where the
glutton's dogs licked his sores: and such as indeed

16   *inquire me out*: search out.
contracted bachelors: men
engaged to be married; announcements
of intended marriages were made in
church (the 'banns' were 'asked') on
three occasions before the wedding
could take place.
18   *commodity*: collection.
warm slaves: cowards with plenty
of money.
had as lief: would rather.
19   *the . . , caliver*: the bang of a gun.
20   *struck*: wounded.
21   *toasts-and-butter*: weaklings.
22   *bellies*: bodies.
23   *bought . . . services*: bought
themselves out of the service (i.e.
bribed Falstaff to release them).
24   *charge*: company (the soldiers he
commands).
ancients: ensigns (the lowest rank
of officer).
25   *gentlemen of companies*: men who
were neither common soldiers nor
officers.
26   *Lazarus*: the beggar in the
parable of Dives (St Luke's Gospel,
16: 19–31; see also *Act 3*, Scene 3, lines
32–3).
painted cloth: cloths painted with
pictures were a cheap substitute for
tapestry.
27   *the glutton*: i.e. Dives.
28–9   *discarded . . . men*: dishonest
servants who had lost their jobs (been
'discarded').
29   *younger . . . brothers*: in English
law, the eldest son inherited his father's
property; his younger brother could
hope for little—and the younger son of
this brother would have no
expectations.
29–30   *revolted tapsters*: inn-servants
who have broken their
apprenticeships—as Hal teasingly
suggests to Francis in *Act 2* Scene 4.

were never soldiers, but discarded unjust servir
men, younger sons to younger brothers, revolt
30 tapsters, and ostlers trade-fallen, the cankers o
calm world and a long peace, ten times m
dishonourable-ragged than an old fazed ancie
And such have I to fill up the rooms of them
have bought out their services, that you wou
35 think that I had a hundred and fifty tatter
prodigals lately come from swine-keeping, fr
eating draff and husks. A mad fellow met me
the way, and told me I had unloaded all the gibb
and pressed the dead bodies. No eye hath se
40 such scarecrows. I'll not march through Coven
with them, that's flat. Nay, and the villains mar
wide betwixt the legs as if they had gyves on,
indeed I had the most of them out of prisc
There's not a shirt and a half in all my compa1
45 and the half shirt is two napkins tacked togetl
and thrown over the shoulders like a herald's co

trade-fallen: unemployed because trade is poor.

cankers: parasites.

-31 *a calm . . . peace*: the Elizabethans believed that war was useful in creating jobs for men who could find no employment in a time of peace.

dishonourable-ragged: ragged in a dishonourable way.

fazed: tattered.

ancient: ensign—the flag carried into battle.

fill . . . rooms: take the places.

-7 *prodigals . . . husks*: the parable of the Prodigal Son is told in St Luke's Gospel (15:16): the son wasted his inheritance, and then found a job guarding pigs; he was so hungry that he ate the food of the swine ('draff and husks').

-9 *unloaded . . . bodies*: taken the bodies from the gallows and conscripted them into his regiment.

flat: certain.

-2 *march . . . gyves on*: march with their legs wide apart, as though they were in chains ('gyves') (i.e. like convicts chained together).

had: got.

tacked: roughly stitched.

a herald's coat: a tabard.

my host: the inn-keeper.

that's all one: that doesn't matter.

linen . . . hedge: Elizabethan housewives spread their washing on the hedges to dry (and Falstaff will encourage his men to steal).

blown . . . quilt: Hal makes two puns: 'blown' = out of breath *and* swollen; 'Jack' is *both* a familiar form of 'John' *and* the word for a soldier's padded (quilted) jacket.

wag: joker.

cry you mercy: beg your pardon.

had . . . Shrewsbury: would have been at Shrewsbury by this time.

without sleeves; and the shirt to say the truth stolen from my host at Saint Albans, or the red-nose innkeeper of Daventry. But that's all one, 50 they'll find linen enough on every hedge.

Enter the Prince *and the* Lord of Westmoreland

Prince

How now, blown Jack? How now, quilt?

Falstaff

What, Hal! How now, mad wag? What a devil dost thou in Warwickshire? My good Lord of Westmoreland, I cry you mercy; I thought your 55 honour had already been at Shrewsbury.

Westmoreland

Faith, Sir John, 'tis more than time that I were

57   *powers*: soldiers.

58   *looks for*: is expecting.

59   *away all night*: march throughout the night.

60   *never fear me*: don't worry about me.

        vigilant: alert and ready.

62-3   *I think ... butter*: I think you must certainly have been stealing cream—that is what has made you so fat (butter is made from cream).

64   *come after*: are following.

67   *toss*: i.e. on the pikes of the enemies.

        food for powder: cannon-fodder (good enough to be shot at).

68   *they'll ... better*: their dead bodies can be thrown into a pit as well as those of better men.

69   *mortal men*: human beings who have got to die some time.

71   *bare*: ragged; *and* thin.

72   *had*: got.

73   *bareness*: thinness.

75-6   *three ... ribs*: fat on the ribs as thick as three fingers.

77   *in the field*: prepared for battle.

78   *is ... encamped*: has the King set up his camp.

81-3   *To ... guest*: a proverbial saying.
81   *fray*: fight.
83   *dull*: unwitting.
        keen: eager.

there, and you too, but my powers are ther
already; the King I can tell you looks for us all; w
must away all night.

Falstaff

60 Tut, never fear me: I am as vigilant as a cat to stea
cream.

Prince

I think, to steal cream indeed, for thy theft hat
already made thee butter. But tell me, Jac
whose fellows are these that come after?

Falstaff

65 Mine, Hal, mine.

Prince

I did never see such pitiful rascals.

Falstaff

Tut, tut, good enough to toss, food for powde.
food for powder; they'll fill a pit as well as bette:
Tush, man, mortal men, mortal men.

Westmoreland

70 Ay, but, Sir John, methinks they are exceedin
poor and bare, too beggarly.

Falstaff

Faith, for their poverty I know not where they ha
that; and for their bareness I am sure they neve
learned that of me.

Prince

75 No, I'll be sworn, unless you call three fingers i
the ribs bare. But sirrah, make haste; Percy
already in the field.   [*Ex*

Falstaff

What, is the King encamped?

Westmoreland

He is, Sir John; I fear we shall stay too long.
                                                  [*Ex*

Falstaff

80 Well,
To the latter end of a fray, and the beginning of
feast
Fits a dull fighter and a keen guest.   [*Ex*

Act 4 Scene 3
Hotspur is eager to start fighting at
once, but his friends try to dissuade
him. Their discussion is interrupted by
Sir Walter Blunt, who brings a message
of peace from the King. Hotspur does
not want peace, and he recites the list of
the rebels' grievances and the King's
broken promises; but he agrees to wait
until morning before sending his reply
to the King.

    You . . . advantage: Douglas
argues that a delay will be an advantage
to the King.

    whit: bit.

    Looks . . . supply: isn't he
expecting reinforcements (extra
troops).

    counsel: advise.

    maintain . . . life: prove my
courage by giving up my life.

    well-respected: well-considered.

    bid me on: tells me to go out and
fight.

    I . . . with: take as little notice of.

    leading: experience.

    Drag . . . expedition: prevent us
from moving fast.

    horse: cavalry.

    not . . . himself: not one of the
horses has a fraction of its usual
strength.

Scene 3 *Shrewsbury : the Rebel Camp*

      Enter Hotspur, Worcester, Douglas,
      Vernon

    Hotspur
We'll fight with him tonight.
    Worcester   It may not be.
    Douglas
You give him then advantage.
    Vernon   Not a whit.
    Hotspur
Why say you so? Looks he not for supply?
    Vernon
So do we.
    Hotspur   His is certain, ours is doubtful.
    Worcester
5 Good cousin, be advis'd, stir not tonight.
    Vernon
Do not, my lord.
    Douglas   You do not counsel well.
You speak it out of fear and cold heart.
    Vernon
Do me no slander, Douglas; by my life—
And I dare well maintain it with my life—
10 If well-respected honour bid me on,
I hold as little counsel with weak fear
As you, my lord, or any Scot that this day lives;
Let it be seen tomorrow in the battle
Which of us fears.
    Douglas   Yea, or tonight.
    Vernon   Content.
    Hotspur
15 Tonight, say I.
    Vernon
Come, come, it may not be. I wonder much,
Being men of such great leading as you are,
That you foresee not what impediments
Drag back our expedition: certain horse
20 Of my cousin Vernon's are not yet come up;
Your uncle Worcester's horse came but today,
And now their pride and mettle is asleep,
Their courage with hard labour tame and dull,
That not a horse is half the half himself.

26   *journey-bated*: tired with travelling.
    brought low: in poor condition.
27   *full of rest*: well rested.
29   *stay . . . in*: wait until everyone has arrived.
29sd   *sounds a parley*: calls to summon them to a discussion.
31   If you will agree to listen and take notice of what I say.
33   *of our determination*: on our side.
35   Are reluctant to praise you and give you the honour ('good name') that you deserve.
36   *of our quality*: on our side.
37   *stand against*: oppose.
38   *defend*: forbid.
    still: always.

Hotspur

25 So are the horses of the enemy
In general journey-bated and brought low.
The better part of ours are full of rest.

Worcester

The number of the King exceedeth ours.
For God's sake, cousin, stay till all come in.

                    [*The trumpet sounds a parl*

Enter Sir Walter Blunt

Blunt

30 I come with gracious offers from the King,
If you vouchsafe me hearing and respect.

Hotspur

Welcome, Sir Walter Blunt: and would to God

out of limit: beyond the bounds
your allegiance.

true rule: proper conduct.

to my charge: let me say what I
ve been commanded to say.

griefs: grievances.

whereupon: for what reason.

conjure: call up (as though by
agic).

the . . . peace: the hearts of peace-
ving citizens.

duteous land: law-abiding nation.

your good deserts: the good deeds
u have done which should be
warded.

And he admits that there are very
any of these (the 'good deserts').

your . . . interest: all that you
nt—and more.

absolute: unconditional.

these . . . suggestion: those who
ve been led astray through your
fluence.

kind: Hotspur is sarcastic.

well . . . pay: we know how the
ng makes promises which he never
eps.

royalty: the title of 'king', the
own.

he was . . . strong: he had no more
an 26 supporters.

sick: poor.

regard: opinion.

unminded: ignored.

came . . . Lancaster: see p. v.

but: only.

sue his livery: ask for the
liverance of his lands.

terms of zeal: declarations of
cerity.

in . . . mov'd: out of the kindness
his heart and because he was sorry
him.

Promised to give him help, and
l help him.

lean to him: take his side (against
chard II).

The more and less: both high and
w (the nobles and the common
ople).

with cap and knee: taking off their
ts and bowing (in sign of respect).

You were of our determination!
Some of us love you well, and even those some
35 Envy your great deservings and good name,
Because you are not of our quality,
But stand against us like an enemy.

Blunt

And God defend but still I should stand so,
So long as out of limit and true rule
40 You stand against anointed majesty.
But to my charge. The King hath sent to know
The nature of your griefs, and whereupon
You conjure from the breast of civil peace
Such bold hostility, teaching his duteous land
45 Audacious cruelty. If that the King
Have any way your good deserts forgot,
Which he confesseth to be manifold,
He bids you name your griefs, and with all speed
You shall have your desires with interest,
50 And pardon absolute for yourself and these
Herein misled by your suggestion.

Hotspur

The King is kind, and well we know the King
Knows at what time to promise, when to pay.
My father, and my uncle, and myself
55 Did give him that same royalty he wears;
And when he was not six and twenty strong,
Sick in the world's regard, wretched and low,
A poor unminded outlaw sneaking home,
My father gave him welcome to the shore;
60 And when he heard him swear and vow to God
He came but to be Duke of Lancaster,
To sue his livery, and beg his peace,
With tears of innocency and terms of zeal,
My father, in kind heart and pity mov'd,
65 Swore him assistance, and perform'd it too.
Now when the lords and barons of the realm
Perceiv'd Northumberland did lean to him,
The more and less came in with cap and knee,
Met him in boroughs, cities, villages,

70   *Attended*: waited for.
      in lanes: in rows (so Bolingbroke
could walk between them).
71   *proffer'd . . . oaths*: swore oaths of
allegiance.
72   *Gave . . . pages*: i.e. the noblemen
sent their sons to attend Bolingbroke as
pageboys (a sign of their allegiance).
73   *Even . . . heels*: close behind him.
      golden: richly dressed; *and*
promising success.
74   *presently*: immediately.
      as . . . itself: as he began to
recognize his power.
75   *Steps . . . higher*: climb a bit
above.
76   *blood*: spirit.
      poor: humble.
77   *naked*: barren.
78   *forsooth*: indeed.
79   *certain*: particular.
      strait: strict.
81   *Cries out upon*: exposes.
82   *by this face*: with this appearance.
83   *This . . . justice*: pretending to be
concerned with justice.
84   *angle for*: fish for, try to catch.
87   *In deputation*: as substitutes to
rule for him (see p. iv).
88   *was personal in*: went himself to.
92   *in the neck of*: immediately after.
      task'd: taxed.
93   *suffer'd*: allowed.
      March: the Earl of March
(Mortimer).
94   *if . . . plac'd*: if everyone had his
proper title.
95   *his king*: see p. 126.
      engag'd: held prisoner.
96   To be kept there, unredeemed,
because no ransom was paid.
97   *Disgrac'd*: discredited.
      happy: splendid.
98   *intelligence*: secret information
(provided by spies).
99   *Rates*: dismissed with abuse.
103   *head of safety*: army in self-
defence.
      withal: also.
103-4   *to pry . . . title*: to investigate his
claim to the throne.

70 Attended him on bridges, stood in lanes,
   Laid gifts before him, proffer'd him their oath
   Gave him their heirs as pages, follow'd him
   Even at the heels in golden multitudes.
   He presently, as greatness knows itself,
75 Steps me a little higher than his vow
   Made to my father while his blood was poor
   Upon the naked shore at Ravenspurgh;
   And now, forsooth, takes on him to reform
   Some certain edicts and some strait decrees
80 That lie too heavy on the commonwealth;
   Cries out upon abuses, seems to weep
   Over his country's wrongs; and by this face,
   This seeming brow of justice, did he win
   The hearts of all that he did angle for;
85 Proceeded further—cut me off the heads
   Of all the favourites that the absent King
   In deputation left behind him here,
   When he was personal in the Irish war.
      Blunt
   Tut, I came not to hear this.
      Hotspur   Then to the poi
90 In short time after, he depos'd the King;
   Soon after that depriv'd him of his life;
   And in the neck of that, task'd the whole state
   To make that worse, suffer'd his kinsman Mar
   (Who is, if every owner were well plac'd,
95 Indeed his king) to be engag'd in Wales,
   There without ransom to lie forfeited;
   Disgrac'd me in my happy victories,
   Sought to entrap me by intelligence,
   Rated mine uncle from the Council-board;
100 In rage dismiss'd my father from the court;
    Broke oath on oath, committed wrong on wror
    And in conclusion drove us to seek out
    This head of safety, and withal to pry
    Into his title—the which we find
105 Too indirect for long continuance.
       Blunt
    Shall I return this answer to the King?
       Hotspur
    Not so, Sir Walter. We'll withdraw awhile.
    Go to the King, and let there be impawn'd

too indirect: not in a sufficiently straight line of descent (see p. vi); *and* morally doubtful (see p. v).

for . . . continuance: to last long.

8-9   *let . . . again*: let someone (from the King's army) remain with us as a pledge ('be impawn'd' as 'surety') that my uncle shall return safely.

mine uncle: i.e. Worcester.

Bring . . . purposes: go to the King and tell him our intentions.

I would: I wish.

Some surety for a safe return again,
110 And in the morning early shall mine uncle
Bring him our purposes—and so, farewell.
  Blunt
I would you would accept of grace and love.
  Hotspur
And may be so we shall.
  Blunt   Pray God you do. [*Exeunt*

Act 4 Scene 4
The Archbishop of York (who supports the rebels against the King) is sending letters to his friends, asking for assistance. He explains that the rebels are not as powerful as they had hoped to be, and he is afraid that they will be defeated by the King's army.

Hie: hurry.

sealed brief: letter with the Archbishop's seal.

winged haste: as fast as if you could fly.

the Lord Marshal: Thomas Mowbray, Duke of Norfolk.

my cousin Scroop: several members of the Scroop family supported the rebels' cause; the Archbishop himself was Lord Scroop.

directed: addressed.

How . . . import: how important they are.

tenor: purpose.

bide the touch: be tested.

quick-raised power: an army which has been very quickly formed.

Lord Harry: Hotspur (Lord Harry Percy).

Whose army was the largest.

rated sinew: valuable source of strength.

comes not in: will not be joining the rebels.

o'er-rul'd by prophecies: deterred by evil omens.

Scene 4 *York: the Archbishop's Palace*

  Enter the Archbishop of York *and* Sir
  Michael

  Archbishop
Hie, good Sir Michael, bear this sealed brief
With winged haste to the Lord Marshal;
This to my cousin Scroop; and all the rest
To whom they are directed. If you knew
5 How much they do import, you would make haste.
  Sir Michael
My good lord,
I guess their tenor.
  Archbishop   Like enough you do.
Tomorrow, good Sir Michael, is a day
Wherein the fortune of ten thousand men
10 Must bide the touch; for, sir, at Shrewsbury,
As I am truly given to understand,
The King with mighty and quick-raised power
Meets with Lord Harry: and I fear, Sir Michael,
What with the sickness of Northumberland,
15 Whose power was in the first proportion,
And what with Owen Glendower's absence
  thence,
Who with them was a rated sinew too,
And comes not in, o'er-rul'd by prophecies,

wage: fight.
instant: immediate.

head: army.

8   *drawn . . . together*: assembled
the finest army of the country.

mo: more.
corrivals: partners.
dear: noble.
estimation: high reputation.
command in arms: experienced
warriors.
they . . . oppos'd: their opponents
will fight well.
needful 'tis: it is necessary.
thrive not: does not conquer.
ere: before.
our confederacy: our plotting with
the rebels.
make strong: defend ourselves
strongly.

I fear the power of Percy is too weak
20 To wage an instant trial with the King.
    Sir Michael
Why, my good lord, you need not fear,
There is Douglas, and Lord Mortimer.
    Archbishop
No, Mortimer is not there.
    Sir Mortimer
But there is Mordake, Vernon, Lord Harry Percy,
25 And there is my Lord of Worcester, and a head
Of gallant warriors, noble gentlemen.
    Archbishop
And so there is; but yet the King hath drawn
The special head of all the land together:
The Prince of Wales, Lord John of Lancaster,
30 The noble Westmoreland, and warlike Blunt,
And many mo corrivals and dear men
Of estimation and command in arms.
    Sir Michael
Doubt not, my lord, they shall be well oppos'd.
    Archbishop
I hope no less, yet needful 'tis to fear;
35 And to prevent the worst, Sir Michael, speed.
For if Lord Percy thrive not, ere the King
Dismiss his power he means to visit us,
For he hath heard of our confederacy,
And 'tis but wisdom to make strong against him:
40 Therefore make haste. I must go write again
To other friends; and so, farewell, Sir Michael.
                                    [*Exeunt*

Act 5

Act 5 Scene 1
The King's army has gathered at
Shrewsbury. The Earl of Worcester
comes from the rebel camp and
reminds the King of the rebels'
grievances. The Prince of Wales sends
a challenge to Hotspur, offering to fight
him in single combat rather than risk
the lives of thousands of men in a full
battle. The King offers peace and
forgiveness if the rebels will yield. The
scene ends with the parting of Hal and
Falstaff, and Falstaff's meditation on
the subject of honour.

1–3   *How . . . distemp'rature*: in
England, a red sky at sunrise is often a
sign that the day will be wet or stormy.

2   *yon*: yonder.

3   *distemp'rature*: disorder.
    The southern wind: the south
wind brings stormy weather in
England.

4   *play . . . purposes*: blows like a
trumpet to announce the coming events
(as a herald would do).
    his: i.e. the sun's.

10   *upon such terms*: in such a
relationship (i.e. as enemies).

12   *doff*: throw off.
    easy: comfortable.

15   *unknit*: untangle.

16   *churlish*: brutal.
    all-abhorred: utterly hateful,
hated by everyone.

17   The King compares the rebels to
stars, which should each move in a
fixed orbit ('obedient orb').

19   *exhal'd*: displaced.

20   *prodigy of fear*: fearful monster.

21   Of trouble that has exploded
now and will affect future generations.

Scene 1 *Shrewsbury : the King's Camp*

> *Enter the* King, Prince of Wales, Lo[
> John of Lancaster, Sir Walter Blu[
> Falstaff

King

How bloodily the sun begins to peer
Above yon bulky hill! The day looks pale
At his distemp'rature.

Prince   The southern wi[
Doth play the trumpet to his purposes,
5 And by his hollow whistling in the leaves
Foretells a tempest and a blust'ring day.

King

Then with the losers let it sympathize,
For nothing can seem foul to those that win.

> [*The trumpet soun[*

> *Enter* Worcester *and* Vernon

How now, my Lord of Worcester! 'Tis not we[
10 That you and I should meet upon such terms
As now we meet. You have deceiv'd our trust,
And made us doff our easy robes of peace
To crush our old limbs in ungentle steel:
This is not well, my lord, this is not well.
15 What say you to it? Will you again unknit
This churlish knot of all-abhorred war,
And move in that obedient orb again
Where you did give a fair and natural light,
And be no more an exhal'd meteor,
20 A prodigy of fear, and a portent
Of broached mischief to the unborn times?

Worcester

Hear me, my liege:

24   *lag-end*: last days.
26   *I . . . sought*: I did not want.
        dislike: enmity.
29   *chewet*: jackdaw (= chatterbox).
32   *remember*: remind.
34–5   *For you . . . time*: when
Worcester joined the rebels, he gave up
the stewardship of Richard II's
household and broke the white rod
(which was the symbol of this office).
35   *posted*: galloped.
36   *kiss your hand*: as a sign of
allegiance.
37–8   When you were still very much
inferior to me.
37   *yet*: still, as yet.
        place: status, position.
        account: public opinion.
38   *Nothing*: nothing like.
43   *did . . . 'gainst*: had no hostile
intentions against.
44   *further*: more.
        new-fall'n right: what had
recently become your right (by the
death of his father, John of Gaunt).
45   *seat*: property.
46   *space*: time.
49   *the absent king*: Richard II was
not in England when Bolingbroke
returned from exile.
50   *injuries*: abuses.
        wanton: badly governed.
51   *seeming sufferances*: apparent
hardships.
52   *contrarious*: contrary.
54   *repute*: believe.
56   *woo'd*: persuaded.
57   *gripe*: grab.
        general sway: rule of the whole
kingdom.
59–61   *you . . . sparrow*: you made use of
us in the same way that the young
cuckoo—a wretched nestling ('gull')—
makes use of the sparrow. (The cuckoo
does not build a nest, but lays its eggs
in the nests of smaller birds, such as the
sparrow; eventually the young cuckoo
pushes the sparrow's own young out of
the nest—or it might even eat them.)

For mine own part, I could be well content
To entertain the lag-end of my life
25 With quiet hours. For I protest
I have not sought the day of this dislike.
            King
You have not sought it? How comes it, then?
        Falstaff
Rebellion lay in his way, and he found it.
        Prince
Peace, chewet, peace!
        Worcester
30 It pleas'd your Majesty to turn your looks
Of favour from myself and all our house;
And yet I must remember you, my lord,
We were the first and dearest of your friends:
For you my staff of office did I break
35 In Richard's time, and posted day and night
To meet you on the way, and kiss your hand,
When yet you were, in place and in account,
Nothing so strong and fortunate as I.
It was myself, my brother, and his son,
40 That brought you home, and boldly did outda
The dangers of the time. You swore to us,
And you did swear that oath at Doncaster,
That you did nothing purpose 'gainst the state
Nor claim no further than your new-fall'n right
45 The seat of Gaunt, dukedom of Lancaster.
To this we swore our aid. But in short space
It rain'd down fortune show'ring on your head
And such a flood of greatness fell on you,
What with our help, what with the absent Kin
50 What with the injuries of a wanton time,
The seeming sufferances that you had borne,
And the contrarious winds that held the King
So long in his unlucky Irish wars
That all in England did repute him dead:
55 And from this swarm of fair advantages
You took occasion to be quickly woo'd
To gripe the general sway into your hand;
Forgot your oath to us at Doncaster;
And being fed by us, you us'd us so
60 As that ungentle gull, the cuckoo's bird,
Useth the sparrow—did oppress our nest,

our love: we who loved you.
durst: dare.
swallowing: being swallowed.
head: army.
Whereby: because of this (i.e.
Bolingbroke's behaviour as a 'cuckoo's
bird').
    opposed: in conflict with each
other.
    by such means: for such reasons.
    forg'd: created (Worcester speaks
as though the King had himself made
the weapons—swords—with which
they now fight.)
    unkind: discourteous; *also*
unnatural.
    dangerous countenance:
threatening appearance.
    troth: trust.
    younger: earlier (i.e. the plan to
recover his own property).
    articulate: announced.
    market crosses: the stone cross in
the centre of the market-place was the
general meeting-point for citizens,
where they would hear most of the
news and official announcements.
    face: decorate.
    colour: excuse (as well as the
word's usual sense).
    fickle changelings: those who
easily change their allegiances.
    poor discontents: wretches who
are never satisfied with anything.
    gape: stand open-mouthed.
    rub the elbow: hug themselves
with delight (it was believed that joy
made the elbows itch).
    hurlyburly innovation: a
revolution which will turn things
upside down.
    want: lack.
    water-colours: i.e. weak excuses
('water-colours' are paints that can
easily be washed away).
    impaint: paint.
    his: its.
    moody: sullen.
    pellmell: riotous.
    they ... trial: the armies engage
in battle.

Grew by our feeding to so great a bulk
That even our love durst not come near your sight
For fear of swallowing; but with nimble wing
65 We were enforc'd for safety sake to fly
Out of your sight, and raise this present head;
Whereby we stand opposed by such means
As you yourself have forg'd against yourself
By unkind usage, dangerous countenance,
70 And violation of all faith and troth
Sworn to us in your younger enterprise.
        King
These things, indeed, you have articulate,
Proclaim'd at market crosses, read in churches,
To face the garment of rebellion
75 With some fine colour that may please the eye
Of fickle changelings and poor discontents,
Which gape and rub the elbow at the news
Of hurlyburly innovation;
And never yet did insurrection want
80 Such water-colours to impaint his cause,
Nor moody beggars, starving for a time
Of pellmell havoc and confusion.
        Prince
In both your armies there is many a soul
Shall pay full dearly for this encounter,
85 If once they join in trial. Tell your nephew,

87   *hopes*: i.e. of salvation after death.
88   If we forget this responsibility ('set off his head') for the present business.
89   *braver*: finer.
90   *active-valiant*: valiant in action (i.e. courageous in war).
        valiant-young: valiant (courageous) in his youth.
92   *latter*: modern.
93   *I . . . shame*: I am ashamed to have to say this.
94   I have been absent from the heroic world of chivalry (as a schoolboy is absent from school—playing 'truant').
95   *account me*: consider me (i.e. as a 'truant').
96   Yet let me say this in front of His Majesty the King, my father.
97   *odds*: advantages.
98   *estimation*: reputation.
100   *Try fortune*: risk my chances.
101–3   The King would have confidence in his son, but he can see too many political difficulties in such a single combat.
102   *Albeit*: yet on the other hand.
        considerations infinite: an infinite number of considerations.
103   *make against it*: make it undesirable.
104   *even . . . love*: we love even those.
105   Who are misguided enough to fight on your relation's side ('cousin' here has its vague, non-specific, meaning of 'relative').
106   *will they take*: if they will accept.
        grace: pardon.
107   *yea*: indeed.
111   *dread correction*: dreadful punishment.
        wait on us: are in my power.
112   *do their office*: be used appropriately.
114   We are making a fair offer; think about it carefully.
117   Think they can fight against the whole world.

The Prince of Wales doth join with all the wor
In praise of Henry Percy: by my hopes,
This present enterprise set off his head,
I do not think a braver gentleman,
90 More active-valiant or more valiant-young,
More daring or more bold, is now alive
To grace this latter age with noble deeds.
For my part (I may speak it to my shame),
I have a truant been to chivalry,
95 And so I hear he doth account me too;
Yet this before my father's majesty—
I am content that he shall take the odds
Of his great name and estimation,
And will, to save the blood on either side,
100 Try fortune with him in a single fight.
        King
And, Prince of Wales, so dare we venture thee,
Albeit considerations infinite
Do make against it. No, good Worcester, no!
We love our people well—even those we love
105 That are misled upon your cousin's part—
And will they take the offer of our grace,
Both he, and they, and you, yea, every man
Shall be my friend again, and I'll be his:
So tell your cousin, and bring me word
110 What he will do. But if he will not yield,
Rebuke and dread correction wait on us,
And they shall do their office. So, be gone;
We will not now be troubled with reply:
We offer fair; take it advisedly.
                [*Exit* Worcester, *with* Vern
        Prince
115 It will not be accepted, on my life:
The Douglas and the Hotspur both together
Are confident against the world in arms.

charge: regiment.
on their answer: as soon as they reply.
set on: attack.
as: to the extent that.
bestride: stand over (i.e. protect).
so: that will please me.
a point of friendship: your duty as my friend.
Colossus: the gigantic statue that once stood on the harbour walls at Rhodes.
thou . . . death: a proverbial saying (with the sense of 'you must die some day').
'Tis . . . yet: it is not yet time to pay the debt (Falstaff picks up the metaphor of 'owest').
forward with: prompt to pay.
calls not: is making no demands.
pricks: urges, spurs.
-31 prick me off: kills me (by pricking—or stabbing—with a sword).
-2 set to a leg: set (mend) a broken leg.
grief: pain.
-6 A trim reckoning: a fine summing-up.
-7 a-Wednesday: last Wednesday.
'Tis insensible: it cannot be perceived by any of the five senses.
Detraction: slander.
suffer: allow.
-41 I'll none of it: I won't have anything to do with it.
a mere scutcheon: nothing more than the drapery at a funeral (the churches were hung with special heraldic banners).
catechism: a form of teaching by oral questions and answers; it was used particularly for religious instruction.

King
Hence, therefore, every leader to his charge;
For on their answer will we set on them,
120 And God befriend us as our cause is just!
[Exeunt all but the Prince and Falstaff
Falstaff
Hal, if thou see me down in the battle and bestride me, so; 'tis a point of friendship.
Prince
Nothing but a Colossus can do thee that friendship. Say thy prayers, and farewell.
Falstaff
125 I would 'twere bed-time, Hal, and all well.
Prince
Why, thou owest God a death.   [Exit
Falstaff
'Tis not due yet: I would be loath to pay him before his day—what need I be so forward with him that calls not on me? Well, 'tis no matter, 130 honour pricks me on. Yea, but how if honour prick me off when I come on, how then? Can honour set to a leg? No. Or an arm? Or take away the grief of a wound? No. Honour hath no skill in surgery then? No. What is honour? A word. What is in 135 that word 'honour'? What is that honour? Air. A trim reckoning! Who hath it? He that died a-Wednesday. Doth he feel it? Doth he hear it? No. 'Tis insensible, then? Yea, to the dead. But will it not live with the living? No. Why? 140 Detraction will not suffer it. Therefore I'll none of it. Honour is a mere scutcheon—and so ends my catechism.   [Exit

Act 5 Scene 2
Worcester has returned to the rebel
camp, but he is unwilling to tell
Hotspur that the King has made an
offer of peace. War is declared.

3   *undone*: ruined.
5   *keep . . . us*: be friends with us as
he promised.
7   *this offence*: i.e. the rebellion.
8   *Supposition*: suspicion;
Worcester imagines a monster with
many eyes, watching the rebels for the
rest of their lives.
10   *lock'd up*: kept in a cage.
11   *a wild . . . ancestor*: the habit of
his wild ancestors.
12   *or . . . or . . .*: whether . . . or . . .
13   Our appearances will be
misinterpreted and wrongly reported.
14   *at a stall*: kept in the stable (i.e.
being fattened for the butcher).
15   *still*: always.
16   *may . . . forgot*: may well be
forgotten.
18   *an adopted name*: a nickname (i.e.
'Hotspur').
       of privilege: which gives him the
privilege of being hot-tempered.
19   *hare-brain'd*: rash, thoughtless.
       spleen: impulsiveness.
20   *live*: lie; Worcester believes that
he and Northumberland will be blamed
for Hotspur's faults.
21   *train him on*: lead him on,
encourage him.
22   *corruption*: wickedness.
       ta'en: caught (like an infection).
23   *spring*: source.
25   *In any case*: whatever happens.
26   *Deliver . . . will*: give them
whatever message you like.

28   *Deliver up*: release (apparently
the Earl of Westmoreland had been
kept as the hostage demanded in *4,
3*,109).

30   *bid you battle*: challenge you to
fight.
       presently: immediately.

Scene 2 *Shrewsbury : the Rebel Camp*

Enter Worcester *and* Sir Richard
Vernon

Worcester
O no, my nephew must not know, Sir Richard,
The liberal and kind offer of the King.
Vernon
'Twere best he did.
Worcester   Then are we all undone
It is not possible, it cannot be,
5 The King should keep his word in loving us;
He will suspect us still, and find a time
To punish this offence in other faults:
Supposition all our lives shall be stuck full of eyes
For treason is but trusted like the fox,
10 Who, never so tame, so cherish'd and lock'd up
Will have a wild trick of his ancestors.
Look how we can, or sad or merrily,
Interpretation will misquote our looks,
And we shall feed like oxen at a stall,
15 The better cherish'd still the nearer death.
My nephew's trespass may be well forgot,
It hath the excuse of youth and heat of blood,
And an adopted name of privilege—
A hare-brain'd Hotspur, govern'd by a spleen.
20 All his offences live upon my head
And on his father's. We did train him on,
And, his corruption being a ta'en from us,
We as the spring of all shall pay for all.
Therefore, good cousin, let not Harry know
25 In any case the offer of the King.
Vernon
Deliver what you will; I'll say 'tis so.
Here comes your cousin.

Enter Hotspur *and* Douglas

Hotspur   My uncle is return'd
Deliver up my Lord of Westmoreland.
Uncle, what news?
Worcester
30 The King will bid you battle presently.

Douglas
Defy him by the Lord of Westmoreland.
Hotspur
Lord Douglas, go you and tell him so.
Douglas
Marry, and shall, and very willingly.   [*Exit*
Worcester
There is no seeming mercy in the King.
Hotspur
35 Did you beg any? God forbid!
Worcester
I told him gently of our grievances,
Of his oath-breaking—which he mended thus,
By now forswearing that he is forsworn.
He calls us rebels, traitors, and will scourge
40 With haughty arms this hateful name in us.

Enter Douglas

Douglas
Arm, gentlemen, to arms! for I have thrown
A brave defiance in King Henry's teeth,
And Westmoreland that was engag'd did bear it,
Which cannot choose but bring him quickly on.
Worcester
45 The Prince of Wales stepp'd forth before the
   King,
And nephew, challeng'd you to single fight.
Hotspur
O, would the quarrel lay upon our heads,
And that no man might draw short breath today
But I and Harry Monmouth! Tell me, tell me,
50 How show'd his tasking? Seem'd it in contempt?
Vernon
No, by my soul, I never in my life
Did hear a challenge urg'd more modestly,
Unless a brother should a brother dare
To gentle exercise and proof of arms.
55 He gave you all the duties of a man,
Trimm'd up your praises with a princely tongue,
Spoke your deservings like a chronicle,
Making you ever better than his praise
By still dispraising praise valu'd with you;
60 And, which became him like a prince indeed,

Defy him: return his challenge.

no seeming mercy: apparently no forgiveness.

mended: corrected (the tone is sarcastic).
By swearing falsely *now* that he ever swore false in the past.

engag'd: held as hostage.
Which can only make him advance quickly.
would: I wish.
lay . . . heads: was our responsibility.
draw short breath: pant (with fighting).
How show'd: how did it look.
tasking: challenge.
urg'd: presented.
proof of arms: test of skill with weapons.
all . . . man: all that is due to a man.
Trimm'd up: elaborated, gave a good description of.
Described your merits as though he were writing your life-story ('chronicle' = history book).
Always saying that he knew no words good enough to praise you properly.
ever: always.
still: constantly.
praise: i.e. words of praise.
valu'd: compared.
became him: showed him that he was.

61   He gave an account ('cital') of himself, blushing with shame.

62   *chid*: reproached.
      truant: disobedient (see the Prince's words in 5, 1,94).

63-4 Vernon thinks that the Prince showed the ability to teach and the ability to learn, both at the same time.

63   *master'd*: was in possession.

64   *instantly*: simultaneously.

65   *There . . . pause*: he stopped there (i.e. did not say any more).

66   *outlive*: survives.
      envy: hostility, warfare.

67   *owe*: own, possess.

68   *misconstru'd . . . wantonness*: misunderstood because of his wild behaviour.

69-70 *thou . . . follies*: you have fallen in love with his crazy ways.

70-71 *Never . . . liberty*: I have never heard of a king's son who was so irresponsible.

72   *be . . . will*: whatever he is like.
      ere: before.

74   So that he will not be so great when I have finished with him.
      courtesy: Hotspur is ironic—the 'courtesy' of his 'soldier's arm' will (he threatens) kill Prince Hal.

76-8 You should think about what you have to do rather than listen to me, because I can't speak well enough to inspire you with my words of persuasion.

77   *gift of tongue*: eloquence.

78   *lift . . . up*: excite you.

82-4 *To spend . . . hour*: if there were only one hour to live, it would be too long if we were to spend that hour in a dishonourable way.

83   *a dial's point*: the hand of a clock.

87   *for*: as for.

87-8 *the arms . . . just*: it is right to make war (bear arms) when there is a good reason ('intent') for fighting.

89   *apace*: fast.

90   *cuts . . . tale*: shortens my speech.

91   *I profess not talking*: I don't claim to be a good speaker.

He made a blushing cital of himself,
And chid his truant youth with such a grace
As if he master'd there a double spirit
Of teaching and of learning instantly.
65 There did he pause. But let me tell the world—
If he outlive the envy of this day,
England did never owe so sweet a hope
So much misconstru'd in his wantonness.

Hotspur
Cousin, I think thou art enamoured
70 On his follies. Never did I hear
Of any prince so wild a liberty.
But be he as he will, yet once ere night
I will embrace him with a soldier's arm,
That he shall shrink under my courtesy.
75 Arm, arm with speed! And fellows, soldiers, friends,
Better consider what you have to do
Than I, that have not well the gift of tongue,
Can lift your blood up with persuasion.

Enter a Messenger

Messenger
My lord, here are letters for you.

Hotspur
80 I cannot read them now.
O gentlemen, the time of life is short!
To spend that shortness basely were too long
If life did ride upon a dial's point,
Still ending at the arrival of an hour.
85 And if we live, we live to tread on kings;
If die, brave death when princes die with us!
Now, for our consciences, the arms are fair
When the intent of bearing them is just.

Enter another Messenger

Messenger
My lord, prepare, the King comes on apace.

Hotspur
90 I thank him that he cuts me from my tale,
For I profess not talking: only this—
Let each man do his best; and here draw I

temper: steel (tempering is a process in the hardening of steel).

withal: with.

Esperance! Percy! the battle-cry of the Percy family; the final *e* of 'Esperance' (= Good Hope, Good Luck) is pronounced.

set on: start fighting.

lofty . . . war: i.e. the martial trumpets.

by: to the sound of.

heaven to earth: the odds are as high as heaven is from earth.

A sword whose temper I intend to stain
With the best blood that I can meet withal
95 In the adventure of this perilous day.
Now, Esperance! Percy! and set on.
Sound all the lofty instruments of war,
And by that music let us all embrace,
For, heaven to earth, some of us never shall
100 A second time do such a courtesy.
    [*Here they embrace; the trumpets sound, exeunt*

Act 5 Scene 3
The fighting has begun. We learn that several noblemen are disguised to look like the King; and we see how one of these is killed. Prince Hal is looking for Hotspur, but Falstaff claims that he has killed him.

crossest: oppose.

Upon my head: by killing me.

haunt: follow.

-8   Looking like you has today been very expensive for the Earl of Stafford; Douglas believes that Blunt really is the King.

him: i.e. his life.

Scene 3 *Shrewsbury : the Field of Battle*

> *Enter the* King *with his army. Alarum to the battle. Then enter* (*on opposite sides*) Douglas, *and* Sir Walter Blunt (*disguised as the* King

Blunt
What is thy name that in the battle thus
Thou crossest me? What honour dost thou seek
Upon my head?
            Douglas   Know then my name is Douglas,
And I do haunt thee in the battle thus
5 Because some tell me that thou art a king.
    Blunt
They tell thee true.
    Douglas
The Lord of Stafford dear today hath bought
Thy likeness, for instead of thee, King Harry,
This sword hath ended him: so shall it thee
10 Unless thou yield thee as my prisoner.
    Blunt
I was not born a yielder, thou proud Scot,
And thou shalt find a king that will revenge
Lord Stafford's death.
                [*They fight.* Douglas *kills* Blunt

Enter Hotspur

Hotspur
O Douglas, hadst thou fought at Holmedon thus

15   I would never have beaten the Scots (Douglas and Hotspur were on opposite sides at the Battle of Holmedon—see *1*, *1*,55).

16   *breathless*: i.e. lifeless.

19   *full*: very.

21   *Semblably furnish'd*: dressed in the same way.

22   May the name of 'fool' accompany your soul, wherever it has gone (to heaven or hell); Douglas speaks to Blunt's body.

23   Pretending to be someone else (the King) has cost you too much.

25   *many*: i.e. many men.
      coats: sleeveless tunics ('surcoats') with heraldic devices, worn over the armour so that the wearer could be easily identified.

29   *stand . . . day*: have a very good chance of victory.

30   *scape shot-free*: escape without being wounded; *and* avoid paying the bill.

31   *shot*: bullets—or arrows.
      scoring: a pun on 'hitting' *and* 'charging the bill'.
      pate: head.

32   *Soft*: look at this.

32–3   *there's . . . you*: Falstaff recalls his 'catechism' on honour in *Act 5*, Scene 1.

33   *Here's no vanity*: this (the dead body) is the real thing.

34–5   *molten*: melted.
      God . . . me: God save me from gunshot (made of lead).

36   *bowels*: i.e. body.
      led: sent (Falstaff would not have marched with his soldiers).

37   *peppered*: massacred (Falstaff can now keep the money which should have been the soldiers' pay).
      not: no more than.

38–9   *they . . . life*: they will have to sit at the entrance to the town and beg for the rest of their lives; (the soldiers are badly wounded).

42.   *vaunting*: boastful.

15   I never had triumph'd upon a Scot.
      Douglas
      All's done, all's won: here breathless lies the King
      Hotspur
      Where?
      Douglas
      Here.
      Hotspur
      This, Douglas? No, I know this face full well,
20   A gallant knight he was, his name was Blunt,
      Semblably furnish'd like the King himself.
      Douglas
      A fool go with thy soul, whither it goes!
      A borrow'd title hast thou bought too dear.
      Why didst thou tell me that thou wert a king?
      Hotspur
25   The King hath many marching in his coats.
      Douglas
      Now, by my sword, I will kill all his coats;
      I'll murder all his wardrobe, piece by piece,
      Until I meet the King.
      Hotspur   Up and away
      Our soldiers stand full fairly for the day. [*Exeun*

      Alarum. Enter Falstaff
      Falstaff
30   Though I could scape shot-free at London, I fea
      the shot here; here's no scoring but upon the pate
      Soft! who are you? Sir Walter Blunt—there'
      honour for you! Here's no vanity! I am as hot a
      molten lead, and as heavy too—God keep lead ou
35   of me, I need no more weight than mine ow
      bowels. I have led my ragamuffins where they ar
      peppered; there's not three of my hundred an
      fifty left alive, and they are for the town's end, t
      beg during life. But who comes here?

      Enter the Prince
      Prince
40   What, stands thou idle here? Lend me thy swor
      Many a nobleman lies stark and stiff
      Under the hoofs of vaunting enemies,

breathe awhile: get my breath
back, have a short rest.

Turk Gregory: the name of
'Turk' was applied to any particularly
cruel man; and by 'Gregory' Falstaff
probably refers to Pope Gregory XIII,
who was associated with the vicious
Massacre of St Bartholomew's Day in
1572.

in arms: in fighting.

paid: killed.

Percy: i.e. Hotspur.

made him sure: made certain that
he is dead.

He is indeed: Hal pretends to
think that 'sure' = 'safe'.

case: holster (instead of being
ready for shooting).

'tis hot: i.e. after shooting
(Falstaff pretends that he has put away
his pistol until it cools).

4   there's . . . city: there is enough to
conquer a whole city. Falstaff makes a
pun on 'sack' = 'conquer' and 'sack'—
the drink his holster contains.

Whose deaths are yet unrevenged. I prithee lend
  me thy sword.

Falstaff

O Hal, I prithee give me leave to breathe awhile—
45 Turk Gregory never did such deeds in arms as I
have done this day; I have paid Percy, I have made
him sure.

Prince

He is indeed, and living to kill thee: I prithee lend
me thy sword.

Falstaff

50 Nay, before God, Hal, if Percy be alive thou gets
not my sword; but take my pistol if thou wilt.

Prince

Give it me: what, is it in the case?

Falstaff

Ay, Hal, 'tis hot, 'tis hot; there's that will sack a
city.

[The Prince *draws it out, and finds
it to be a bottle of sack*

55   *dally*: fool around.

56   *pierce*: the word was pronounced
     as 'perse'; Falstaff makes a pun with
     'Percy'.

57   *so*: that will be fine.

     if he . . . in his: if he does not
     come in my way, and if I get in his way.

58   *carbonado*: grilled steak (which
     was slashed with a knife before being
     cooked).

59–61   If I can save my life, that will be
        good; and if I can't save it, then I shall
        get honour without making an effort—
        and that's all there is to it.

Act 5 Scene 4
The battle continues, Prince Hal is
slightly wounded, but he refuses to stop
fighting and he is able to save his
father's life when the King is in danger.
At last the Prince encounters Hotspur.

1   *withdraw thyself*: go back to your
    tent.

4–5   *make up . . . friends*: go up to the
      front of the battle, or else your
      supporters will think you have
      retreated and be worried.

5   *retirement*: withdrawal, retreat.
    amaze: distress, worry.

12   *stain'd*: dishonoured (by being
     defeated); *and* bloodstained.
     nobility: noble men.

13   *rebels' arms*: the fighting rebels.

14   *breathe*: rest.

Prince

55 What, is it a time to jest and dally now?
          [*He throws the bottle at* Falstaff. *Ex*
     Falstaff
     Well, if Percy be alive, I'll pierce him. If he c
     come in my way, so: if he do not, if I come in h
     willingly, let him make a carbonado of me. I lil
60 not such grinning honour as Sir Walter hath. Gi
     me life—which if I can save, so: if not, hono
     comes unlooked for, and there's an end.   [*Ex*

Scene 4 *The Battlefield*

          Alarum. Excursions. Enter the King, t
          Prince, Lord John of Lancaster, Earl
          Westmoreland

     King
     I prithee, Harry, withdraw thyself, thou bleed'
       too much.
     Lord John of Lancaster, go you with him.
          Lancaster
     Not I, my lord, unless I did bleed too.
          Prince
     I beseech your Majesty, make up,
5   Lest your retirement do amaze your friends.
          King
     I will do so. My Lord of Westmoreland,
     Lead him to his tent.
          Westmoreland
     Come, my lord, I'll lead you to your tent.
          Prince
     Lead me, my lord? I do not need your help;
10 And God forbid a shallow scratch should drive
     The Prince of Wales from such a field as this,
     Where stain'd nobility lies trodden on,
     And rebels' arms triumph in massacres!
          Lancaster
     We breathe too long: come, cousin Westmorelan
15 Our duty this way lies: for God's sake, come.
          [*Exeunt* Lancaster *and* Westmorelan

lord . . . spirit: possessed such courage.

19 Until today I loved you because you were my brother, but now I have very great respect for you.

at the point: i.e. the point of his sword.

lustier maintenance: greater tenacity.

look for: expect to see.
ungrown: inexperienced.
Lends mettle: inspires.

Prince

By God, thou hast deceiv'd me, Lancaster,
I did not think thee lord of such a spirit.
Before, I lov'd thee as a brother, John,
But now I do respect thee as my soul.

King

20 I saw him hold Lord Percy at the point
With lustier maintenance than I did look for
Of such an ungrown warrior.

Prince   O, this boy

Lends mettle to us all!   [*Exit the* Prince

Enter Douglas

Douglas
Another king! They grow like Hydra's heads!
25 I am the Douglas, fatal to all those
That wear those colours on them. What art thou
That counterfeit'st the person of a king?
King
The King himself, who, Douglas, grieves at heart
So many of his shadows thou hast met,
30 And not the very King. I have two boys
Seek Percy and thyself about the field;
But seeing thou fall'st on me so luckily
I will assay thee, and defend thyself.
Douglas
I fear thou art another counterfeit,
35 And yet, in faith, thou bearest thee like a king;
But mine I am sure thou art, who'er thou be,
And thus I win thee.
[They fight; the King is in danger

Enter Prince of Wales

Prince
Hold up thy head, vile Scot, or thou art like
Never to hold it up again! The spirits
40 Of valiant Shirley, Stafford, Blunt are in my arms
It is the Prince of Wales that threatens thee,
Who never promiseth but he means to pay.
[They fight: Douglas flies
Cheerly, my lord. How fares your grace?
Sir Nicholas Gawsey hath for succour sent,
45 And so hath Clifton—I'll to Clifton straight.
King
Stay and breathe a while:
Thou hast redeem'd thy lost opinion,
And show'd thou mak'st some tender of my life
In this fair rescue thou has brought to me.
Prince
50 O God, they did me too much injury
That ever said I hearken'd for your death.
If it were so, I might have let alone
The insulting hand of Douglas over you,
Which would have been as speedy in your end

24   *Hydra*: a snake (in classical mythology) which grew two new heads each time a head was cut off.
26   *wear those colours*: are disguised in the King's surcoats (see note to 5, 3,25).
29   *shadows*: imitators (the word is often used by Shakespeare to refer to actors).
30   *very*: real.
       two boys: i.e. his sons, Prince Hal and Lord John.
32   *fall'st*: has found me.
33   *assay*: tackle you myself.

35   *bearest thee*: behave.
36   *mine*: i.e. my victim (or conquest).

38   *like*: likely.

40   *Shirley, Stafford, Blunt*: the noblemen killed by Douglas.

43   *Cheerly*: don't worry, cheer up.
44   *succour*: assistance, reinforcements.
45   *I'll to*: I will go to.
       straight: immediately.
46   *breathe*: rest.
47   *opinion*: reputation.
48   *mak'st . . . of*: have some care for.

51   *hearken'd for*: was looking forward to.
52   *let alone*: not interfered with.
53   *insulting*: conquering.
54   *as . . . end*: killed you as quickly.

And saved your son from having
do a treacherous job.
Make up: go to help.

55 As all the poisonous potions in the world,
And sav'd the treacherous labour of your son.
King
Make up to Clifton; I'll to Sir Nicholas Gawsey.
[*Exit* King Henry

Enter Hotspur

Hotspur
If I mistake not, thou art Harry Monmouth.
Prince
Thou speak'st as if I would deny my name.
Hotspur
60 My name is Harry Percy.
Prince   Why then I see

rebel: when Hal speaks this word,
is a term of insult—with the sense,
most, of 'coward' (so that 'valiant
ebel' is a paradox).

In the Ptolemaic system of the
niverse, the earth is at the centre and
e planets ('stars') circle around ('keep
eir motion'), each one in its own orbit
r 'sphere'.

brook: tolerate.
the one of us: the life of one of us.
would: I wish.
name in arms: reputation for
ghting.

crest: helmet; in 3, 2,142 Hal
eaks of the 'honour sitting on his
lotspur's) helm'.

brook: endure.
vanities: boasting.

A very valiant rebel of that name.
I am the Prince of Wales, and think not, Percy,
To share with me in glory any more:
Two stars keep not their motion in one sphere,
65 Nor can one England brook a double reign
Of Harry Percy and the Prince of Wales.
Hotspur
Nor shall it, Harry, for the hour is come
To end the one of us; and would to God
Thy name in arms were now as great as mine!
Prince
70 I'll make it greater ere I part from thee,
And all the budding honours on thy crest
I'll crop to make a garland for my head.
Hotspur
I can no longer brook thy vanities.   [*They fight*

Enter Falstaff

Falstaff
Well said, Hal! To it, Hal! Nay, you shall find no
75 boy's play here, I can tell you.

you . . . here: this isn't child's
lay, you know (Falstaff speaks to
lotspur).

Enter Douglas; *he fights with* Falstaff,
who falls down as if he were dead. Exit
Douglas. *The* Prince *mortally wounds*
Hotspur

Hotspur
O Harry, thou hast robb'd me of my youth!
I better brook the loss of brittle life

78   *proud*: glorious.
        won of me: won from me.
79–80   *thought's . . . life*: i.e. 'life'
controls 'thought' as a master controls a
slave.
80   *life . . . fool*: life is made a fool by
time—because it is restricted to a
certain time.
81–2   *time . . . stop*; even time, that
commands ('takes survey of') all the
world, will end.
82   *prophesy*: the Elizabethans
believed that prophecies were often
spoken by dying men.

Than those proud titles thou hast won of me;
They wound my thoughts worse than thy sw⌐
my flesh:
80 But thought's the slave of life; and life, time's fo⌐
And time, that takes survey of all the world,
Must have a stop. O, I could prophesy,
But that the earthy and cold hand of death
Lies on my tongue. No, Percy, thou art dust,
85 And food for—   [D

Hal compares Hotspur's mis-
directed ambition to badly-woven ('Ill-
weav'd') cloth which has shrunk
because it was not well made.

bound: limit.

stout: brave.

If I thought you could ('wert
sensible of') tell what I am doing, I
would not make such an emotional
expression of my feelings.

my favours: the plumes from his
helmet (Hal covers Hotspur's face).

in thy behalf: on your behalf.

May your shame (for his part in
the rebellion) be buried with you, and
not mentioned in your epitaph.

heavy: sorrowful (and a reference
to Falstaff's weight).

miss: loss.

vanity: frivolity, foolishness.

dearer: more valuable.

Embowell'd: disembowelled: the
human intestines were removed before
the body was embalmed—and the
entrails of a hunted deer were taken out
before the meat was 'powdered' with
spices to preserve it.

in blood: in the bloodshed of
battle; the phrase 'in blood' was also
used to describe a live deer in good
condition (as Falstaff is in fact).

powder: preserve with spices.

termagant: bloodthirsty.

had paid me: would have killed
me.

scot . . . too: Falstaff refers to the
phrase 'to pay scot and lot' (= to pay
completely), making word-play out of
the double meanings of both 'pay' and
'scot'.

Prince

For worms, brave Percy. Fare thee well, great
  heart!
Ill-weav'd ambition, how much art thou shrunk!
When that this body did contain a spirit,
A kingdom for it was too small a bound;
90 But now two paces of the vilest earth
Is room enough. This earth that bears thee dead
Bears not alive so stout a gentleman.
If thou wert sensible of courtesy
I should not make so dear a show of zeal.
95 But let my favours hide thy mangled face;
And even in thy behalf I'll thank myself
For doing these fair rites of tenderness.
Adieu, and take thy praise with thee to heaven!
Thy ignominy sleep with thee in the grave,
100 But not remember'd in thy epitaph!
          [*He sees* Falstaff *on the ground*
What, old acquaintance, could not all this flesh
Keep in a little life? Poor Jack, farewell!
I could have better spar'd a better man.
O, I should have a heavy miss of thee
105 If I were much in love with vanity!
Death hath not struck so fat a deer today,
Though many dearer, in this bloody fray.
Embowell'd will I see thee by and by,
Till then in blood by noble Percy lie.   [*Exit*

Falstaff *rises up*

Falstaff

110 Embowelled? If thou embowel me today, I'll give
  you leave to powder me and eat me too tomorrow.
  'Sblood, 'twas time to counterfeit, or that hot
  termagant Scot had paid me, scot and lot too.

Counterfeit? I lie, I am no counterfeit: to die is
115 be a counterfeit, for he is but the counterfeit o
man, who hath not the life of a man: but
counterfeit dying, when a man thereby liveth, is
be no counterfeit, but the true and perfect image
life indeed. The better part of valour is discretic
120 in the which better part I have saved my li
'Zounds, I am afraid of this gunpowder Perc
though he be dead! How if he should counterf
too, and rise? By my faith, I am afraid he wou
prove the better counterfeit; therefore I'll ma
125 him sure, yea, and I'll swear I killed him. W
may not he rise as well as I? Nothing confutes i
but eyes, and nobody sees me: therefore, sirr
[stabs him], with a new wound in your thigh, cor
you along with me.

[He takes up Hotspur on his ba

Enter Prince *and* Lord John
Lancaster

Prince
130 Come, brother John, full bravely hast thou flesh
Thy maiden sword.
Lancaster   But soft, whom have we her
Did you not tell me this fat man was dead?
Prince
I did, I saw him dead,
Breathless and bleeding on the ground. Art th
alive?
135 Or is it fantasy that plays upon our eyesight?
I prithee speak—we will not trust our eyes
Without our ears: thou art not what thou seem'
Falstaff
No, that's certain, I am not a double-man: but i
be not Jack Falstaff, then am I a jack: there
140 Percy [throws the body down]! If your father w
do me any honour, so: if not, let him kill the n
Percy himself. I look to be either earl or duke
can assure you.
Prince
Why, Percy I kill'd myself; and saw thee dead
Falstaff
145 Didst thou? Lord, Lord, how this world is giv

117   *thereby*: as a result (Falstaff is alive now only because he pretended to be dead in his fight with Douglas).

119   *The better . . . discretion*: a proverbial saying, meaning that commonsense should accompany bravery; but Falstaff seems to imply that the two are separate—and that his 'discretion' (i.e. in pretending to be dead) was better than the 'valour' of continuing to fight.

121   *gunpowder*: explosive, dangerous.

122   *how if*: what would happen if.

124–5 *make him sure*: make certain he is dead.

126–7 *Nothing . . . eyes*: I could only be called a liar by someone who can see what I am doing.

130   *full*: very.
       flesh'd: used for the first time.

131   *maiden*: new, never used.
       soft: wait.

134   *Breathless*: not breathing.

135   *fantasy that plays*: imagination playing tricks.

138   *double-man*: deceiver; *and* ghost (also, Falstaff appears to be two men because he is carrying the body of Hotspur).

139   *a jack*: a rascal.

141   *do me*: reward me with, recognize what I have done.
       so: good.

142   *look to be*: expect to be made.

to lying! I grant you I was down, and out of
breath, and so was he; but we rose both at an
instant, and fought a long hour by Shrewsbury
clock. If I may be believed, so: if not, let them that
150 should reward valour bear the sin upon their own
heads. I'll take it upon my death, I gave him this
wound in the thigh; if the man were alive, and
would deny it, 'zounds, I would make him eat a
piece of my sword.

Lancaster

155 This is the strangest tale that ever I heard.

Prince

This is the strangest fellow, brother John.
Come, bring your luggage nobly on your back.
[*Aside to* Falstaff] For my part, if a lie may do thee
grace,
I'll gild it with the happiest terms I have.
[*A retreat is sounded*
160 The trumpet sounds retreat, the day is ours.
Come, brother, let us to the highest of the field,
To see what friends are living, who are dead.
[*Exeunt* Prince of Wales *and* Lancaster

Falstaff

I'll follow, as they say, for reward. He that rewards
me, God reward him! If I do grow great, I'll grow
165 less, for I'll purge, and leave sack, and live cleanly
as a nobleman should do.
[*Exit, bearing off the body*

Scene 5   *The Battlefield*

> *The trumpets sound. Enter the* King,
> Prince of Wales, Lord John of
> Lancaster, Earl of Westmoreland, *with*
> Worcester *and* Vernon *prisoners*

King

Thus ever did rebellion find rebuke.
Ill-spirited Worcester, did not we send grace,
Pardon, and terms of love to all of you?
And wouldst thou turn our offers contrary?

5   Abuse the nature of the trust
that Hotspur ('thy kinsman') put in
you.
6   *upon our party*: on our side.
7   *A noble earl*: the Earl of Stafford
was killed in this battle.
9   *truly*: honestly.
9–10   *borne . . . intelligence*: carried true
information between our two armies.
11   I did what I thought would be
the safest.

14   *to the death*: to be executed.
15   *pause upon*: decide later what to
do with them.
16   *field*: battle.

18   *quite turn'd from him*: had
completely left him.

20   *Upon . . . fear*: running away in
fear.

22   *took*: captured.

26   *honourable bounty*: noble act.
27–8   *deliver . . . pleasure*: release him
to do whatever he wants.
28   *ransomless*: without having to pay
a ransom.
29   The courage he has shown in
fighting in this battle against us ('upon
our crests').
30   *high*: noble.
31   Even when they are done by
those who are fighting against us.
32   *high courtesy*: great generosity.
33   *give away*: i.e. by releasing
Douglas.
34   *this remains*: this is what is left to
do.
        power: army.
36   *bend you*: direct yourselves.
        dearest: best.
38   *busily in arms*: busy preparing to
fight.

5 Misuse the tenor of thy kinsman's trust?
Three knights upon our party slain today,
A noble earl and many a creature else,
Had been alive this hour,
If like a Christian thou hadst truly borne
10 Betwixt our armies true intelligence.
        Worcester
What I have done my safety urg'd me to;
And I embrace this fortune patiently,
Since not to be avoided it falls on me.
        King
Bear Worcester to the death, and Vernon too:
15 Other offenders we will pause upon.
        [*Exeunt* Worcester *and* Vernon, *guard*
How goes the field?
        Prince
The noble Scot, Lord Douglas, when he saw
The fortune of the day quite turn'd from him,
The noble Percy slain, and all his men
20 Upon the foot of fear, fled with the rest,
And falling from a hill, he was so bruis'd
That the pursuers took him. At my tent
The Douglas is; and I beseech your Grace
I may dispose of him.
        King   With all my hea
        Prince
25 Then, brother John of Lancaster, to you
This honourable bounty shall belong;
Go to the Douglas and deliver him
Up to his pleasure, ransomless and free:
His valours shown upon our crests today
30 Have taught us how to cherish such high deeds
Even in the bosom of our adversaries.
        Lancaster
I thank your Grace for this high courtesy,
Which I shall give away immediately.
        King
Then this remains, that we divide our power:
35 You, son John, and my cousin Westmoreland,
Towards York shall bend you with your dear
        speed
To meet Northumberland and the prelate Scroo
Who, as we hear, are busily in arms.

will: will march.
lose his sway: have no more
ower.
  If it is controlled by another
attle like this one.
fair: successfully.
leave: stop.
till . . . won: until we have
ompletely finished the job.

Myself and you, son Harry, will towards Wales,
40 To fight with Glendower and the Earl of March.
Rebellion in this land shall lose his sway,
Meeting the check of such another day;
And since this business so fair is done,
Let us not leave till all our own be won. [*Exeunt*

The Historical Background

Henry IV, Part 1 is not a history lesson. Shakespeare did not intend
teach his audience the facts about the rebellion against King Hen
IV in 1402. His play is based on historical truth: but it is n
historically accurate. The dramatist omits to mention much tha
historian would consider important; he adds much that is pu
invention (the character of Falstaff, and all the scenes in which
appears); and he alters some historical facts to suit his drama
purposes.

The greatest alteration affects the character of Hotspur, 'You
Harry Percy', who is constantly contrasted with King Henry's son,
own 'young Harry'. The King even wishes

> that it could be prov'd
> That some night-tripping fairy had exchang'd
> In cradle-clothes our children where they lay.

Shakespeare clearly intends us to think that the two 'children' are
the same age. But the real Hotspur was born in 1364; and Prince H
was born in 1387. At the battle of Shrewsbury in 1402 the you
Prince of Wales (aged fifteen) fought bravely; but it was not he w
killed the famous Hotspur.

Another character who was not – historically – what he seems
be is the Earl of March, Edmund Mortimer. In Act 1, Scene 3 K
Henry speaks scornfully of 'the foolish Mortimer' who apparen
'betray'd The lives of those that he did lead to fight' against the We
and who then married the daughter of 'that great magician, dam
Glendower'. The King refuses to pay a ransom for Mortimer, a
Worcester explains the reason for Henry's hatred and fear: Mortin
was the true heir to the throne of England, 'the next of blood'
Richard II.

The family tree of the Plantagenets on page vi shows Edmu
Mortimer, son of Roger Mortimer, whose descent from Lionel Du
of Clarence gave him the right to the throne after the death
Richard II (who had no children). As the son of Roger Mortimer,
took the title 'Earl of March' after his father's death in 1398. But
was born in 1391; and so he was only eleven years old at the ti
Shakespeare's play opens.

The family tree of the Mortimers and the Percys on page vii, however, solves the problem: there were two historical figures with the same name: one was the child heir to the throne, who did become Earl of March; and the other was his uncle, the 'revolted Mortimer' who appears in the play with his Welsh wife. Perhaps Shakespeare himself was confused?

Modern historians also accuse Shakespeare of confusing two *rebellions*; it now appears that the 'indenture tripartite' which is so important to the rebels (Act 3, Scene 1) belongs to the year 1405 – two years after the death of Hotspur at Shrewsbury (when Shakespeare's play ends). For this confusion, however, Shakespeare is not to blame: his authority was the sixteenth-century historian, Raphael Holinshed, whose work *The Chronicles of England, Scotland, and Ireland* was the chief (but not the only) source for this play.

Shakespeare never worried about the minor details which are often so important to a modern director (especially those in charge of television drama) who is keen to give his production 'period' accuracy. In the play *Julius Caesar*, for instance, Shakespeare's ancient Romans tell the time by clocks, and cover their heads with hats, just as the Elizabethans did. In *Henry IV Part 1* there are similar anachronisms. Prince Hal describes the Earl of Douglas as 'He rides at high speed, and with his pistol kills a sparrow flying'. In fact the pistol was not invented until the sixteenth century in Italy. But what Prince Hal is doing is showing respect for Douglas' skill, and at the same time showing scorn for the energy wasted on such a trivial achievement. It is more important that we should appreciate Hal's attitude than that we should object to a fourteenth-century Scottish earl using a sixteenth-century Italian pistol: the fact is irrelevant.

Selections from The Chronicles of England, Scotland, and Ireland

By Raphael Holinshed

The Percys' Rebellion

Owen Glendower, according to his accustomed manner of robbing and spoiling within the English borders, caused all the forces of the shire of Hereford to assemble together against them, under the conduct of Edmund Mortimer, Earl of March. But coming to try the matter by battle . . . the English power was discomfited, the Earl taken prisoner, and above a thousand of his people slain in the place. The shameful villainy used by the Welshwomen towards the dead carcasses was such as honest ears would be ashamed to hear . . .

The King was not hasty to purchase the deliverance of the Earl of March, because his title to the crown was well enough known, and therefore suffered him to remain in miserable prison, wishing both the Earl and his lineage out of this life . . .

About the mid of August the King, to chastise the presumptuous attempts of the Welshmen, went with a great power of men into Wales to pursue the captain of the Welsh rebel Owen Glendower, but in effect he lost his labour, for Owen conveyed himself out of the way into his known lurking places; and (as was thought) through art magic he caused such foul weather of winds, tempest, rain, snow, and hail, to be raised for the annoyance of the King's army, that the like had not been heard of – in such sort that the King was constrained to return home . . .

Archibald, Earl Douglas . . . procured a commission to invade England . . . [but] at a place called Holmedon they were so fiercely assailed by the English, under the leading of the Lord Percy surnamed Henry Hotspur . . . that with violence of the English shot they were quite vanquished and put to flight, on the Rood day in harvest, with a great slaughter made by the Englishmen . . .

Henry Earl of Northumberland, with his brother Thomas Earl of Worcester and his son the Lord Henry Percy (surnamed Hotspur) who were to King Henry in the beginning of his reign both faithful friends and earnest aiders, began now to envy his wealth and felicity; and especially they were grieved because the King demanded of the Earl and his son such Scottish prisoners as were taken at Holmedon . . .

[Hotspur and his father] came to the King unto Windsor . . . and there required of him, that either by ransom or otherwise he would cause to be delivered out of prison Edmund Mortimer Earl of March, their cousin . . . The King began not a little to muse at this request, and not without cause; for indeed it touched him somewhat near, sith this Edmund . . . at King Richard's going into Ireland was proclaimed heir apparent to the crown and realm . . . The King, when he had studied on the matter, made answer . . . he would neither ransom him nor redeem him . . .

[In great anger, Hotspur and his father departed], minding nothing more than to depose King Henry from the high type of his royalty, and to place in his seat their cousin Edmund Earl of March, whom they did not only deliver out of captivity, but also (to the high displeasure of King Henry) entered in league with the foresaid Owen Glendower. Herewith, they by their deputies, in the house of the Archdeacon of Bangor, divided the realm amongst them, causing a tripartite indenture to be made and sealed with all their seals, by the covenants whereof all England from Severn and Trent, south and eastward, was assigned to the Earl of March; all Wales and the lands beyond Severn, westward, were appointed to Owen Glendower; and all the remnant, from Trent northward, to the Lord Percy.

This was done (as some have said) through a foolish credit given to a vain prophecy, as though King Henry was the moldwarp, cursed of God's own mouth, and they three were the dragon, the lion, and the wolf – which should divide this realm between them . . .

King Henry . . . gathered a great army to go again into Wales; . . . Northumberland and his son . . . raised all the power they could make, and sent to the Scots, which before were taken prisoners at Holmedon, for aid of men . . .

The Percies, to make their part seem good, devised certain articles, by the advice of Richard Scroope, Archbishop of York, brother to the Lord Scroope whom King Henry had caused to be beheaded at Bristow. These articles being showed to divers noblemen and other states of the realm moved them to favour their purpose, insomuch that many of them did not only promise to the Percies' aid and succour by words, but also by their writings and seals confirmed the same. Howbeit when the matter came to trial, the most part of the confederates abandoned them, and at the day of conflict left them alone . . .

The Earl of Northumberland himself was not with them; but being sick, had promised upon his amendment to repair unto them (as some write) with all convenient speed . . .

King Henry, advertized of the proceedings of the Percies forthwith gathered about him such power as he might . . . [and passed forward with such speed that he was in sight of his enemies lying in camp near to Shrewsbury, before they were in doubt of any such thing; for the Percies thought that he would have stayed at Burton-upon-Trent . . .

Forthwith the Lord Percy (as captain of high courage) began to exhort the captains and soldiers to prepare themselves to battle, sith the matter was grown to that point that by no means it could be avoided; so that (said he) this day shall either bring us all to advancement and honour, or else, if it shall chance us to be overcome, shall deliver us from the King's spiteful malice and cruel disdain. For playing the men (as we ought to do) better it is to die in battle for the commonwealth's cause, than through cowardlike fear to prolong life, which after shall be taken from us by sentence of the enemy . . .

Now when the two armies were encamped, the one against the other, the Earl of Worcester and the Lord Percy with their complices sent the articles . . . to King Henry, under their hands and seals; which articles in effect charged him with manifest perjury in that (contrary to his oath received . . . at Doncaster, when he first entered the realm after his exile) he had taken upon him the crown and royal dignity, imprisoned King Richard, caused him to resign his title, and finally to be murdered . . .

It was reported for a truth, that now when the King had condescended unto all that was reasonable at his hands to be required, and seemed to humble himself more than was meet for his estate, the Earl of Worcester (upon his return to his nephew) made relation clean contrary to that the King had said, in such sort that he set his nephew's heart more in displeasure towards the King than ever it was before, driving him by that means to fight, whether he would or not.

Then suddenly blew the trumpets – the King's part crying 'Saint George!' upon them, the adversaries cried '*Esperance Percy!*' And so the two armies furiously joined . . .

The prince that day holp his father like a lusty young gentleman; for although he was hurt in the face with an arrow, so that divers noblemen that were about him would have conveyed him forth of the field, yet he would not suffer them so to do, lest his departure from amongst his men might haply have stricken some fear into their hearts; and so, without regard of his hurt, he continued with his men and never ceased either to fight where the battle was most hot, or to encourage his men where it seemed most need . . .

At length the King . . . adventured so far that (as some write) the Earl Douglas strake him down, and at that instant slew Sir Walter Blunt and three others apparelled in the King's suit and clothing, saying 'I marvel to see so many kings thus suddenly arise, one in the neck of another'. The King indeed was raised, and did that day many a noble feat of arms, for (as it is written) he slew that day with his own hands six and thirty persons of his enemies. The other on his part, encouraged by his doings, fought valiantly, and slew the Lord Percy, called Sir Henry Hotspur . . .

To conclude, the King's enemies were vanquished and put to flight; in which flight the Earl of Douglas . . . was taken – and for his valiantness of the King frankly and freely delivered.

Henry IV and the Prince of Wales

The Lord Henry, Prince of Wales, eldest son to King Henry, got knowledge that certain of his father's servants were busy to give information against him, whereby discord might arise betwixt him and his father; for they put into the King's head not only what evil rule (according to the course of youth) the prince kept, to the offence of many, but also what great resort of people came to his house, so that the court was nothing furnished with such a train as daily followed the Prince. These tales brought no small suspicion into the King's head, lest his son would presume to usurp the crown (he being yet alive); through which suspicious jealousy it was perceived that he favoured not his son as in times past he had done.

The Prince . . . wrote his letters into every part of the realm, to reprove all such slanderous devices of those that sought his discredit. And to clear himself the better . . . he came to the court . . . [which] was then at Westminster . . . He . . . was straight admitted to the presence of the King . . . [and] kneeling down before his father, said:

> 'Most redoubted and sovereign lord and father, I am at this time come to your presence as your liege man, and as your natural son, in all things to be at your commandment. And where I understand you have in suspicion my demeanour against your grace, you know very well that if I knew any man

within this realm of whom you should stand in fear, my d
were to punish that person, thereby to remove that grief fr
your heart. Then how much more ought I to suffer death,
ease your grace of that grief which you have of me ... A
therefore I beseech you ... to ease your heart of all su
suspicion as you have of me, and to dispatch me here, bef
your knees, with this same dagger ...'

The King, moved herewith, cast from him the dagger, and, embrac
the Prince, kissed him and (with shedding tears) confessed t
indeed he had him partly in suspicion – though now (as
perceived) not with just cause; and therefore from henceforth
misreport should cause him to have him in mistrust ...

So by his great wisdom was the wrongful suspicion which
father had conceived against him removed, and he restored to
favour ...

Indeed he was youthfully given, grown to audacity, and I
chosen him companions agreeable to his age, with whom he sp
the time in such recreations, exercises, and delights as he fancied. I
yet it should seem (by the report of some writers) that his behavic
was not offensive or at least tending to the damage of anybody, s
he had a care to avoid doing of wrong, and to tedder his affecti
within the tract of virtue, whereby he opened unto himself a re
passage of good liking among the prudent sort, and was beloved
such as could discern his disposition, which was in no degree
excessive as that he deserved in such vehement manner to
suspected. In whose dispraise I find little, but to his praise very mu

Background

England in *c*. 1592

When Shakespeare was writing *Henry IV Part 1*, many people still believed that the sun went round the earth. They were taught that this was the way God had ordered things, and that – in England – God had founded a Church and appointed a Monarchy so that the land and people could be well governed.

'The past is a foreign country; they do things differently there.'
L.P. Hartley

Government

For most of Shakespeare's life, the reigning monarch of England was Queen Elizabeth I. With her counsellors and ministers, she governed the nation from London, although fewer than half a million people out of a total population of six million lived in the capital city. In the rest of the country, law and order were maintained by the land-owners and enforced by their deputies. The average man had no vote, and women had no rights at all.

Religion

At this time, England was a Christian country. All children were baptized, soon after they were born, into the Church of England; they were taught the essentials of the Christian faith, and instructed in their duty to God and to humankind. Marriages and funerals were conducted only by the licensed clergy and according to the Church's rites and ceremonies. Attending divine service was compulsory; absences (without a good medical reason) could be punished by fines. By such means, the authorities were able to keep some control over the population – recording births, marriages, and deaths; being alert to anyone who refused to accept standard religious practices, who could be politically dangerous; and ensuring that people received the approved teachings through the official 'Homilies' which were regularly preached in all parish churches.

Elizabeth I's father, Henry VIII, had broken away from the Church

of Rome, and from that time all people in England were able to hea
the church services *in their own language* rather than in Latin. Th
Book of Common Prayer was used in every church, and an Englis
translation of the Bible was read aloud in public. The Christia
religion had never been so well taught before!

Education

School education reinforced the Church's teaching. From the age c
four, boys might attend the 'petty school' (its name came from th
French '*petite école*') to learn reading the writing along with a fe
prayers; some schools also included work with numbers. At the age c
seven, boys were ready for the grammar schools (if their fathers wei
willing and able to pay the fees).

Grammar schools taught Latin grammar, translation work an
the study of Roman authors, paying attention as much to style as t
content. The art of fine writing was therefore important from earl
youth. A very few students went on to university; these were eithe
clever boys who won scholarships, or else the sons of rich noblemei
Girls stayed at home, and learned domestic and social skills
cooking, sewing, perhaps even music. The lucky ones might learn t
read and write.

Language

At the start of the sixteenth century the English had a very poc
opinion of their own language: there was little serious writing i
English, and hardly any literature. Latin was the language c
international scholarship, and the eloquent style of the Romans wa
much admired. Many translations from Latin were made, and in th
way writers increased the vocabulary of English and made i
grammar more flexible. French, Italian, and Spanish works were als
translated and, for the first time, there were English versions of th
Bible. By the end of the century, English was a language to be prou
of: it was rich in vocabulary, capable of infinite variety and subtlet
and ready for all kinds of work-play – especially *puns*, for whic
Elizabethan English is renowned.

Drama

The great art-form of the Elizabethan and Jacobean age was i
drama. The Elizabethans inherited a tradition of play-acting fro

the Middle Ages, and they reinforced this by reading and translating the Roman playwrights. At the beginning of the sixteenth century plays were performed by groups of actors. These were all-male companies (boys acted the female roles) who travelled from town to town, setting up their stages in open places (such as inn-yards) or, with the permission of the owner, in the hall of some noble house. The touring companies continued outside London into the seventeenth century; but in London, in 1576, a new building was erected for the performance of plays. This was the Theatre, the first purpose-built playhouse in England. Other playhouses followed, including the Globe, where most of Shakespeare's plays were performed, and English drama reached new heights.

There were people who disapproved, of course. The theatres, which brought large crowds together, could encourage the spread of disease – and dangerous ideas. During the summer, when the plague was at its worst, the playhouses were closed. A constant censorship was imposed, more or less severe at different times. The Puritans, a religious and political faction who wanted to impose strict rules of behaviour, tried to close down the theatres. However, partly because the royal family favoured drama, and partly because the buildings were outside the city limits, they did not succeed until 1642.

Theatre

From contemporary comments and sketches – most particularly a drawing by a Dutch visitor, Johannes de Witt – it is possible to form some idea of the typical Elizabethan playhouse for which most of Shakespeare's plays were written. Hexagonal (six-sided) in shape, it had three roofed galleries encircling an open courtyard. The plain, high stage projected into the yard, where it was surrounded by the audience of standing 'groundlings'. At the back were two doors for the actors' entrances and exits; and above these doors was a balcony – useful for a musicians' gallery or for the acting of scenes 'above'. Over the stage was a thatched roof, supported on two pillars, forming a canopy – which seems to have been painted with the sun, moon, and stars for the 'heavens'.

Underneath was space (concealed by curtains), which could be used by characters ascending and descending through a trapdoor in the stage. Costumes and properties were kept backstage in the 'tiring house'. The actors used the most luxurious costumes they could find, often clothes given to them by rich patrons. Stage properties were

important for showing where a scene was set, but the dramatist's o
words were needed to explain the time of day, since all performan
took place in the early afternoon.

A replica of Shakespeare's own theatre, the Globe, has been b
in London, and stands in Southwark, almost exactly on the Banks
site of the original.

William Shakespeare, 1564–1616

Elizabeth I was Queen of England when Shakespeare was born in 1564. He was the son of a tradesman who made and sold gloves in the small town of Stratford-upon-Avon, and he was educated at the grammar school in that town. Shakespeare did not go to university when he left school, but worked, perhaps, in his father's business. When he was eighteen he married Anne Hathaway, who became the mother of his daughter, Susanna, in 1583, and of twins in 1585.

There is nothing exciting, or even unusual, in this story: and from 1585 until 1592 there are no documents that can tell us anything at all about Shakespeare. But we have learned that in 1592 he was known in London, and that he had become both an actor and a playwright.

We do not know when Shakespeare wrote his first play, and indeed we are not sure of the order in which he wrote his works. If you look on page 161 at the list of his writings and their approximate dates, you will see how he started by writing plays on subjects taken from the history of England. No doubt this was partly because he was always an intensely patriotic man – but he was also a very shrewd businessman. He could see that the theatre audiences enjoyed being shown their own history, and it was certain that he would make a profit from this kind of drama.

The plays in the next group are mainly comedies, with romantic love-stories of young people who fall in love with one another, and at the end of the play marry and live happily ever after.

At the end of the sixteenth century the happiness disappears, and Shakespeare's plays become melancholy, bitter, and tragic. This change may have been caused by some sadness in the writer's life (one of his twins died in 1596). Shakespeare, however, was not the only writer whose works at this time were very serious. The whole of England was facing a crisis. Queen Elizabeth I was growing old. She was greatly loved, and the people were sad to think she must soon die; the were also afraid, for the queen had never married, and so there was no child to succeed her.

When James I came to the throne in 1603, Shakespeare continued to write serious drama – the great tragedies and the plays based on Roman history (such as *Julius Caesar*) for which he is most famous. Finally, before he retired from the theatre, he wrote another set of

comedies. These all have the same theme: they tell of happin
which is lost, and then found again.

Shakespeare returned from London to Stratford, his home tov
He was rich and successful, and he owned one of the biggest hou
in the town. He died in 1616. Although several of his plays w
published separately, most of them were not printed until 1623, i
collection known as 'the First Folio'.

Shakespeare also wrote two long poems, and a collection
sonnets. The sonnets describe two love-affairs, but we do not kn
who the lovers were. Although there are many public docume
concerned with his career as a writer and a businessman, Shakespe
has hidden his personal life from us. A nineteenth-century po
Matthew Arnold, addressed Shakespeare in a poem, and wrote "
ask and ask – Thou smilest, and art still'.

There is not even a trustworthy portrait of the world's great
dramatist.

Approximate Dates of Composition of Shakespeare's Works

Period	Comedies	History plays	Tragedies	Poems
I before 1594	Comedy of Errors Taming of the Shrew Two Gentlemen of Verona Love's Labour's Lost	Henry VI, part 1 Henry VI, part 2 Henry VI, part 3 Richard III King John	Titus Andronicus	Venus and Adonis Rape of Lucrece
II 1594–1599	Midsummer Night's Dream Merchant of Venice Merry Wives of Windsor Much Ado About Nothing As You Like It	Richard II King John Henry IV, part 1 Henry IV, part 2 Henry V	Romeo and Juliet	Sonnets
III 1599–1608	Twelfth Night Measure for Measure All's Well That Ends Well Pericles		Julius Caesar Hamlet Othello Timon of Athens King Lear Macbeth Antony and Cleopatra Coriolanus Troilus and Cressida	
IV 1608–1613	Cymbeline The Winter's Tale The Tempest	Henry VIII		

Exploring Henry IV Part 1 *in the Classroom*

One of Shakespeare's history plays, *Henry IV Part 1* has princes, battles, and valiant soldiers as well as comical rogues and highwaymen. If students don't appreciate the ideals of honour and leadership, they will probably revel in some of the worst insults in any of Shakespeare's plays.

This section will suggest a range of approaches in the classroom, to help bring the text to life and to engender both enjoyment and understanding of the play.

Ways into the Play

Students may feel an antipathy towards the study of Shakespeare. The imaginative and enthusiastic teacher, with the help of this edition of the play, will soon break this down!

Family trees

Families and connections are important in this play. Ask students to track and write their own family tree. Encourage them to present it as imaginatively as they can: for example, as a scroll or with thumbnail sketches of people on it. Next ask them to compare their family tree with the Plantagenet family tree on page vi, discussing what differences they notice (e.g. titles, and the distance it goes back in time).

Every picture tells a story

Falstaff is one of Shakespeare's most famous comedy characters and a favourite of Elizabeth I. Ask students to look at the pictures of Falstaff on the Shakespeare Illustrated website (see Further Reading and Resources below). Encourage them to explore and discuss what the pictures tell us about the character and what they expect Falstaff will be like. If they keep a note of their observations, they can compare them as they meet the character in the play.

Navigating the play

Your students may need some help and practice in finding their way around a Shakespeare play. After explaining the division into acts, scenes and lines, challenge them to look up some references – such as those below – as quickly as possible. Ask them to discuss the possible meaning of the lines and to use them to guess some of the elements of the plot.

Act 1, Scene 2, lines 2–6	(*Thou art so fat-witted with drinking of old sack, and unbuttoning thee after supper, and sleeping upon benches after noon, that thou hast forgotten to demand that truly which thou wouldst truly know.*)
2, Scene 4, lines 370–4	(*But tell me, Hal, art not thou horrible afeard? Thou being heir apparent, could the world pick thee out three such enemies again, as that fiend Douglas, that spirit Percy, and that devil Glendower?*)
ct 5, Scene 2, lines 85–6	(*And if we live, we live to tread on kings; If die, brave death when princes die with us!*)
Act 5, Scene 4, line 119	(*The better part of valour is discretion*)

Improvisation

Working on one of these improvisations may help students to access some of the ideas behind the drama.

a) Ask students to work in pairs, A and B. A owes someone some money and must pay it back straightaway. A asks B for a loan. B has paid A's bills many times in the past and is getting fed up with doing so. How does A persuade B this time?

b) Ask students to work in pairs. One takes on the role of a parent who runs a successful business. The other takes the role of the teenage child who has only been interested in friends and partying. The young person now wants to work in the company. The parent is disappointed in the young person. Can the young person persuade the parent to take him/her seriously?

c) Ask students to work in groups of four on an improvisation looking at two gangs. Two of them are from one gang and the other two are from an enemy gang. The pairs do not trust each other. They meet to talk about sorting out the differences between

the two gangs and bringing about peace. Improvise t▌
discussions between the four to try to make peace. Then separa▌
the pairs and improvise the conversations that take place aft▌
their meeting with each other over whether they can trust t▌
others and the decisions made.

Setting the Scene

Historical background

Shakespeare bases his play on historical events, but it is n▌
historically factual because he adapts people and events as well▌
making his own dramatic additions to the story. In this play he loo▌
at an unstable part of the country's development and history, tv▌
hundred years before the play was written. It's part of a series of fo▌
plays dealing with the rise of the House of Lancaster, starting wi▌
Henry Bolingbroke usurping the throne in *Richard II* and leading▌
the successful establishment of Henry in *Henry V*.

Ask students to research this period of history, looking at t▌
historical details of those involved. Encourage them to look at t▌
different divisions within what is now Britain. They could prese▌
their research in the form of a display.

The battle

The battle at Shrewsbury, and in particular the duel between ▌
and Hotspur, provides the climax to the play. The second half of A▌
5 sees the frenzy of battle as men pass to and fro in comb▌
Challenge students to become set designers and to create a suital▌
set for the battle that will enhance the exciting and electrifyi▌
conclusion to the play, as well as allowing for the actions that ta▌
part in the final scenes. Students should create a presentati▌
explaining their ideas, which might be a model, art work o▌
PowerPoint presentation. Their ideas might consider scene▌
props, lighting, sound, and visual media.

Thieves and highwaymen

The play gives us a window onto one of the familiar crimes of the ▌
– being robbed while travelling. Reading Act 2, Scenes 1 and 2 will ▌
only illuminate some of this seedier side of Shakespeare's day, ▌

will give students insight into some of the occupations of the day (e.g. carrier and ostler). Students might consider the modern-day equivalents of the jobs (e.g. lorry driver and garage attendant).

Ask students to read the scenes closely and then to write a set of guidelines for travellers in Shakespeare's day, warning them of the possible dangers (e.g. 'pick-purse', 'foot-landrakers', and 'long-staff sixpenny strikers'). They might also produce a 'wanted' poster for a notorious thief like Gadshill.

Keeping Track of the Action

It is important to give students opportunities to 'digest' and reflect upon their reading, so that they may take ownership of the play.

Reading journal

As you read through the play, help students to trace and understand the story by asking them to keep a journal in which they record what happens. They can also record their reactions and thoughts about the action and the characters. Their responses can remained focused through specific questions (from the teacher) to answer.

Falstaff's blog

Students can keep a computer blog or written diary of the events of the play from Falstaff's viewpoint. At the start of the drama, he is part of the wilder and dissolute side of Prince Hal's life, and knows how to benefit from this. He also observes the change in Hal's character, and will have particular views about what he thinks about that. Students should attempt to maintain a blog that reflects the actions of the play from Falstaff's own self-interested viewpoint.

News reports

Students can create a series of news reports, either for press or television, which track the wider picture, including matters of state and issues of public interest. The reports will describe the political and military developments of the play, including the state of the royal family and their control over events, spotlights on the main players such as the rebels Hotspur and Worcester, and the build-up and outcomes of the military campaign.

Cartoon-strip versions

Ask students to choose a significant moment from the play and to create a cartoon-strip version of it. In order to do this they will need to look at the order of events, contributions by individuals, and the words of the characters. They should aim to retell a short episode – for example, the conning of Falstaff over the theft – and all or part of the battle scene. The cartoon strip should include pictures, captions and word bubbles.

Characters

Students of all ages need to come to an understanding of the characters – their motivations, their relationships, and their development.

Game cards

In the tradition of card games such as 'Top Trumps', ask students to create a series of game cards on the characters in the play. On each card, students will need to include a brief description and picture of the character. They will then list facts and qualities about each character. Facts might be age and relationships (e.g. king, son of . . . wife of . . .); qualities in this case might be honour, honesty, bravery ruthlessness, popularity. For each quality they will need to award the characters marks out of ten. Once they have created their cards, they can play a brief game with them.

Prince Hal

Hal undergoes a transformation during the play, changing from jack-the-lad to a successful soldier and responsible prince. The transformation is by no means complete but he already shows signs of becoming the heroic leader that comes to fruition in *Henry V*.

Help students to explore his development by creating an outline drawing on the wall to represent the prince, and then asking them for comments on his character at different moments in the action. Students can write their comments on sticky notes that can be placed on the picture. You might use two different colour sticky notes to represent positive and negative qualities.

Obituary

Hotspur is spoken of in glowing terms throughout the drama. He is brave and honourable and King Henry wishes he was his own son at one point. Explain the purpose and conventions of an obituary, and perhaps show one from a newspaper. Ask students to write an obituary for Harry Hotspur.

Themes

Honour

Honour is one of the important themes of the play. It is a difficult quality to define (ask students to try). Different characters in the play show honour in various ways: for example, Hotspur considers honour is to do with bravery on the battlefield, and Prince Hal shows his honour when he pardons Douglas after the battle.

Ask students to discuss how honour is shown by the characters (or not shown in the case of Falstaff). Then ask for volunteers to take the roles of the main characters – Henry IV, Prince Hal, Hotspur, Blunt, and Falstaff. 'Hot seat' the characters, allowing the rest of the class to question them on their idea of honour.

Young and old

There is a clear contrast between sons and their fathers in the play. Hotspur is ready to fight while his father is ill in bed, and Hal has to save his father in the heat of battle. Challenge students to find evidence in the play of the different qualities displayed by young and old, both positive and negative. Which character do they think shows a good mix of such qualities? Ask them to consider why Shakespeare focuses on this theme.

Great pretenders

Quite a lot of pretence and deception occurs in the play. Students can look for examples (e.g. Poins and the prince robbing Falstaff and the others, Worcester keeping the king's offer from Hotspur, Falstaff pretending to be dead). Ask students to find other examples, and to discuss what the incidences tell us about the characters involved.

Shakespeare's Language

Prose and verse

There is a clear distinction between the two worlds of the play: the inn (and the characters that frequent it) and the courtly life of the King. Shakespeare emphasizes this with his use of language, generally using prose for the more lowly characters and verse (iambic pentameter) for the nobility.

Prince Hal straddles both worlds, and students can investigate how the way the Prince talks tells us about his role and condition within the play. What does his ease at speaking in both spheres suggest about the Prince? Challenge students to write their own verse in iambic pentameter – perhaps in rhyming couplets – summing up the change in the character of Prince Hal.

Imagery

Both Prince Hal and his father use the image of the sun, stars, and planets to talk about kingship and influence. Ask students to look for examples (e.g. Act 1, Scene 2, line 175; Act 3, Scene 2, lines 79–80; Act 5, Scene 4, line 64) and discuss the effectiveness of the images used.

Insults

Some of Shakespeare's coarsest and most potent insults occur in *Henry IV Part 1*, emanating from the rough-and-ready world of the commoner and the inn, including 'clay-brained guts' and 'bull pizzle'. Challenge students to find as many of these insults as they can in order to compile a collection of insults which they might like to try out on each other!

Exploring with Drama

Book the hall or push back the desks, because the best way to study a great play is through drama. Students of all ages will benefit from a dramatic encounter with *Henry IV Part 1*. They will enjoy the opportunity to act out a scene or two, or to explore the situation through improvisation: for example, by putting a character in the 'hot seat' for questioning by others.

Stirring speeches

Hotspur admits that he does not have the 'gift of tongue', so the speech he gives to rouse his troops and supporters and lead them into battle is not as effective as it might be. Students should read the speech (Act 5, Scene 2, lines 75–100) and look for its strengths and weaknesses. They should look at how the speech is also undermined by interruptions.

If possible, give students access to the renowned speech ('Once more unto the breech . . .', from *Henry V*, Act 3, Scene 1, lines 1–34) by Henry V, the man who is Prince Hal in *Henry IV Part 1*, where he leads his men into a famous victory at Agincourt. Once they have compared the two speeches, ask them to give a performance of each – contrasting the approach of both.

Forum theatre

Ask a group of volunteers to act out a section of the drama: for example, Hotspur's discussion with Glendower (Act 3, Scene 1, lines 1–60) or Falstaff recounting being robbed (Act 2, Scene 4, lines 177–236). Everyone else watches the performance. At appropriate moments, freeze the action and ask the rest of the class to offer contributions either about performance (e.g. where characters would be best placed at that moment) or about the character's thoughts and development (e.g. how does that character feel now?).

Writing about *Henry IV Part 1*

If your students have to write about *Henry IV Part 1* for coursework or for examinations, you may wish to give them this general guidance:

- Read the question or task carefully, highlight the key words, and answer all parts of the question.

- Planning is essential. Plan what will be in each paragraph. You can change your plan if necessary.

- Avoid retelling the story.

- *Henry IV Part 1* is a play – so consider the impact or effect on the audience.

- Use the Point, Evidence, Explanation (PEE) structure to expla points.

- Adding Evaluation (PEEE!) will gain you higher marks.

- Keep quotations short.

- Avoid referring to a film version of the play, unless this is part your task.

Further Reading and Resources

General

Fantasia, Louis, *Instant Shakespeare: A Practical Guide for Actors, Directors and Teachers* (A & C Black, 2002).

Greer, Germaine, *Shakespeare: A Very Short Introduction* (Oxford, 2002).

Hall, Peter, *Shakespeare's Advice to the Players* (Oberon Books, 2003).

Holden, Anthony, *Shakespeare: His Life and Work* (Abacus, 2002).

Kneen, Judith, *Teaching Shakespeare from Transition to Test* (Oxford University Press, 2004).

McConnell, Louise, *Exit, Pursued By a Bear – Shakespeare's Characters, Plays, Poems, History and Stagecraft* (Bloomsbury, 2003).

McLeish, Kenneth, and Unwin, Stephen, *A Pocket Guide to Shakespeare's Plays*, (Faber and Faber, 1998).

Muirden, James, *Shakespeare in a Nutshell: A Rhyming Guide to All the Plays* (Constable, 2004).

Wood, Michael, *In Search of Shakespeare* (BBC, 2003).

Children's/Students' Books

Ganeri, Anita, *What They Don't Tell You About Shakespeare* (Hodder, 1996).

Garfield, Leon, *Shakespeare Stories* (Puffin, 1997).

Garfield, Leon, *Shakespeare: The Animated Tales* (Egmont, 2002).

Lamb, Charles and Mary, *Tales from Shakespeare* (Puffin, 1987).

Websites

The Complete Works of Shakespeare
http://the-tech.mit.edu/Shakespeare/

Elizabethan pronunciation
Including information on insults.
http://www.renfaire.com/Language/index.html

Encyclopaedia Britannica – Shakespeare and the Globe: Then and Now
Information about the Globe and the theatre in Shakespeare's times.
http://search.eb.com/shakespeare/index2.html

The Royal Shakespeare Company website
As well as information on the theatre company, there are resource
on the plays and the life and times of Shakespeare.
http://www.rsc.org.uk/home/default.aspx

The Shakespeare Birthplace Trust
Information on his works, life and times.
http://www.shakespeare.org.uk/homepage

Shakespeare's Globe
Information on The Globe Theatre, London.
http://www.shakespeares-globe.org/

Shakespeare Illustrated
An excellent source of paintings and pictures based on Shakespeare
plays.
http://www.emory.edu/ENGLISH/classes/Shakespeare_Illustrated/
Shakespeare.html

Spark Notes: Henry IV Part 1
An online study guide.
http://www.sparknotes.com/shakespeare/henry4pt1/

Mr William Shakespeare and the Internet
A comprehensive guide to Shakespeare resources on the Internet.
http://shakespeare.palomar.edu/

Film, video, DVD and audio

Henry IV Part 1, BBC TV Shakespeare Collection, 1979
The Complete Arkangel Shakespeare: Henry IV, Part 1 (Audi
Cassette) 2004